Teaching Learners Who Struggle with Mathematics

Systematic Intervention and Remediation

Second Edition

Helene J. Sherman
University of Missouri–St. Louis

Lloyd I. Richardson
University of Missouri–St. Louis

George J. Yard
University of Missouri–St. Louis, Emeritus

Merrill
is an imprint of

Upper Saddle River, New Jersey
Columbus, Ohio

Library of Congress Cataloging-in-Publication Data

Sherman, Helene J.
Teaching learners who struggle with mathematics: systematic intervention and remediation/Helene J. Sherman, Lloyd I. Richardson, George J. Yard.—2nd ed.
p.cm.
Originally published: Teaching children who struggle with mathematics. Upper Saddle River, N.J.: Pearson/Merrill/Prentice Hall, © 2005
Includes bibliographical references and index.
ISBN 978-0-13-613577-7
1. Mathematics—Study and teaching (Elementary)—United States.
I. Richardson, Lloyd I. II. Yard, George J. III. Sherman, Helene J. Teaching learners who struggle with mathematics IV. Title
QA 135.6.S483 2009
372.7—dc22 2007038925

Vice President and Executive Publisher: Jeffery W. Johnston
Publisher: Kevin M. Davis
Editor: Meredith D. Fossel
Editorial Assistant: Maren Vigilante
Senior Project Manager: Linda Hillis Bayma
Production Coordination: Norine Strang, S4Carlisle Editorial Services
Design Coordinator: Diane C. Lorenzo
Cover Designer: Bryan Huber
Cover Image: Corbis
Operations Specialist: Susan Hannahs
Director of Marketing: Quinn Perkson
Marketing Coordinator: Brian Mounts

This book was set in Bookman by S4Carlisle Publishing Services. It was printed and bound by Bind-Rite Graphics. The cover was printed by Phoenix Color Corp.

Pearson Education Ltd.
Pearson Education Singapore Pte. Ltd.
Pearson Education Canada, Ltd.
Pearson Education—Japan
Pearson Education Australia Pty. Limited
Pearson Education North Asia Ltd.
Pearson Educación de Mexico, S.A. de C.V.
Pearson Education Malaysia Pte. Ltd.

Merrill
is an imprint of

10 9 8 7 6 5 4 3 2 1
ISBN-13: 978-0-13-613577-7
ISBN-10: 0-13-613577-3

To Carl, Craig, and Ellen for the positive and loving support they have always provided me and to the late Adeline Wagman Kohn for her lifelong love of learning and unfailing encouragement.

Helene J. Sherman

This book is dedicated to Judith, Ira, and Zoe for their encouragement and unconditional support throughout this project.

Lloyd I. Richardson

To my wife, Carole Thornbloon Yard, who stood beside me during my career and knew there was a book inside me and encouraged me to find it; and to my shining stars: my daughters Michelle Yard and Tammy McCracken.

To the memory of my parents, Glenn and Edna Yard, who took great pride in my accomplishments.

George J. Yard

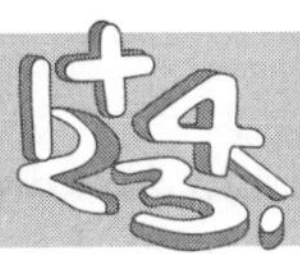

About the Authors

Helene J. Sherman

Helene J. Sherman, Ed.D., is a professor and the associate dean for undergraduate education in the College of Education at the University of Missouri–St. Louis. She has taught at the elementary, middle school mathematics, community college, and university levels, and she teaches undergraduate and graduate courses in K–8 mathematics teaching methods. Dr. Sherman has had her work published in numerous professional educational journals and has coauthored three books for teaching metric measurement across the curriculum. She has directed and codirected federal and statewide grant projects in St. Louis area school districts, focusing on classroom applications of mathematics teaching methods. She presents workshops throughout the country on methods for teaching mathematics to elementary and middle-grade students. Dr. Sherman has won several teaching awards, among which are the 2003 Missouri Governor's Award for Excellence in Teaching, the 2000 College of Education Distinguished Teaching Award, the 1998 Emerson Electric Outstanding Teaching Award, and the 1997 Distinguished Alumni Award from the University of Missouri–St. Louis.

Lloyd I. Richardson

Lloyd I. Richardson received his Ph.D. in mathematics education from Vanderbilt University's Peabody College. He has 38 years of teaching experience at the middle school, high school, and university levels. His experiences include serving as chair of a high school mathematics department, director of the Center for Excellence in Metropolitan Education at University of Missouri–St. Louis, director of the NSF Summer Science Camp, and director of numerous other federally funded precollegiate programs in mathematics education. He has taught in the mathematics department at three universities. He currently holds joint appointments in the College of Education and the College of Arts and Sciences at the University of Missouri–St. Louis as distinguished teaching professor in education and mathematics. He is the author or coauthor of two books, eleven monographs, and numerous professional journal articles. He has also produced a commercial mathematics readiness test and a manipulative fraction kit. He is a recreational woodworker and fisherman.

George J. Yard

George J. Yard received his Ph.D. in special education from St. Louis University. During his 28 years at the University of Missouri–St. Louis, he taught in the field of behavior disorders while serving in a number of leadership positions, including area leader of special education, coordinator of graduate studies, and chair of the department of behavioral studies. Dr. Yard has authored and coauthored numerous articles and monographs and has served as editor of *The Journal of the National Association of Adults with Special Learning Needs.* He has conducted research addressing the curricular aspect of serving children with disabilities, served as consultant to school districts throughout the Midwest, and was an advisor to law firms and the federal district court system on issues involving individuals with disabilities. Dr. Yard currently lives in Houston, Texas, where he continues to teach at the college level and serves as a certified mediator for issues involving the Americans with Disabilities Act. He was named associate professor emeritus by the University of Missouri–St. Louis in 2000.

Preface

Me . . . math? That was always my worst subject.

I stopped taking math as soon as I could.

Is there much math required for this course/job/game/question?

I'm just not a math person.

I understood math until I got to algebra and geometry.

I never really thought I needed math.

My mother wasn't good at math, either.

When asked about understanding and appreciating mathematics, people often reply that their comprehension is limited and their attitude is less than satisfactory. In fact, with little prompting, many individuals readily confess that they "never understood math," "never saw the use of it," and "got by" by taking the minimum number of courses to graduate from high school or college. Students such as those so described are termed *dissimilar learners* in this book. They are not necessarily identified as learners who have special needs and they may or may not have been provided extra resources despite making unsatisfactory progress. These pupils require well-designed alternative approaches to being taught and learning mathematics.

The purpose of this book is to address the mathematics teaching and learning of and by underachieving students. They are those who do not understand mathematical concepts sufficiently and/or are not as skillful as they could or would like to be in terms of executing math rules and symbolic computations. The authors believe that satisfactory achievement can be attained by adapting instruction to address influential classroom learning factors that affect dissimilar learners. Lessons and remediation must be designed in terms of developmental instructional strategies that promote thoughtful, active learning and connections to earlier concepts. Recognizing how learners adapt to learning environments and classroom organization in terms of preferences for reinforcement and methods for completing work are also critical learning factors. When teachers and parents focus on how their students learn best, rather than repeatedly offering the same or very similar instructional methods and materials, progress can be made. Students can move from believing they "can't do mathematics" to real achievement and confidence because instruction is targeted and effective.

Features of This Text

Unique to this book is a systemic approach designed to deal with variables that contribute to mathematics success. The authors created a data analysis sheet (DAS), a template for considering learning characteristics and variables. These include the physical environment, the curriculum and current course of study, methods, strategies, and tools that students prefer for accepting and expressing information, academic behaviors, and responses from the environment that cause inappropriate or appropriate behavior to recur.

After considering the learner's strengths and areas of concern, including the content to be taught, teachers complete a mathematics improvement plan (MIP). With a learner's academic and behavioral characteristics in mind, specific instructional approaches are planned to fit the daily schedule. Because these approaches are appropriate to those identified factors that best promote individual student learning, mathematics content improvement can occur.

The approach to learners' error patterns is another unique feature of this book. Each chapter deals with a different mathematics topic—from place value to problem solving—including whole numbers, fractions, decimals, and time and money. A variety of errors made by typical learners are described in a case study format. The reader can therefore examine patterns in terms of each child's learning and environmental characteristics. For example, José makes a number of decimal fraction errors described in the decimal/fractions chapter. Remediation strategies for addressing his misunderstandings are described in specific detail and in the context of the mathematical content and his case study, which highlights his academic and behavioral strengths as well as areas of concern.

Organization of This Text

In Chapters 1 through 8, the error patterns are based upon the same or very similar set of problem examples. In this way, readers can analyze a variety of errors in the same context and focus clearly on the mathemetical patterns, rather than on the exercises. The authors chose problem sets for each chapter, in which a series of patterned errors is demonstrated. Using problem sets provides the opportunity to analyze multiple patterns in detail. The reader needs to identify distinctive patterns because, quite often, errors look similar even though they are based on very different misunderstandings. Students may make addition regrouping errors by not correctly recording the regrouped numeral if they do not know where to write it. However, other learners may also make addition regrouping errors by starting to add from left to right and by confusing the notation. The learner's work in each chapter is representative of many different types of patterns of errors. Thus, the text explains how teachers can systematically assess student work in order to appropriately base diagnosis, prescription, and remediation decisions.

Interactive instructional games and activities included in Chapters 2 through 8 and Chapter 10 extend and deepen instruction. They make it possible for teachers to encourage learners to actively develop their conceptual understanding and/or practice skills.

An important theme of the book is that long-term retention is based upon a strong conceptual foundation of numbers as well as a well-designed learning environment. The reader will find detailed, step-by-step strategies for addressing each mathematical topic so that it can be understood and remembered. By analyzing and understanding why and how their students make errors, teachers can design appropriate remediation to habituate the process with practice that is meaningful.

Although Chapter 9, "Problem Solving," contains no error patterns, it does describe effective instructional strategies for assisting struggling students. The reader will find information related to common mistakes and methods for fostering success.

Each chapter contains fundamental content background information for the mathematical topic of concern. These explanations serve to remind readers of the content upon which the topic is based and can assist teachers in discussions with students.

Lessons and activities designed to take into consideration not only the learning context but also students' specific mathematical misunderstandings or missteps lead to increased mathematics achievement. Dissimilar learners, those who find themselves frustrated by traditional teaching methods, respond well to alternative approaches carefully designed to address their overall educational needs. The strategies and techniques in this book will make it possible for learners to steadily progress, within a guided discovery teaching and learning environment, to higher levels of comprehension and skill.

This book addresses mathematics education in a manner that encourages positive content growth and attitude for both teachers and students. Almost everyone, at one time or another, is a dissimilar mathematics learner, and this book enables each of us to succeed far beyond the status quo and one's expectations for achievement.

Acknowledgments

The authors wish to thank our reviewers for their invaluable comments and encouragement. We are grateful to Jane K. Bonari, California University of Pennsylvania; Janet Bosnick, University of Northern Florida; Yolanda De La Cruz, Arizona State University; John W. Dougherty, Lindenwood University; Janice K. Ewing, Colby Sawyer College; Betty K. Hathaway, University of Arkansas at Little Rock; Hiram D. Johnston, Georgia State University; Lisa Kirtman, California State University, Fullerton; Charles E. Lamb, Texas A&M University; Ann L. Lee, Bloomsburg University of Pennsylvania; Anne L. Madsen, University of New Mexico; Eula Ewing Monroe, Brigham Young University; Daniel C. Orey, California State University, Sacramento; Kay Reinke, Oklahoma State University; Anne M. Rule, Saint Louis University; and Karen A. Verbeke, University of Maryland, Eastern Shore.

The authors would also like to thank the reviewers of the second edition: Christyn Luce, University of North Carolina, Charlotte; Sueanne McKinney, Old Dominion University; and Trena L. Wilkerson, Baylor University.

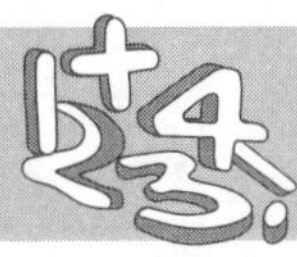

Brief Contents

Contents

Note: Every effort has been made to provide accurate and current Internet information in this book. However, the Internet and information posted on it are constantly changing, and it is inevitable that some of the Internet addresses listed in this textbook will change.

Chapter 1

The Dissimilar Learner and Mathematics Instruction

A fourth-grade student approached me one day while I was visiting his classroom. He told me proudly that he now "got math." Excitedly, I asked him what he meant. He replied, "I know that whatever I think will be wrong. So now I don't think or say anything. I just wait for the teacher to tell me what to do and if I do it, then I know I'll be right."

A Problem and a Solution

Two important questions a teacher of mathematics often asks are: "How do I successfully teach mathematics concepts and skills so they are understood and remembered?" and "How can I effectively teach this math content?" Rather than focusing solely on content, instructional questions must also relate to the needs of the child. The child must be the focus of any pedagogical decision being made because a learner's cognitive, emotional, and physical needs vary widely and have great impact on achievement. For learners to succeed, teachers must assess students' individual abilities and characteristics and choose appropriate and effective instructional strategies accordingly.

The purpose of this book is to address the cognitive needs of first- through sixth-grade students who underachieve when learning mathematics. Certainly, all students do not find success when taught with uniform instructional approaches or within the same behavioral model. The educational system may have "given up" on these students. We propose that a mathematics improvement plan (MIP), based on a targeted, functional assessment of learners' strengths and areas of concern, can be a proactive instructional tool. It serves to guide a wide range of intervention strategies to increase achievement.

The Learner-Centered Approach

The principle of "learner at the center" implies that more than one teaching approach is necessary to achieve desired results. The term *dissimilar learner* was developed for students who have not succeeded when engaged in "one size fits all" instruction (Cooper, Lingg, Puricelli, & Yard, 1995). Dissimilar learners do not fit the traditional instructional mold. They are often rebellious and dysfunctional in a learning environment that does not adequately address various teaching options and learning styles. They lack *resilience* (Bernard, 1995), which is defined as the "capacity to successfully overcome personal vulnerabilities and environmental stressors, to be able to 'bounce back' in the face of potential risks, and to maintain well-being" (Wang, 1998, p. 12).

Research in the nature of resilience has identified certain factors, including school-related factors, that can counteract these risks—termed *protective factors* (Bernard, 1995, p. 3). Bernard found that schools fostering resilience also provide opportunities for children to develop the internal assets necessary for resilience, such as problem-solving skills, autonomy, a purposeful, constructive, and optimistic outlook on the future, and effective communication and relationship skills. The author further summarized the contributions to these external protective factors made by schools and teachers under three main categories: caring and supportive relationships, positive and high expectations, and opportunities for meaningful participation.

Werner and Smith (1998) also address protective factors in the school setting. They emphasize the need for including all students in the decisions that affect them. Teachers should offer such opportunities for student involvement in all areas and activities. Caring, promoting positive expectations, participation, and acceptance of a broad range of learning styles that builds from perceptions of students' strengths and interests are important features of protective factors. Werner and Smith identified school personnel whose characteristics show genuine personal interest in students and who are positive role models and mentors. Further research emphasized acknowledgment of achievements in sports, music, and art as well as academics as an important protective factor.

Absence of the teacher characteristics just described can result in lack of academic success for students and can set in motion a cycle of inaccurate diagnosis and remediation and, sometimes, withdrawal from the educational system. "Dissimilarity in no way reflects presence or absence of capacity within the developmental domains. The student will, however, most likely exhibit certain characteristics that are common in special learners. Although these characteristics may exist in different degrees, they place these children at risk in the conventional educational system" (Cooper et al., 1995, p. 36). The primary characteristics of dissimilar learners are represented in several areas and listed in Figure 1.1. The types of support characteristics are listed in Figure 1.2.

Systematic Instruction

The most effective pedagogical approach that benefits the dissimilar learner is both multidimensional and systematic. It examines all the conditions within and surrounding the child, such as the curriculum content, context of the classroom, academic and social behavior, and ways in which students process information and respond to feedback. A comprehensive approach to teaching and remediating mathematics specifies and systematizes a number of factors to be applied in an orderly and logical manner. If any one of these components is ignored or overlooked, academic success is jeopardized. The problems that teachers and students experience when handling any of these factors are interrelated and may negatively affect the teacher's attempts to bring about positive change. A system that considers all factors when designing and targeting teaching approaches is most advantageous for students.

- Concrete in thought processes
- Physical or direct confrontation yields negative results
- The visual modality is the primary intake style for learning
- Tactile involvement with the environment
- Communication style is high in word usage, low in word meaning
- Adverse to written language
- Prefers group performance rather than individual performance
- Low sense of self-security, especially when environment is radically different from his or her norm
- Views educational system as a threat to self-preservation
- Reacts negatively to rigid order
- Emotionally fragile and volatile
- Loyalties are strong but bonding is slow

FIGURE 1.1
Primary Characteristics of Dissimilar Learners

Home Problems
- Lack of learning structure in the home
- Lack of respect for parents on the part of student
- Parents lack respect for educational system

Visual Learner
- Does not like to read
- Prefers hands-on activities
- Thought processes are more concrete than abstract

Low Skill Development
- Social skills are low
- Dissimilar learners are verbally impaired—have difficulty effectively communicating feelings

Aggressive—Verbally and Physically
- Aggressive toward adults and peers
  - Verbal explosions
  - Abusive language
- Physically aggressive toward peers and teachers
  - Fights
  - Throws objects
  - Makes inappropriate gestures
  - Reacts violently to being touched

Poor Personal Habits
- Poor hygiene
- Poor nutrition
- Misses classes, tardy
- Disorganized
- Complains of physical discomfort

Tactile
- Seeks excessive physical attention
- Can't keep hands or feet to self

Poor Peer Relationships
- Has difficulty making friends
- Teases other students
- Prefers to interact with older or younger age groups
- Often prefers to be alone
- Isolated by peers
- Physically threatens peers

Poor Work Habits
- Has trouble working independently
  - Needs frequent attention from the teacher
  - Needs directions to be repeated
  - Wants demands to be met immediately
  - Needs constant supervision and reminders
- Complains and whines about tasks
- Varies in rate of work completion
- Wants to monopolize class activities
- Rarely participates in class activities
- Shows inappropriate response/behavior
  - Talks in class
  - Sleeps in class

(continued)

FIGURE 1.2
Support Characteristics of Dissimilar Learners

High Risk
- Fears are translated into aggression
- Emotionally fragile
  - Cries
  - Withdrawn, avoids interactions with people
  - Low sense of security in relationships; does not generalize; must accept you first
- Feelings of insecurity
  - Thinks people are unfair
  - Denies behavior
  - Blames others
  - Responds inappropriately to constructive criticism
  - Reacts inappropriately in competitive situations or to the success of others

Poor Attitude
- Negativism—especially as a reaction to a rigid system
- Defensive
- Lack of motivation
- Acts impulsively
- Seeks to control the environment
- Lack of respect for authority
  - Questions directions and argues with corrections
  - Inappropriate comments, talks out
  - Verbally threatens authority figures
  - Physically threatens authority figures
- Defies rules, presents a continuing discipline problem
- Engages in self-destructive behavior
- Abuses property of others
  - Steals
  - Cheats

Hyperactive
- Nervous
- Very active (eg., taps pencils, makes noises, moves body)
- Daydreams, draws, doodles
- Has difficulty staying in seat
- Leaves the room
- Continues inappropriate behavior after request to stop

FIGURE 1.2
(Continued)

Teachers must recognize that no one tool will be effective in every circumstance or environment. Therefore, planning for maximum flexibility, manageable units of classroom time periods, and incorporating all teaching and behavioral approaches *must be the rule* rather than the exception.

Why Do Students Struggle with Mathematics?

A major component of the child-centered, systematic teaching approach is content. The discipline of mathematics presents many challenges to dissimilar learners. Mathematics has often been termed the "gatekeeper" of success or failure for high school graduation and career success (National Research Council [NRC], 1989). It is essential that "mathematics . . . become a pump rather than filter in the pipeline of American education" (NRC, 1989, p. 7). A lack of sufficient mathematical skill and understanding affects one's ability to make critically important educational, life, and career decisions.

Students fall below their expected level of mathematics achievement for a variety of reasons. When asked why they were not as successful in learning mathematics, many people reply that they "never understood math," or "never liked it because it was too abstract and did not relate to them." These reasons and others can be categorized, in general, as environmental or personal, individualized factors.

Environmental Factors

Instruction: Mathematics instruction must provide many opportunities for concept building, relevant challenging questions, problem solving, reasoning, and connections within the curriculum and real-world situations. Students who are taught in a way that relies too heavily on rote memorization isolated from meaning have difficulty recognizing and retaining math concepts and generalizations.

Curricular Materials: Spiraling the curriculum provides opportunities for learners to deal with content developmentally over time. Concepts can be built upon and related to previous learning throughout the curriculum as students become more proficient and experienced in mathematics. However, it is critical that the same content not be taught year after year, in almost the same manner of delivery. Students who do not "get it" the first time are not likely to "get it" the next several times it is taught in the usual manner. Moreover, underachieving students are frequently assigned repetitious and uninteresting skill-and-drill work each year in order to teach them "the basics." This type of work often represents a narrow view of mathematical foundations and a low level of expectation of students' abilities. It limits opportunities to reason and problem solve.

The Gap Between Learner and Subject Matter: When the mathematics content being taught is unconnected to students' ability level and/or experiences, serious achievement gaps result. This situation may occur if students are absent frequently or transfer to another school during the academic year. A student may find the mathematics curriculum to be more advanced or paced differently than what was being taught in the previous school. Without intervention strategies, students could remain "lost" for the duration of their education.

Too few life experiences, such as trips to neighborhood stores or opportunities to communicate with others about numbers through practical life examples, can make math irrelevant for students. Gaps exist, therefore, not only in the curriculum but between the learner and perceived usefulness of the subject matter.

Personal or Individualized Factors

Locus of Control: Some students believe that their mathematical achievement is mainly attributable to factors beyond their control, such as luck. These students think that if they scored well on a mathematics assignment, they did so only because the content happened to be easy. These students do not attribute their success to understanding or hard work. Their locus is external because they believe achievement is due to factors beyond their control and do not acknowledge that diligence and a positive attitude play a significant role in accomplishment. Students might also believe that failure is related to either the lack of innate mathematical inability or level of intelligence. They view their achievement as accidental and poor progress as inevitable. In doing so, they limit their capacity to study and move ahead (Beck, 2000; Phillips & Gully, 1997).

Memory Ability: Some students lack well-developed mental strategies for remembering how to complete algorithmic procedures and combinations of basic facts.

However, strategies to improve capacities for remembering facts, formulas, or procedures can be taught. Repetition games such as calling out fact combinations and having students solve them and then repeat those that were called before their turn can help. For example, the teacher would call out "3 × 5" and a student would respond with "15." That student would then ask a number question such as "7 − 5" of the group. The responder would reply, "3 × 5 = 15 and 7 − 5 = 2." The game continues as each player calls out a new fact and each responder answers with all the previous combinations and the new answer. Students' ability to organize their thinking and use it to recall data will affect success throughout the curriculum.

Attention Span: Students may be mentally distracted and have difficulty focusing on multistep problems and procedures. Dealing with long-term projects or a number of variables or pieces of information at one time can interfere with achievement. Effective teachers should use attention getters such as drawings and learning aids. Students who work in pairs can help each other stay on task.

Understanding the Language of Mathematics: Students are confused by words that also have special mathematical meaning, such as "volume," "yard," "power," and "area." Lack of understanding of mathematical terms such as "divisor," "factor," "multiple," and "denominator" seriously hampers students' abilities to focus on and understand terms and operations for algorithms and problem solving. Memorizing these terms without meaning and context is not productive.

How Is Mathematics Taught Effectively for All Students?

Developing Mathematics Proficiency

Students who complete algorithms with little understanding quickly forget or confuse the procedures. An algorithm is a "finite, step-by-step procedure for accomplishing a task that we wish to complete" (Usiskin, 1998, p. 7), such as the rules needed to solve a long-division problem. Understanding is the underpinning of skill work (Clements, 1997; Piaget, 1965). Suppose, for example, students cannot recall if they are supposed to divide the denominator into the numerator, or the reverse, to find a decimal equivalent. They can carry out the procedure and long divide either way but do not understand why the process yields a decimal number and cannot explain their reasoning. Similarly, students may understand the concept of decimal numbers but may have trouble remembering the steps to complete the division algorithm. Long-term understanding and skill achievement are established together when students successively build upon concepts in a guided discovery process (Bruner, 1977).

Understanding fundamental concepts and accurately completing algorithms contribute to becoming numerate (mathematically proficient). These terms describe "what it means for anyone to learn mathematics successfully" (NRC, 2001, p. 4). More broadly, according to a national review of all relevant research on mathematics learning (NRC, 2001), mathematics learning is composed of five interrelated strands of thought: "the comprehension of ideas (conceptual understanding), flexible and accurate skills and procedures (procedural fluency), ability to formulate and solve problems (strategic competence), capacity to reflect and evaluate one's knowledge and ability to reason (adaptive reasoning), [and] a habitual inclination to make sense of and value what is being learned (productive disposition)" (NRC, 2001, p. 5).

The dissimilar learner is one who has experienced little success in all five strands or may, in fact, lack development of an entire strand. However, mathematical proficiency can be expected and achieved as adaptations are made to the curriculum in light of the learners' characteristics, such as relating problems to daily life interests or providing more time for cooperative strategic thinking.

Students reach higher levels of proficiency when they engage in lessons that are developmentally structured. The rate of time taken to move from one step to another varies according to students' progress, and two steps may be combined in one lesson. The general framework is as follows.

Structuring Lessons for Success

Step 1 Learners connect new concepts to those with which they are familiar and are actively engaged at a concrete level of understanding. Objects such as counters and base-10 blocks are manipulated to solve questions that represent authentic and interesting problems. For example, students are asked to demonstrate how many more cookies need to be baked for a class party if eight are already baked for the class of 15 students (each student is to get one cookie). When studying multiplication, learners gain a conceptual understanding of the operation by forming three groups of four counters, each representing Halloween candy collected by children. Connections are also made to previous lessons, such as relating long division to the mathematical idea of repeated subtraction. Questions are asked and students discuss their understanding of these mathematical concepts.

Step 2 Students represent their understanding with pictures or diagrams. For example, the sets of cookies appear as follows:

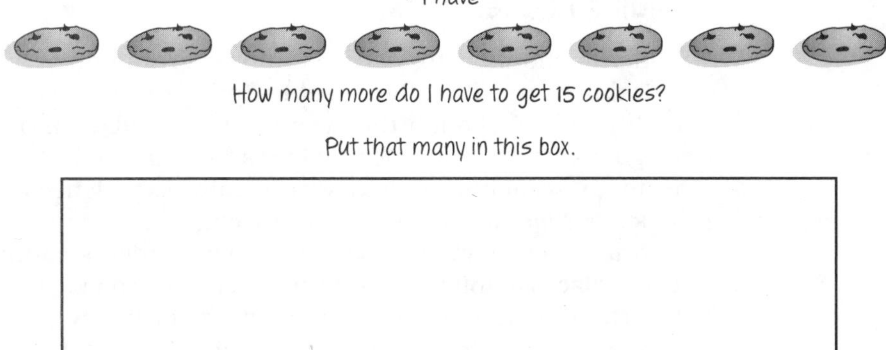

Three sets of four may be drawn like this:

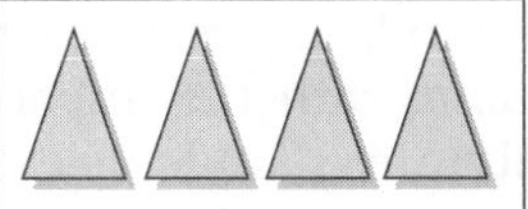 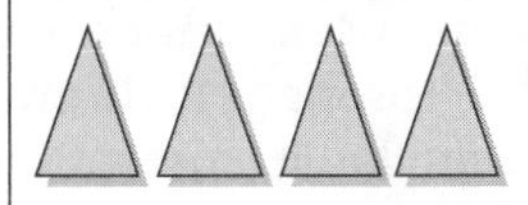 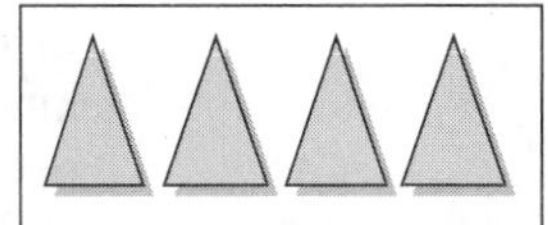

Twelve divided by four is related to repeated subtraction in a diagram such as:

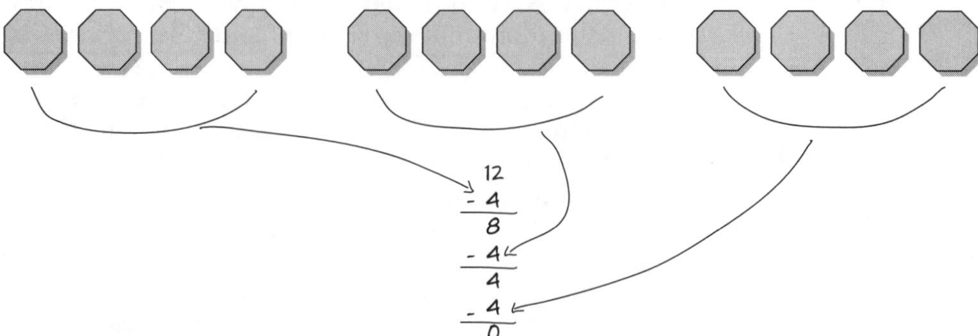

Step 3 Students attach numerals and number sentences to the drawings in this way:

A) 8 + □ = 15
□ = 7

because I need
7 more than
8 to get 15

B) 3 X 4 = 12
groups in each group

4 X 3 = 12
groups in each group

C) 4)12 → 3 groups of 4
in each group; in all

Step 4 Students practice skills and algorithmic procedures through a variety of activities and reinforcement lessons. The teacher provides continuous and targeted feedback at each learning step, so that errors of misunderstanding or procedure can be corrected quickly and effectively.

Valuing Mathematics

Students should also learn to value learning and the use of mathematics in their daily lives. Too often, people find it socially acceptable to say, "I am not a math person." Though they would find it embarrassing to claim that they are not good readers, innumeracy is readily admitted. Problems and examples that relate to students' interests and daily experiences establish relevance and value, particularly for students disengaged from studying mathematics. Presenting concepts in situations to which students connect, such as sports, currency, places of interest, and their own classrooms and schools, establishes the importance of mathematics on a personal level. Students will more readily participate and inquire when they care about content.

Meeting Standards for Dissimilar Learners

The National Council of Teachers of Mathematics' (NCTM) *Principles and Standards for School Mathematics* "provides a guide for focused, sustained efforts to improve students' school mathematics education" (NCTM, 2000, p. 5). The document presents a comprehensive set of standards for teaching mathematics from kindergarten through 12th grade. Dealing with the importance of meeting the needs of dissimilar learners, the Council states, "students exhibit different talents, abilities, achievements, needs, and interests in mathematics . . . [Nevertheless], all students must have access to the highest-quality mathematics instructional programs" (NCTM, 2000, p. 4).

Further, the *Principles and Standards* identify six principles, which are statements "reflecting basic precepts that are fundamental to a high-quality mathematics education" and are "perspectives on which educators can base decisions that affect school mathematics" (NCTM, 2000, p. 16). Principles include Equity, Curriculum, Teaching, Learning, Assessment, and Technology. Three (Equity, Teaching, and Learning) have particular relevance to dissimilar learners in a systems model for assessment and instructional purposes.

The Equity Principle: The Equity Principle states "excellence in mathematics education requires equity—high expectations and strong support for all students" (NCTM, 2000, p.11). The key and the theme of this book—is that all children can learn mathematics and deserve the opportunity to do so. Equity "demands that reasonable and appropriate accommodations be made as needed to promote access and attainment" (NCTM, 2000, p. 12).

Accommodations to make learning equitable should include:

- alternative approaches with manipulatives
- a wide variety of divergent questions
- games
- authentic materials such as calculators, menus, maps, spinners, and measuring tools
- more time on task
- peer tutoring

A more comprehensive list of suggestions to increase achievement is found in Appendix A, including ideas for affecting the content, behavior, and emotional environment for learners. Teachers can adapt the environment and deal with the wide range of abilities and experience in such a way that one or a combination of methods will stimulate achievement.

The Teaching Principle: "Effective mathematics teaching requires understanding what students know and need to learn and then challenging and supporting them to learn it well" (NCTM, 2000, p. 17). The Teaching Principle highlights the practice of designing instruction from students' point of view (a child-focused model). Teachers connect concepts and procedures that are new to students to what is already known. Instruction begins where children are, in terms of their ability to understand the language and the foundational ideas and experiences being taught. Conceptual development is guided and established by the instructional sequence. It assists all students with well-designed and connected lessons, step by step, toward deeper understanding and proficient skill.

Dissimilar learners are often those who are presented only with practice materials, in an effort to make certain they know "the basics." These students are negatively affected. They typically lack credible foundational concepts, so they have difficulty working with reinforcement practice materials that assume understanding. Lacking those concepts, students often forget procedures and then are remediated with more of the same misunderstood work, repeating a cycle of inaccurate or soon-forgotten practice of uninteresting skill-based assignments. The learner is not the center of instruction in terms of needs; rather, the drill and practice is the focus, which does not provide much long-term success.

The Teaching Principle is implemented when students engage in authentic, interesting, and challenging work. It stimulates interest and relates to real academic needs. Learners build a strong foundation on understanding "the basics."

The Learning Principle: The Learning Principle is closely related to the Teaching Principle. The Learning Principle calls for students to "learn mathematics with understanding, actively building new knowledge from experience and prior knowledge" (NCTM, 2000, p. 20). Presenting students with alternative approaches to learning the content of mathematics provides valuable opportunities to build upon those that are most closely related to students' thinking and previous experiences. For example, students are given place value blocks to bundle in groups of tens when modeling the regrouping necessary to subtract 9 from 35. When the hundreds place is introduced in the problem 235 – 79, students again work with place value blocks to actively connect the previous lesson with the new concept of regrouping hundreds to groups of tens.

The cognitive foundation, often found missing in the experiences of "dissimilar learners," is thus established and can be called upon in future lessons. Students are often able to invent and utilize their algorithms because they are making sense of mathematics for themselves. Discussions of concepts and answers to questions about thinking patterns and strategies provide further exploration into a variety of problem-solving methods.

Most important, teachers can support the principles by working with dissimilar learners to help them build a solid foundation of understanding by developing skill proficiency, the ability to reason, and to make sense of their work. Establishing an environment of trust in which novel ideas and alternative ways of thinking are acceptable is essential. The ultimate goal is to find strategies directly related to the students' assessed learning characteristics and to use that knowledge to build understanding, skill proficiency, and confidence for mathematical success.

The recent publication *Curriculum Focal Points for Prekindergarten Through Grade 8 Mathematics: A Quest for Coherence* (NCTM, 2006) provides guidelines for specifying the most significant mathematical concepts and skills at each grade level. The document also deals with issues related to students who struggle with learning mathematics by emphasizing that "instruction focused on a small number of key areas of emphasis provides extended experience with core concepts and skills" (NCTM, 2006, p. 5). Teachers and learners benefit from organized instruction, as identified by the focal points, that "assumes that the learning of mathematics is cumulative, with work in the later grades building on and deepening what students have learned in the earlier grades, without repetitious and inefficient re-teaching. A curriculum built on focal points also has the potential to offer opportunities for the diagnosis of difficulties and immediate intervention" (NCTM, 2006, p. 13). The NCTM *Principles and Standards* and *Curriculum Focal Points* stress the importance of establishing relevance, need, and number sense and connecting mathematics teaching and learning to related content and everyday experiences. The data analysis sheet (DAS) and mathematics improvement plan (MIP) included in this text are designed to guide teachers in their work to focus on students' assessed needs and provide a coherent, integrated mathematics curriculum for learners.

Identifying and Meeting the Needs of Dissimilar Learners

The authors of this text have created a three-step systematic approach to improving dissimilar learners' mathematics achievement. These three steps include the following components, completed in this order:

1. assessing the learner's strengths and weaknesses
2. completing a data analysis sheet (DAS)
3. designing a mathematics improvement plan (MIP) based on collected information

Step 1: Assessing strengths and areas of concern The first step in planning for instructional needs is to conduct a current-status assessment. Mathematics content knowledge, environmental factors that may affect learning, learning style, behavior, and the manner in which reinforcement typically occurs are considered. Assessment data is gathered from anecdotal records of daily observations; performance on classroom assignments; informal classroom mathematics tests, quizzes, and homework; and in-class work and/or formal standardized test results. This information is recorded on a DAS, a collection tool for assessment data that represents all major factors impacting a student's progress. The value of assessment, in general, is that it leads to an overall perception of the functional abilities of a learner's strengths and areas of concern. Data collected for a DAS informs instruction and prescribes a more accessible environment to influence future learning. A template for the DAS is found in Table 1.1. A brief description of the areas in the table follows:

- ***Context:*** Refers to the physical environment in which students exist. The setting would include the classroom, hallway, lunch room,

TABLE 1.1 A Sample Data Analysis Sheet

Data Analysis Sheet						
Student Name:						
Team Members:						
Data Analysis Record						
Context	**Content Assessment**	**Process**		**Behavior**		**Reinforcement**
		Input	Output	Academic	Social	
+	+	+	+	+	+	+
–	–	–	–	–	–	–

Note: The + symbols indicate strengths and the – symbols indicate areas of concern.

art room, gym, and bus. The contextual environment includes all environments in which the school holds administrative authority over the child.

- ***Content:*** Includes the curriculum and the current course of study in which the child is engaged.
- ***Process:*** Refers to methods, strategies, and tools that students prefer for accepting and expressing information, such as listening, speaking, writing, or drawing.
- ***Behavior:*** Includes academic and social behaviors such as whether the student enjoys learning through print material and/or in group settings, does or does not like to correct and complete assignments, is willing to ask questions of other students in a group, and is willing to socialize, communicate, and work well with teachers and classmates.
- ***Reinforcement:*** Refers to responses from the environment that cause inappropriate or appropriate behavior to reoccur (Sperbar, Premack, & Premack, 1996).

Recording Behavior Patterns: High probable behavior is described as a behavior that is likely to occur and will occur on a consistent basis. It might include the desire to play mathematics games or use the computer. Low probable behavior describes behavior that is very likely to occur below an average rate or at a very minimal level (Sperber et al., 1996). Low probable behavior could be the students' rate of studying alone or studying with others; completing drill pages or solving problems are also examples of behaviors that occur less often in dissimilar learners.

For example, a classroom climate context that is conducive to student achievement would be classified as a "+" symbol. However, if a student is having difficulty in the physical environment of the classroom, the teacher would mark this category with a "−" symbol. Likewise, students' unacceptable classroom behavior during the mathematics lesson is coded as a "−." Collecting and reviewing this information assists the teacher in recognizing which classroom activities foster high probable behavior and which do not. Also, teachers can focus on a low-occurring positive behavior in content, for example, as a starting point for lesson planning. If bundling tens during place value lessons is unfamiliar to students and is coded as a "−," teachers should begin with reviewing a skill that could be considered a "+," such as counting.

An additional dimension of this assessment approach is that context refers to all environments that students use in a typical school day. Often, the teacher records behavior only in the classroom, yet it is widely known that low-occurring behaviors most often occur outside of the room (Sperber et al., 1996). Student actions in all environments are reflective of learning achievement. Social and emotional behaviors, language usage, spatial awareness, and other academic functions recorded in any part of a school environment provide valuable assessment data. A significant purpose of the DAS is that it generates a large bank of strengths (plusses), which become available to teachers when looking for reinforcers in academic endeavors. Anything that the student likes to do and does well in the learning environment is a reinforcer and, conversely, anything the student does at a low rate of occurrence is something the student will avoid. This data collection provides the information for the actual DAS.

Step 2: Completing the DAS DAS information provides teachers with current behavioral data, collected from a real environment, and an informed foundation upon which to diagnose difficulties. The DAS process evaluates the child against herself and generates diagnostic and prescriptive information that is ready to use. The result frames the remediation plan for the MIP.

Utilizing the data listed for each of the areas—context, content, process, behavior, and reinforcement—the DAS is prepared for each student several times during the school year as learning conditions and/or a child's characteristics change. High- and low-probable-occurring behaviors (HPBs, LPBs) are reviewed and recorded for each category.

Completing the DAS: Instructions for completing the DAS are as follows:

1. Identify the data as collected.
2. Record the data for each category as a strength, an HPB or an LPB, including information from all environments. Define what a student does rather than what is not done. For example, record that a student "can count to 10" rather than "child cannot count to 10 or higher quantities."
3. Record behavioral terminology, including more than one data sample; for example, record that a student raised his hand, worked well in a group, or received feedback favorably as a "+," and record examples of inappropriate behaviors as a "−."
4. Record reinforcement activities such as giving oral praise or stickers for feedback.

A column becomes a "+" when it contains more cells with a "+" for high probable behavior than a "−" for low probable behavior. A sample DAS, with collected data, is shown in Table 1.2.

Case studies that contain additional examples of completed DAS forms are included in each chapter.

Step 3: Designing the MIP Mathematics instruction should focus on all factors that affect learning, while building on students' mathematical strengths and recognizing students' error patterns. As discussed, this information is gathered systematically on a DAS as an organizing tool for individualizing instructional needs. The teacher considers the DAS information, noting the particular type of classroom or learning environment (i.e., works best alone or with groups), reinforcement, and other factors that will affect the mathematics lesson to be designed. Based on recognizing how students learn in the classroom, the MIP is developed to recognize and generate more HPBs than LPBs in remediation activities that address error patterns. It is the totality of the mathematics instruction that must be considered rather than a repetition of lessons not learned well without a change in approach. A template for the MIP is given in Table 1.3.*

Completing the MIP Form: To complete an MIP, teachers must:

1. Review DAS information related to the learner's environment.
2. Diagnose a mathematics error pattern for a concept or skill within a particular topic, such as place value, whole-number computation, rational numbers, and problem solving.
3. Prescribe mathematics remediation strategies that encourage high-occurring behaviors and build upon low-occurring behaviors, including any content error patterns. If a student is regrouping whole numbers

*For your use, a second MIP template is provided in Appendix B.

The following is an example of typical information teachers might record under each column.

TABLE 1.2 How to Fill in the Data Analysis Sheet

Data Analysis Sheet						
Student:						
Team Members:						
Context	**Content Assessment**	**Process**		**Behavior**		**Reinforcement**
		Input	Output	Academic	Social	
+	+	+	+	+	+	+
Information should cover the strengths (+) and areas of concern (–) of a student's environment and his or her reactions to it, such as: • Works well when sitting by the window, alone at desk, with a peer, by the teacher, in the classroom, in the hallway, in the gym, on a bus, or in a group of peers • Open and friendly with peers, quietly working alone, anxious to work with teacher • Enjoys group activities, likes being paired with peers or working with teacher • Likes being in front of the class, by the teacher, alone at desk	*Information should cover the strengths (+) and areas of concern (–) representative of specific skills associated with learning mathematics, such as:* ***Learned Concepts I*** • Reads and recognizes numerals • Knows subtraction involving zero • Knows proper alignment of digits ***Learned Concepts II*** • Recognizes sums less than 10 • Knows that place value rules exist • Knows how to borrow across a zero	*Information should cover the strengths (+) and areas of concern (–) in which the student takes in information when learning and puts out the information gained from his or her learning, such as:* • Listens to teacher talk or read, or listens to students read • Follows directions given in outline form, traces math problems with fingers, counts out loud or memorizes quickly • Sits by self or in group, or sits near teacher	• Verbally responds as individual or in groups, enjoys group discussion, or likes giving oral reports • Writes with pencil and paper or types on computer, does team writing, develops outline of work, or develops graphics	*Information should cover the strengths (+) and areas of concern (–) of the student's academic and social behaviors, such as:* • Enjoys learning activities, raises hand to answer questions, or assists others in learning tasks • Wants to complete activities • Shows willingness to hand material in to teacher, to review or to make corrections on work	• Cooperates well with peers or teacher • Enjoys social aspects of school • Is well-liked • Follows school rules • Accepts verbal or visual prompts or accepts corrections of work and continues working • Waits turn for others to respond	*Information should cover the strengths (+) and areas of concern (–) in which the student reacts to reinforcement methods used in learning, such as:* • Likes being with peers or teacher • Enjoys helping adults and being praised • Enjoys rewards such as candy, popcorn, toys, stickers, or free time, or collecting points or stars to earn special privileges • Likes being in front of class or getting to talk with teacher one-on-one
–	–	–	–	–	–	–
• Behaves shyly around adults, around peers, in group situations • Can't sit for a long period of time; doesn't communicate well in groups • Doesn't like to work alone, be in front of class, work with teacher one-on-one, or do group work	***Error Pattern I*** • Records more than a single digit for place value • Unable to express multidigit numerals using place value system ***Error Pattern II*** • Borrows from wrong place • Does not regroup • Does not connect numerals to concept underlying the collecting and trading principles	• Doesn't listen well in class, to directions, or to other peers; does not like to ask for help; does not take time to read directions, or reads directions in a hurry • Does not like reading, group assignments, multitask assignments, or oral reports	• Slow to complete assignments; doesn't complete assignments at all, or completes assignments late • Completes work in a hurry; avoids oral reports or participating in group work	• Can't stay focused, can't complete a written task, or can't stay seated • Doesn't like to make mistakes in front of peers or have mistakes pointed out by teacher • Doesn't pay attention in large-group instruction	• Argues with peers; defiant with teacher; behaves shyly with peers or teacher, or only does well in one-on-one interactions • Becomes frustrated and angry when she makes errors, or upset when others don't do their share of group work • Talks out of turn in class	• Doesn't like made-up work or extra credit work • Doesn't like tangible reinforcements, such as stickers, candy, or free time • Doesn't like being with teacher one-on-one, or doesn't like spending time with peers

Note: The + symbols indicate strengths and the – symbols indicate areas of concern.

TABLE 1.3 A Sample Mathematics Improvement Plan

Time				
Context				
Content				
Process	Input			
	Output			
Behavior	Academic			
	Social			
Reinforcement				

Note: The + symbols indicate strengths and the – symbols indicate areas of concern.

TABLE 1.4 How to Fill in the Mathematics Improvement Plan: Sample (Name of Error Pattern Addressed)

Time		**30 minutes**	**15–20 minutes**	**20–30 minutes**
Context		Close to teacher (+) Small-group setting (–)	With peer (+) Close to teacher (+)	Working independently (–)
Content		Counts to 10 aloud, records and illustrates groups of 10s	Grouping objects in bundles of 10s (+)	Records quantities (+)
Process	Input	Oral instruction by teacher (–)	Tactile material (+)	Tactile materials supported by visuals and graphics (+)
	Output	Oral answers in single words (+) Working on laptop (+)	Oral activities (+) Calculator usage (+)	Reports answers orally to teacher (+)
Behavior	Academic	Completes assignments quickly (–) Work is not carefully completed (–)	Turns in assignments (+) Accepts teacher directions (+)	Staying in seat (–)
	Social	Follows group directions (+) Talks to friends during lessons (–)	Positive response to peers' requests (+)	Monitoring for student use of self-control (–)
Reinforcement		Oral feedback (+)	Allowed movement in classroom (+)	Group activities (+) Sitting with peers (+)

Note: The + symbols indicate strengths and the – symbols indicate areas of concern.

incorrectly when subtracting, the teacher may identify the specific misunderstandings as conceptual errors. Strategies involving manipulatives and drawings, as well as methods to encourage HPBs, such as working in small groups and receiving frequent written reinforcement, are then selected and listed in the MIP.

4. Complete the MIP with plans for each cell that will elicit HPBs. Build each cell's activities on "+" behaviors, which are those behaviors that students can do or will like, in terms of how they learn best. Spend no more than 30 minutes on lessons or activities that will pose a great cognitive mathematics challenge to students.
5. Implement the prescribed remediation strategies in the context of the learning climate and student behavior.

In this way, the MIP is based on the DAS information and serves as a guide for a well-planned, child-centered, focused learning approach. As new topics are introduced, mathematics achievement is again assessed and a new MIP for the content component is written.

See Table 1.4 for a sample of a completed MIP with collected data. A completed MIP form is included in each chapter.

Conclusions

Mathematics achievement has been defined in terms of both understanding and skill levels, the ability to reason and solve problems, and a positive disposition toward learning. Many pupils who have not succeeded as well as they, or their parents or teachers, would expect are "dissimilar learners." They do not progress satisfactorily when taught with traditional, one-dimensional instructional approaches. Environmental and personal reasons for underachievement also affect learning performance. A more targeted and systematic approach that assesses students' needs and abilities, the environment, classroom, behavior, learning style, and means of reinforcement is essential for designing a successful strategy. Strategies that consider all aspects of the learner's instructional needs can more accurately address the needs of dissimilar learners and can lead to a global approach to success.

This book is based on the premise that teachers should utilize a systematic approach to diagnosing their students' specific mathematics error patterns, should prescribe plans of action, and should implement those techniques in the context of the students' learning environment. Mathematics teaching and learning that stresses the relevance of the discipline to students' lives, connects rules to conceptual understanding, offers challenging, authentic, and interesting problems to all students, and encourages students to express their reasoning in a positive classroom climate leads to achievement.

Discussion Questions

1. What are the advantages of addressing the learning needs of dissimilar learners with a systematic instructional approach?
2. What characteristics are often found in students referred to as "dissimilar"?
3. Why is assessment so important in developing a useful DAS or MIP, as in developing an individualized education program, for students?
4. Describe an activity that relates primary (grades K–3) and also upper elementary (grades 4–6) students' everyday experiences to a lesson on the value of learning mathematics.
5. How does focusing mathematics teaching on specific HPBs encourage students to achieve?
6. What mathematical thinking processes do the NCTM publications *Principles and Standards* and *Curriculum Focal Points* recommend be taught through mathematics instruction for all students as well as those who are struggling with mathematics? How do thinking processes enhance and make mathematics learning more effective?
7. Which teaching principles have the most impact, in your experience? Explain your reasoning.
8. Interview three classmates or acquaintances. Ask them if they had difficulty learning mathematics. If so, what reasons could they provide for those experiences? Identify their reasons as environmental or personal. Explain your choices.
9. How does learning mathematics in the context of understanding and then practicing the concepts differ from how you were taught mathematics? Provide specific examples.

References

Arbaugh, F., Lannin, K., Arhauch, F., Barker D. D., & Townsend, B. (2006). Making the most of student errors. *Teaching Children Mathematics*, *13*(3), 182–186.

Beck, R. C. (2000). *Motivation: Theories and principles* (4th ed.). Upper Saddle River, NJ: Merrill/Prentice Hall.

Bernard, B. (1995). Fostering resilience in children. *ERIC/EECE Digest EDO-PS99*, 1–6.

Brownell, W. (1935). Psychological considerations in the learning and teaching of arithmetic. *In the Teaching of Arithmetic.* New York: Bureau of Publications, Teachers College, Columbia University: National Council of Teachers of Mathematics Yearbook, 10.

Bruner, J. (1977). *The process of education.* Cambridge, MA: Harvard University Press.

Clausen-May, Tandi. (2005). *Teaching math to pupils with different learning styles.* Paul Chapman Educational Publishing, A Sages Publications Company, Thousand Oaks California, London, England, New Delhi, India.

Clements, D. H. (1997). (Mis?) constructing constructivism. *Teaching children mathematics, 4*, 198–200.

Cooper, C., Lingg, M., Puricelli, A., & Yard, G. (1995). *Dissimilar learners.* St. Louis, MO: Pegasus Press.

Hatano, G. (1996). A conception of knowledge acquisition and its implications for mathematics education. In L. P. Steffe et al. (Eds.), *Theories of mathematical learning* (pp. 197–217). Mahwah, NJ: Lawrence Erlbaum.

Hiebert, J. (Ed.). 1986. *Conceptual and procedural knowledge: The case of mathematics.* Hillsdale, NJ: Lawrence Erlbaum.

National Council of Teachers of Mathematics. (2000). *Principles and standards for school mathematics.* Reston, VA: Author.

National Council of Teachers of Mathematics. (2006). *Curriculum focal points for prekindergarten through grade 8 mathematics: A quest for coherence.* Reston, VA: Author.

National Research Council. (1989). *Everybody counts: A report to the nation on the future of mathematics education.* Washington, DC: Author.

Oswald, M., Johnson, B., & Howard, S. (2003). Quantifying and evaluating resilience-promoting factors in teachers' beliefs and perceived roles. *Research in Education, 70,* 50–64.

Phillips. J. M., & Gully, S. M. (1997). Role of goal orientation, ability, need for achievement, and locus of control in the self-efficacy and goal-setting process. *Journal of Applied Psychology, 82,* 792–802.

Piaget, J. (1965). *The child's concept of number.* New York: W. W. Norton.

Randolph, T. D., & Sherman H. J. (2001). Alternative algorithms: Increasing options, reducing errors. *Teaching Children Mathematics, 7*(8), 480–484.

Sowder, J. T. (1992). Making sense of numbers in school mathematics. In G. Leinhardt, R. Putnam, & R. A. Hattrup (Eds.), *Analysis of arithmetic for mathematics teaching* (pp. 1–51). Hillsdale, NJ: Lawrence Erlbaum.

Sperbar, D., Premack, D., & Premack, A. J., (Eds.). (1996). *Causal cognition: A multidisciplinary approach.* Cary, NC: Oxford University Press.

Usiskin, Zalman. (1998). Paper and pencil algorithms in a calculator and computer age. In L. J. Morrow & M. J. Kenney (Eds.), *Teaching and learning of algorithms in school.*

VanDevender, E., & Harris, M. J. (1987). Why students make math errors. *Academic Therapy, 23*(1), 79–85.

Wang, M. (1998). Building educational resilience. *Phi Delta Kappa Fastbacks*, 430, 7–61.

Werner, E., & Smith, R. (1998). *Vulnerable but invincible: A longitudinal study of resilient children and youth.* New York: Adams Bannister Cox.

Chapter 2

Place Value

> I know about place value. If I am sitting in my reading group, the ones are on the same side of the room as the clock. If I am sitting in my math group, the ones column is by the door. It all depends on the direction you are looking. But the numbers from 11–19 don't fit any rules at all. You just have to memorize them.
>
> —*Second Grader*

The Impact of Place Value on Mathematics

Place value is perhaps the most fundamental concept imbedded in the elementary and middle school mathematics curriculum. Correctly solving problems that involve computation of whole and rational numbers is dependent upon understanding and expressing multidigit quantities. "It is absolutely essential that students develop a solid understanding of the base ten numeration system and place-value concepts by the end of grade 2. Students need many instructional experiences to develop their understanding of the systems including how numbers are written (NCTM, 2000, p. 81). Yet, knowing when to exchange groups of ones for tens or how to handle a zero in the hundreds place when subtracting, for example, confuses many students who then struggle with algorithms. Learners can correct these and other misunderstandings by solving real-world problems with hands-on materials and learning aids such as counters, base ten manipulatives, and place value charts. "Understanding and fluency are related . . . and there is some evidence that understanding is the basis for developing procedural fluency" (Kilpatrick, Swafford, & Findell, 2001, p. 197). Correctly recording numerals in the quotient when dividing 348 by 30 is an example of demonstrating procedural fluency.

Research indicates that students' experience using physical models to represent hundreds, tens, and ones can be effective in dealing with place value issues early in the curriculum. The materials should "help them [students] think about how to combine quantities and eventually how this process connects with written procedure" (Kilpatrick et al., 2001, p. 198). However, "merely having manipulatives available does not insure that students will think about how to group the quantities and express them symbolically" (NCTM, 2000, p. 80). Rather, students must construct meaning for themselves by using manipulatives to represent groups of tens in classroom discussions and in authentic, cooperative activities.

This chapter will deal with typical multidigit place value errors of both conceptual understanding and procedure. Appropriate remediation activities will be described for each place value error pattern.

What Is Place Value?

Place value systems are also termed positional systems because the value of a number is determined in part by the position or place it holds. In a decimal place value system, for example, each digit represents a group or base of 10. Place value "pertains to an understanding that the same numeral represents different amounts depending on which position it is in" (Charlesworth P. & Lind, 2003, pp. 308–309). The place value concept enables us to represent any value using 10 symbols (0–9) and compute using whole numbers. Other positional or place value systems include those based on groups of 12, as seen in clock time for counting hours, or groups of 60, for minutes in the hour.

The following are examples of regrouping in base-10 and base-12 system in whole-number algorithms. Current literature (Ma, 1999) uses the term "regrouping." It applies to the exchanges of base groups in the four operations of addition, subtraction, multiplication, and division. For example, in

$$\begin{array}{r} 1 \\ 745 \\ +\ 389 \\ \hline 1134 \end{array}$$

10 ones in the sum of the ones column, 14, is regrouped to the tens column as "1 ten."

Likewise, for the following example:

$$\begin{array}{rr} 6\phantom{\text{ ft}} & 14\phantom{\text{ in.}} \\ \not{7}\text{ ft} & \not{2}\text{ in.} \\ -\ 4\text{ ft} & 8\text{ in.} \\ \hline 2\text{ ft} & 6\text{ in.} \end{array}$$

"7 feet" is renamed to "6 feet 12 inches." The quantity of "12 inches" is combined with 2 inches to be named as "14 inches" when computing in a place value system based on groups of 12.

The Hindu-Arabic Numeration System: The Hindu-Arabic place value numeration system is based on the principle of collection and exchange of groups of 10. In this system, 10 ones can be traded and represented by one group of 10, 10 groups of 10 each can be exchanged and represented as 100, 10 groups of 100 each can be regrouped and represented as 1,000, and so on. This mechanism of collection and exchange makes possible a system in which only 10 unique symbols are necessary to express any quantity.

The total value of a number is determined by multiplying each quantity by the value of its position or place and then adding all those values together. The following example indicates how the total value is found for 47 and for 385.

$$(4 \times 10) + (7 \times 1) = 47$$

$$(3 \times 100) + (8 \times 10) + (5 \times 1) = 385$$

Several important properties of the base-10 place value system include:

1. Ten unique symbols (0–9) express any numerical quantity.
2. The value of each base-10 place is multiplied by 10 as the digits move to the left from the ones place.

Quantity:	4	3	2
Place Value:	100	10	1
Total Value:	400	30	2

3. The decimal point is a symbol that enables the system to express parts of numbers. As one moves to the right of the decimal point in a number, the value of each place is divided by 10 (tenths, hundredths, thousandths, and so on). For example, the value of each place is as follows:

0.	2	3	4	5
	.1	.01	.001	.0001

4. The zero symbol (0) is a placeholder that represents a set that has no members or elements and is integral to expressing and computing quantity.

Why Do Students Struggle with Place Value?

Common Errors

Misunderstanding and errors are evident in student work when place value concepts and procedures are learned in isolation from previous knowledge and with little meaning (Baroody, 1990). For example, not remembering from which direction to count over the number of places when multiplying decimals can be a result of not understanding why the decimal point is placed in a specific spot in the product.

Conceptual and Procedural Errors

In general, conceptual misunderstandings occur when students lack fundamental understanding and experience with positional systems (Kamii, 1986). Learners struggle with trading groups for collections of groups, such as regrouping 10 tens for 1 hundred. There is a lack of understanding of the place value structure, that is, multiplying each place value position to the left of a number by the base (such as 10) and dividing each place to the right of the decimal point by the base.

If students' errors are conceptual in nature, remediation begins with using manipulative materials. These might include place value blocks, counters of any type, and place value charts. Use of more than print-based activity is critical for students needing less-traditional approaches (Clausen-May, 2005). When errors

FIGURE 2.1
Common Errors Related to Place Value

- Not regrouping when necessary
- Regrouping every place, whether necessary or not
- Regrouping the incorrect amount
- Regrouping in the wrong column
- Regrouping in the wrong base
- Using the same digits to regroup over and over
- Ignoring "0" as a placeholder

are more procedural in nature, students forget rules and algorithmic steps but do understand how the system works. Remediation activities do not necessarily have to involve manipulative materials in those cases. Lessons are focused on drawing and/or representing objects and then connecting numerals to those figures or making notations as reminders. For example, when subtracting, students can draw an arrow over the "2" if that helps them remember where to start. Or, pupils could circle the ones column in each example, prior to computing, in order to remember to regroup that place and not the tens place.

$$\begin{array}{r} \downarrow \\ 432 \\ -29 \\ \hline \end{array} \qquad \begin{array}{r} 432 \\ -29 \\ \hline \end{array}$$

The most common errors specifically related to place value include those in Figure 2.1.

About the Student: Colin

Colin is a composite picture of a fourth grader with specific learning needs and abilities who demonstrates difficulty with fundamental place value concepts and the procedural skill of expressing quantity.

Colin is a bright fourth grader who likes school. He enjoys learning activities and the social aspect of school. He is open and friendly with peers but is more reticent around adults. He has a very strong sense of fairness and is well liked by both boys and girls. He has excellent coordination and prefers an active life, which makes it difficult for him to sit still for long periods and stay focused on routine tasks. He generally follows school and classroom rules and rarely receives a reprimand. He does not like to make mistakes and is slow to complete assignments because he tries to get everything done perfectly. Rather than turn in incomplete work, he will put it in his desk. Colin does not like to ask for help because he does not want to look "stupid."

His reading skills are appropriate for fourth grade. However, Colin dislikes reading and delays tasks involving reading. When avoidance tactics are unsuccessful, he reads quickly and with little attention to nuances and detail. Consequently, he misses important information. Colin's reading style causes him to misinterpret directions. His reading style also causes him to think he has read one thing when that is not what was written, which results in his answers being incorrect. He then becomes frustrated and angry with himself but does not acknowledge the connection between his approach to reading and the resulting errors in his work.

Colin quickly memorizes math facts. He knows addition, subtraction, and multiplication facts and is learning division facts. Colin's rapid reading and skimming of details causes problems for him in math. He may not attend to all the steps in multistep directions, which results in errors. Colin's poor reading habits make solving word problems difficult. When confronted with his errors he becomes frustrated and makes self-deprecating comments.

Colin enjoys helping his peers, but especially enjoys helping adults. He likes to feel useful, but quickly sees through "made up" jobs. He likes to earn free time, which he usually spends drawing or playing games with friends. Colin does not respond to tangible reinforcers, such as stickers or points, unless the points lead to free time or helping time. Colin prefers learning tasks that require active participation or a hands-on approach. He enjoys class discussion and is an active participant in group work.

Error Patterns: Diagnosis, Prescription, Remediation

The following error patterns are those made by Colin on different days, when he worked on computations that required place value understanding and skills. These mistakes are typical of many children's thought patterns. The next sections include an analysis of each type of error and a diagnosis of its origin as either conceptual or procedural in nature. Based on that information, as well as the factors that affect Colin's learning in general, remediation activities for each error pattern are described.

Place Value Error Pattern I for Colin

The first type of place value error is found in Student Work Sample I for Colin. Colin responded to six questions asking him to express, with numerals, various quantities that are written with number words.

Diagnosing the Error: The teacher examines Colin's work and identifies the type of mistake he is making as conceptual or procedural. Mathematical strengths are also noted. These might include Colin's ability to write numerals, order numerals, identify places correctly, and more. Record your own analysis of the error pattern you detect in the top half of the box and the strengths you see in the bottom half of the box:

Colin's Error Pattern(s):
Colin's Strengths:

A diagnosis of Colin's work reveals that Colin can read and recognize single-digit numerals. However, he does not understand the rules for writing multi-place numerals using place value notation. He expresses each digit as a

STUDENT WORK SAMPLE I FOR COLIN

Express the following number words as numbers:

1. fifty seven

   507

2. six hundred forty two

   60042

3. seven hundred fifty thousand fifty eight

   7005000058

4. four thousand seven hundred twenty eight

   4000700208

5. nine hundred two

   9002

6. two thousand five hundred ninety

   200050090

separate cardinal value rather than multiplying each numeral by its place value (4 × 1000). For example, he writes "50" instead of "5" to indicate the number of tens in "57." Colin lacks a conceptual understanding of place value in that his notation is not connected to any sense of a positional system.

An example of a completed DAS for Colin's error is shown in Table 2.1. Characteristics, both positive and negative, are listed for the context in which Colin learns. The table also contains information about Colin's input and output processes, academic and social behaviors, and the reinforcers that are most effective to promote overall achievement.

Prescription: Colin should work with both nonproportional and proportional materials to build collections of tens to trade and represent with numerals. Nonproportional manipulatives could include pennies, dimes, Popsicle sticks, coffee stirrers, and buttons. These items can be grouped in bundles of 10 to be traded. However, none of the objects is proportionally 10 times the size of the others. Each stick or coin is about the same size. Each single item represents one unit.

TABLE 2.1 Data Analysis Sheet

Student: Colin						
Team Members: Sherman, Richardson, and Yard						
Context	**Content Assessment**	**Process**		**Behavior**		**Reinforcement**
		Input	Output	Academic	Social	
+	+	+	+	+	+	+
• Likes school • Open and friendly with peers • Likes to be clustered with his peers • Enjoys all cooperative learning activities • Enjoys any and all group participatory activities • Likes being in front of class	***Learned Concepts I*** • Reads and recognizes numerals • Reads numerals from left to right • Correctly identifies each place value in numerals ***Learned Concepts II*** • Reads and recognizes numerals • Knows that place value rules exist ***Learned Concepts III*** • Reads and recognizes numerals • Reads numerals from left to right • Correctly identifies each place value in numerals	• Reading skills are grade appropriate • Memorizes quickly • Concrete in his thinking	• Excellent coordination; prefers an active lifestyle • Retains information he has learned • Enjoys group discussions • Is good at putting ideas into written form • Once he gets started he seldom fails to complete his work • Likes giving oral reports	• Enjoys learning activities • Likes concrete activities • Wants to complete his activities	• Enjoys social aspects of school • Strong sense of fairness • Well liked by boys and girls • Follows school rules	• Likes being with peers • Enjoys helping adults • Likes to feel useful • Free time is important to him • Likes drawing and playing games with his friends • Points help if they lead him to free time or helping time • Likes being in front of class
–	–	–	–	–	–	–
• Reticent around adults • Can't sit for a long period of time • Doesn't like to work with his teacher on a one-on-one basis • Doesn't like to work alone • Doesn't like to be isolated in the classroom	***Error Pattern I*** • Unable to express multidigit numerals using place value system ***Error Pattern II*** • Cannot determine order, inequalities, equalities among multidigit numbers ***Error Pattern III*** • Does not regroup in bases of 12 and 60 • Uses groups of 10 incorrectly	• Does not like to ask for help • Does not like reading • Misinterprets directions • Thinks he has read something when he hasn't • Doesn't do well with multitask assignments	• Slow to complete assignments • Refuses to submit incomplete assignments • Reads quickly with little attention to material • Misses important information • Has difficulty reading word problems	• Can't stay focused for a long period of time • Doesn't like to make mistakes • Unable to connect his reading problems to his errors	• Becomes frustrated and angry when he makes errors • Becomes upset when he believes a group member is not doing his share	• Doesn't like made-up work or tangible reinforcers such as stickers and candy • Avoids independent reading • Doesn't like being with teacher one-on-one

Note: The + symbols indicate strengths and the – symbols indicate areas of concern.

The craft sticks shown are bundled in groups of 10. Each stick is identical in size. Groups of 10 can only be represented with these materials when 10 of the sticks, or 10 of the tens groups, are bundled together.

Proportional Materials: In contrast, proportional materials are specifically designed so that one object in the collection is proportionally 10 times the size of another. Place value blocks are proportional materials. A set of these includes unit cubes that represent the ones place, longs that are actually 10 times the length of one unit cube, flats that represent the size of 10 longs, and a block that is the size of 10 hundreds flats stacked in a column. The place value materials are shown below.

Having Colin manipulate materials and cooperate in a group setting will build on his strengths, according to his DAS. Activities should incorporate those characteristics and should progress from using hands-on manipulatives to representing the objects with drawings and numerals. Colin first collects groups of

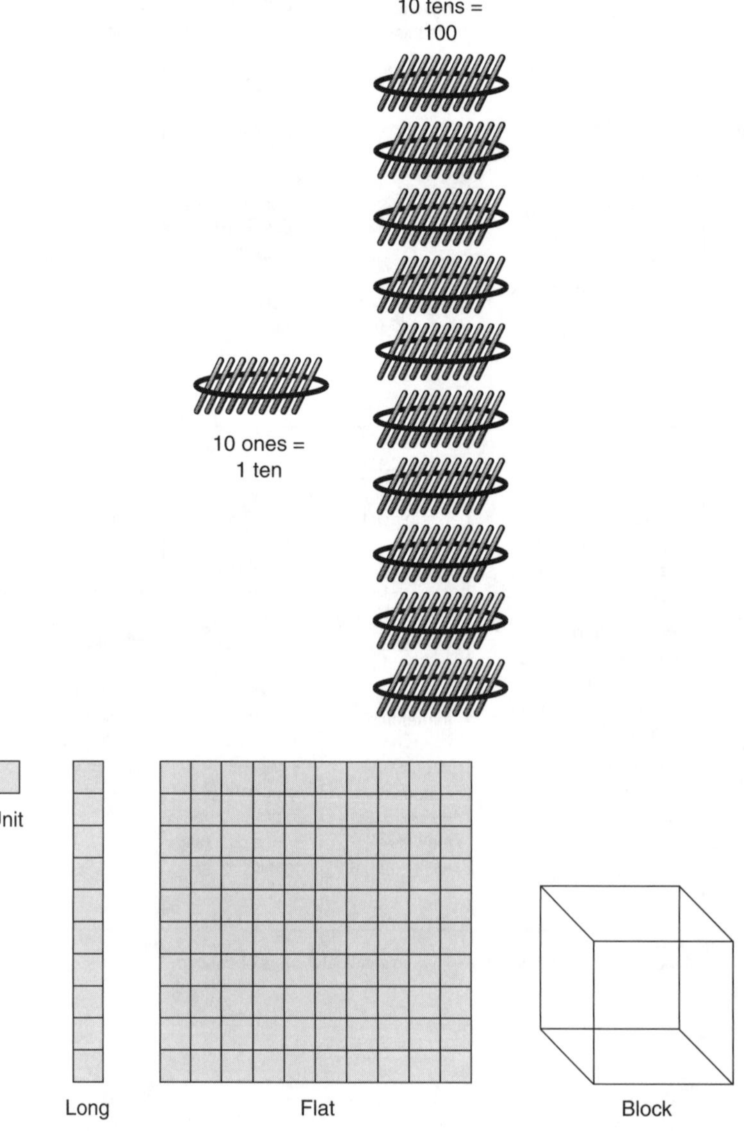

10 ones, then trades them for longs (groups of 10), and continues in this manner with 10 longs traded for a hundreds blocks, and so on. The overall plan for Colin will be to provide opportunities to develop a strong conceptual foundation of place value and number sense by using materials to express amounts in real-world problems posed to him.

Remediation: The following remediation activities, beginning with the use of hands-on materials, are described in this section and listed in the MIP in Table 2.2.

Introductory Activity: The teacher should begin with two-digit numbers in real-world problems to solve, such as:

> Our school is holding a physical fitness day for all students. Our class is supposed to tell the principal how many of us can run one mile in less than a half hour. How can I use the place value chart to help us show the number of students who do that, and also write the correct number for the school office and the awards ceremony?

TABLE 2.2 Mathematics Improvement Plan I for Colin: Writing Multiplace Numerals Using Place Value Notation

Time		30 minutes	20–30 minutes	15–20 minutes
Context		Classroom activities of a cooperative learning style, Colin will work with four of his peers on a group activity (+)	Independent seatwork (+)	Colin will work in the classroom, with a classmate whom he likes, on this activity (+)
Content		Trades nonproportional and proportional blocks of groups of 10 to answer authentic, real-world questions (+)	Independently rolls cubes to fill place value chart reflecting solutions to real-world problems (+)	Works with a student on "Reach the Target" and placing index cards on multidigit numerals to express them correctly (+)
Process	Input	Teacher gives multiple instructions for the task at hand (–)	The work has visual and written examples of the task at hand (+)	The written directions are at grade level and have a singular task (+)
	Output	Group engages in manipulative activities that require a concrete outcome (+)	Is expected to write his results (+)	The words in the word problem will challenge Colin (–)
Behavior	Academic	Group produces a single written project, and all students have input (+)	Completes work for teacher feedback (+)	Teacher encourages student pair to ask questions (+)
	Social	Direct group to work well together and have a sense of responsibility (+)	Could be easily frustrated (–)	His classmate is one whom he likes and he trusts (+)
Reinforcement		If the group does well, members will get free time to play games with a partner (+)	For every problem he gets right he will get to help the teacher with a needed classroom task (+)	Teacher gives oral and written comments (+)

Note: The + symbols indicate strengths and the – symbols indicate areas of concern.

Tens	Ones
Record (Numeral):	Record (Numeral):

Colin is given 27 single Popsicle sticks and the place value chart. He places all 27 in the ones column of the chart, because each represents the quantity of "one," a single unit. Colin is encouraged to then bundle the sticks in groups of 10 to help him visualize what groups of 10 look like.

He should also report situations in which he notices groups of 10 in various authentic, real-world settings, including the fact that he has 10 fingers and that the U.S. currency system uses base-10 groups of coins and paper money.

Colin counts out 10 sticks, puts a rubber band around that group, and places it in the tens section of the place value chart. He sees he made one group of 10 from the 27 with which he began. Colin continues counting by repeating to count and group by 10s and placing the bundle in the 10s column. Leftover single sticks (7) are placed in the ones column.

To record quantity, Colin writes the number of bundles of 10 he sees in the tens column slot and the number of single sticks he has in the ones column area of the place value chart. It would then look like this:

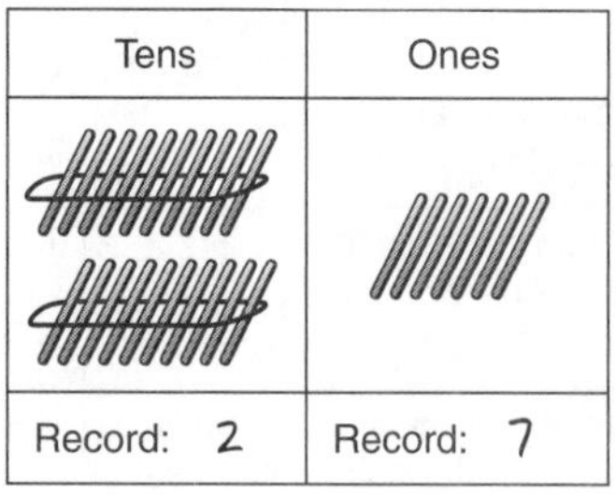

Tens	Ones
Record: 2	Record: 7

Colin reads the number or is helped by the teacher to say "27." The teacher asks Colin why 20 is not written as a "2" and a "0" in the tens column and whether or not the "2" in the tens place represents both digits in the numeral "20."

Using Place Value Blocks: Working with proportional materials, Colin lines up 10 units next to a base-10 long. He gently glides 10 units aside, using the long, so that he has the 1 long in front of him. He writes, in his math journal, "1 ten = 10 ones." He can illustrate the base-10 materials as well to help him remember what that equation means. Colin then trades 10 of the longs for a hundred flat by measuring 10 longs next to the flat. Because the flat and 10 longs take up the same amount of space, he records that "1 hundred = 10 tens," and draws a diagram by tracing them in his journal to show the equivalence:

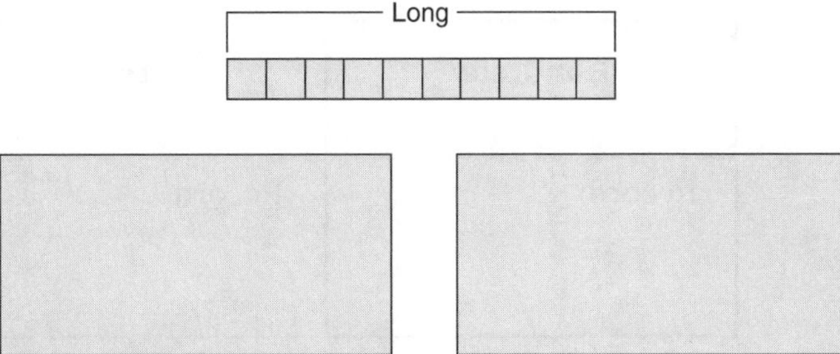

Concept/Skill Building Games: Colin plays the following "Reach the Target" game with the class and teacher to continue with the trading principle using proportional materials. A target number of 27, for example, is announced by the leader and a wooden number cube marked with digits 0 to 5 is rolled. Working with another student to build confidence, Colin and his partner place the number of ones units in the ones column according to the number called. If "3" were called, they would place three single units in the ones column. When 10 units are eventually placed in the ones column by any of the players, they trade them for one rod to be placed in the tens column. The first group that has gathered two longs in the tens column and seven units in the ones column, for example, by virtue of filling the ones column and trading a long for 10 ones, wins. The chart would look as follows:

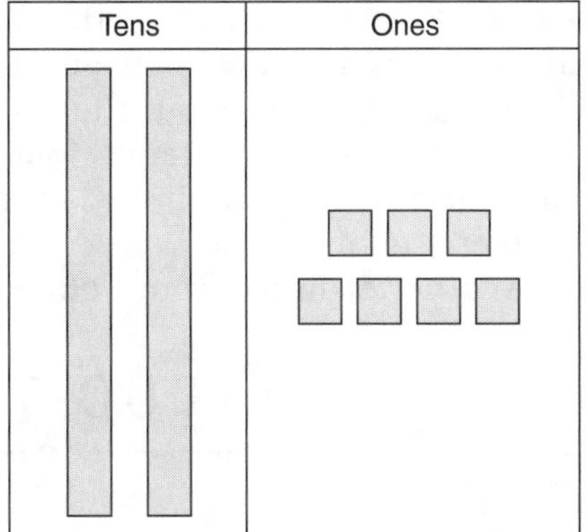

The winning team must record the value of "27" on the board, explaining to the class why "2" in the tens column represents two groups of 10 and the "7" represents 7 ones. The game continues for players to reach additional targets such as 37, 46, and so on.

Target numbers from 11 to 19 should be avoided until several two-digit examples are used. "Fourteen" and "eleven" are unique numeral words, which do not easily lend themselves to the place value system for two-digit numbers. "Twenty-seven" is more clearly associated with the quantity it represents (2 tens and 7 ones). In fact, the teens numbers are expressed in reverse to the base-10 system. Instead of naming the tens digit first, as in "twenty-seven," we say "nineteen," in which case the ones digit is expressed first.

Continue this activity of trading for groups of 10 by extending the place value chart to three places. Students label the chart as before, but include an additional place for the hundreds column.

Hundreds	**Tens**	**Ones**
Record:	Record:	Record:

To reach a target number of 352, for instance, number cubes are again rolled for each team. Players place the indicated number of markers in the ones column, as before. When 10 units are gathered in the ones column, they are traded for one long. When students find they have 10 longs in the center column, the group of 10 tens is traded for a flat. The teacher should pause in the activity, at several points, so that students can report the quantity they have so far grouped and record it. In this way, Colin has to write numbers such as "239" with a numeral in each place, rather than writing each place value separately, as in "200309." Words should also be written and attached to the numerals to form the association of materials to symbols of numerals and words. It is important to record numerals with materials to establish conceptual connections.

Writing Numbers Correctly: Colin writes digits from 0 to 9 on a set of 10 blank index cards. An incorrect response from Student Work Sample I, such as "507" instead of "57," is written on the board or a paper. The number "57" is read aloud to him. Colin now knows that 50 is represented by a 5 in the tens place, and he is asked where to put the card with the "5" on top of the "507" so the "5" can represent a group of tens. Colin should cover the "5" and the "0" with the "5" card, and then place the "7" card on top of the "7." In this way, Colin uses the numeral as it should be recorded so that each digit represents its correct place. Another example from Colin's Student Work Sample I is as follows:

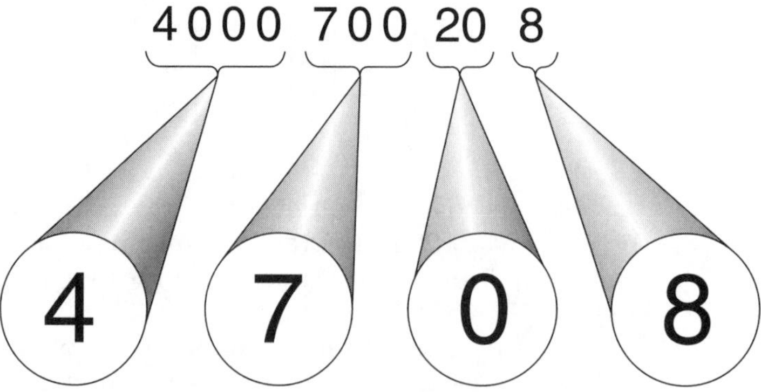

Place Value Error Pattern II for Colin

The second type of place value error is found in Student Work Sample II for Colin. Colin was asked to list quantities in order when presented with a choice of two- or three-digit numbers.

Diagnosing the Error: Examine the mistake Colin is making but also consider his conceptual and procedural strengths. These might include his ability to read two-digit numbers, his understanding of the value of single-digit numbers, and how he writes his numbers. You can list additional information in the following box.

Colin's Error Pattern(s):
Colin's Strengths:

STUDENT WORK SAMPLE II FOR COLIN

Write the correct answer below each question:

1. Which is larger? 13 or 31?

   They are equal

2. Which is larger? 41 or 39

   39

3. Which is larger? 543 or 215

   215

4. Which is larger? 205 or 502

   They are equal

5. Which is smaller? 56 or 35?

   35

6. Which is smaller? 84 or 91

   91

In terms of mathematical error patterns, Colin lacks conceptual understanding of the value of each digit, as determined by its place. He reads a numeral from left to right or right to left, as if the positions of each numeral were interchangeable if the digits in the numbers are identical. He thinks that 13 = 31. To Colin, the value of the 3 in the ones place equals the value of the 3 in the tens place. He also believes that the value of a number is determined by the last digit, reading from left to right, when digits are not identical. Information for this type of error is included in the DAS in Table 2.1.

Prescription: Colin begins with proportional base-10 blocks after completing activities described in the previous section. If he had not done so, he waved begin the following activities with nonproportional materials. The instructional goal is that Colin understands the meaning of each place in a multidigit numeral *and* the total value of the numeral. He needs to understand why one numeral represents a larger quantity than another or whether they are equal.

Remediation: The MIP in Table 2.3 briefly describes the types of remediation activities most beneficial for Colin. The teacher consults Colin's DAS, and in light of Colin's learning style, behavior style, and type of place value error,

TABLE 2.3 Mathematics Improvement Plan II for Colin: Understanding the Value of Each Digit in a Number

Time		20–25 minutes	15–20 minutes	30 minutes
Context		Colin works with a partner	Completes seatwork with a partner (–)	Colin will work in the classroom with a classmate whom he likes (+)
Content		Solves real-world problems using materials for trading with group to order numbers based on problem solutions (+)	Completion of additional authentic problems (+)	Works with a partner to check work and plays the "Shape Game" with a partner (+)
Process	Input	Teacher gives step-by-step instructions for the task at hand (–)	The work has visual and written examples of the task at hand (+)	The written directions are at grade level and have a singular task (+)
	Output	Student pairs are engaged in manipulative activities that require a logical outcome (+)	Writes results and explains to teacher (–)	The words in the word problem will challenge his reading level (–)
Behavior	Academic	Pairs produce written responses for which all students have input (+)	Completes work and explains reasoning (+)	Directed to ask partner questions (–)
	Social	Pairs work well together and all students have a sense of individual responsibility (+)	Directed to solve first few easy examples to build confidence (–)	His classmate is one whom he likes and he trusts (+)
Reinforcement		If each pair does well, they will get free time to play games as partners (+)	For every problem Colin gets right he will get to help the teacher with a needed task (+)	Teacher gives students oral and written comments (+)

Note: The + symbols indicate strengths and the – symbols indicate areas of concern.

selects activities to address the mathematical error pattern. The teacher presents an authentic situation, such as the following.

> My sisters are selling their comic books. One sister sold 25 and the other sister sold 52 books. My brother has been assigned to write a story about his family for the school newspaper. He wants to tell readers which sister sold the most books. Let's help him know which way to record the numerals so that his story is correct.

Assuming Colin can use the base-10 blocks and the place value chart, he models "25" as shown:

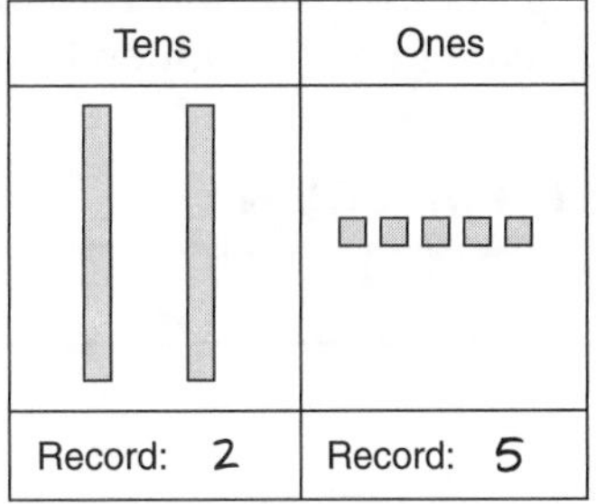

Colin records a "2" beneath the base-10 rods in the tens column and a "5" in the ones column. He reads the numeral aloud.

The next step is to express "52" so that Colin can compare that number to "25." He counts 52 units and trades five groups of 10 for five longs. He places them on the place value chart. A "5" is written below the tens column on the chart. A "2" is recorded in the section below the ones column. Colin writes "52" and reads it aloud. He sees that 52 represents more tens, and therefore is larger than 25. He should continue with additional two-digit numerals.

Playing the "Shape Game": To extend the activity to three-digit numerals, Colin plays the "Reach the Target" game described earlier in this chapter. In a more procedurally or practice-based activity, "The Shape Game," Colin starts by drawing three different shapes in this way:

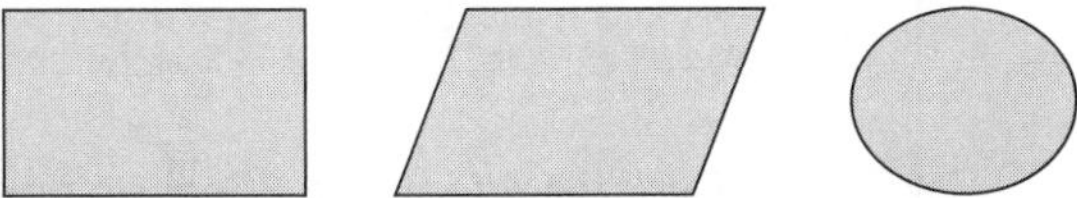

Each player's goal is to record the highest or lowest multidigit number in the class. To begin, the class is told what numbers are written on a wooden cube. Students then decide if the winning combination should be the highest or lowest number made possible with those digits. For example, the teacher/leader indicates that the cube is marked with digits 3 to 8 and the class decides the winning number should be the highest. The cube is rolled and the number seen on the cube is called out. Students write it in one of the three shapes on their paper, trying to form a high three-digit number. The cube is rolled a second time, a digit is written in one of the other shapes, and this procedure is repeated a third time to fill the third shape. Once a number is written in a shape, it cannot be moved to another shape. If numbers 4, 7, and then 5 were rolled, the winners would have written "754" as:

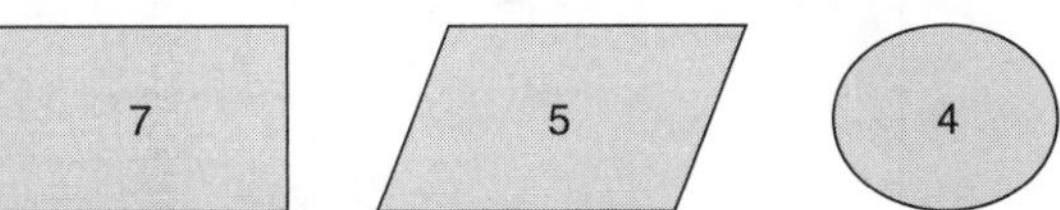

The class should discuss why the winner wrote "7" in the hundreds place rather than the ones place. If the lowest possible number were to be the goal, students would have wanted to record "457." Chance and skill are both important factors in this game.

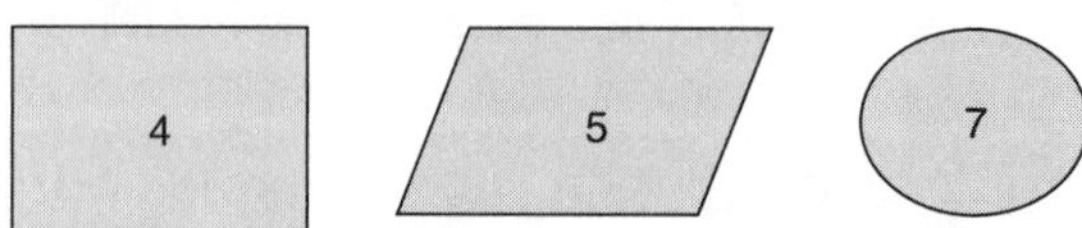

This game helps Colin remember the value of each place because he must carefully consider the values to make his number placement decisions.

STUDENT WORK SAMPLE III FOR COLIN

Fill in the blanks to show a different way to write the amounts:

1. Express 5 hours and 20 minutes as 4 hours and 30 minutes.

2. How much time, in hours and minutes, is between 2:30 and 4:00?

   400
   -230
   170

   1 hour and 70 minutes

3. Express 8 hours and 10 minutes as 7 hours and 20 minutes.

4. Express 4 feet and 7 inches as 3 feet and 17 inches.

5. Express 2 feet and 6 inches as 1 foot and 16 inches.

6. Express 3 feet and 10 inches as 2 feet and 20 inches.

Place Value Error Pattern III for Colin

The third type of place value error is found in Student Work Sample III for Colin. Colin was asked to subtract hours and minutes and feet and inches. These measurement units are built on base-60 and base-12 systems, respectively, and represent the first exercises in which Colin is working with bases other than 10.

Diagnosing the Error: Recognizing that Colin is not working with a base-10 system, think of strengths revealed in his work. Consider the subtraction algorithm and misconceptions that are understandable in light of previous learning.

Colin's other mathematical strengths and error patterns can be recorded in the following chart.

Colin's Error Pattern(s):
Colin's Strengths:

It is evident that Colin understands that renaming the numerals is required to subtract. He knows he must use some type of exchange from one place to another. That is, hours become a different number of hours, and minutes become a different number of minutes; feet become a renamed amount of feet, and inches become a renamed amount of inches. However, he is using 10 as the base number for each renaming of hours to minutes and feet to inches, rather than 60 and 12, respectively. There is no conceptual understanding that different bases, other than 10, exist. Hence, the answers are not reasonable.

An example of a completed DAS for this type of error was shown in Table 2.1.

Prescription: The error is both conceptual and procedural. Although Colin does understand that he should rename numbers, he does not understand how to use or record regrouping principles in non-base-10 place value systems. Working with manipulatives in the context of real-life problems associated with the computation will allow him to conceptualize reasonable answers.

Remediation: The MIP in Table 2.4 contains information related to this specific error. The behaviors and learning styles described for Colin should be taken into consideration when adapting the following activities. They are designed to assist Colin in working with algorithms in non-base-10 units.

Clock activities: Colin begins with handmade clocks and story problems for "time" problems. The clocks are made with paper plates and handmade paper arrows, attached with a paper fastener, for the hands. The clock looks like this one:

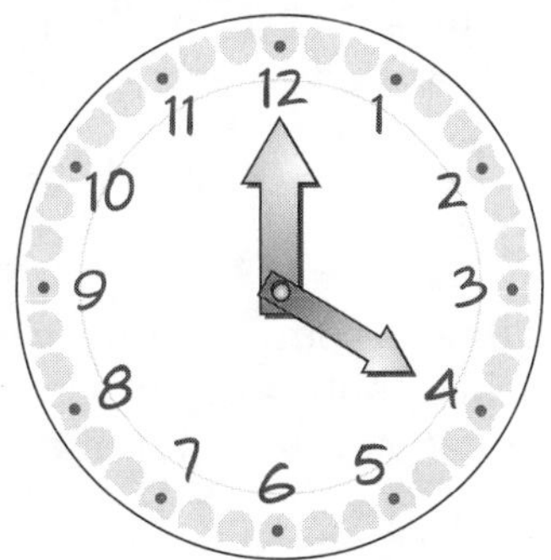

TABLE 2.4 Math Improvement Plan III for Colin: Understanding Bases Other Than Base 10

Time		30–35 minutes	20–25 minutes in pairs	20 minutes
Context		Colin works with one of his peers during a group activity (+)	Works in groups of four to solve measurement problems (–)	Colin will work in the classroom, with a classmate whom he likes, on this activity (+)
Content		Uses clocks to solve real-world problems by counting minutes and hours (+)	Completes measurement problems and algorithms not based in groups of 10s (i.e., 60s, 12s, 16s) (+)	Independent work creating new problems for partner to solve involving measurement and time situations (+)
Process	**Input**	Teacher provides story for students to interpret (–)	The work has visual and written examples of the task at hand (+)	The written directions are at grade level and have a singular task (+)
	Output	Group is engaged in manipulative activities that require a reasonable outcome (+)	Groups are expected to write results and share them with the class (–)	Time and measurement terms are discussed and explained (–)
Behavior	**Academic**	Pairs solve real-world time problems (+)	Groups physically move around class while making explanations (–)	Ask questions to complete tasks (–)
	Social	Pairs work well together and all students have a sense of their responsibility (+)	Colin asks question about how they got their answers (–)	His classmate is one whom he likes and trusts (+)
Reinforcement		If each pair does well, they will get free time to play games as partners (+)	For every problem Colin gets right, he will get to help the teacher with a needed task (+)	Teacher and other students give oral and written comments (–)

Note: The + symbols indicate strengths and the – symbols indicate areas of concern.

Colin is told that his friends and he are in a sports program after school. The activity begins at 3:00, and lasts for 2 hours and 15 minutes. Forty-five minutes of that time is devoted to snacks and breaks. Colin is supposed to find the amount of time that is actually spent in playing the game.

Colin works well with others, and so taking turns in a group, he places the hands at 3:00 on his paper plate clock. He moves the hands around to show 4:00, and that 1 hour has passed, and keeps track of the minutes by counting to 60 (counting by 5s). He records in his mathematics journal that:

60 minutes = 1 hour

Colin counts another 60 minutes to find that the hands now show 5:00. Moving the hands in this way helps Colin know that 2 hours have passed.

Because Colin also knows that 45 minutes were not devoted to sports, he wants to subtract 45 from 2 hours and 15 minutes to determine the actual playing time. To move to the standard algorithm, Colin records

$$\begin{array}{lll} & 2 \text{ hours} & 15 \text{ minutes} \\ - & & 45 \text{ minutes} \\ \hline \end{array}$$

and asks how to complete the algorithm. Because there are not enough minutes from which to subtract 45, Colin has to regroup minutes from the 2 hours. He changes 2 hours to 1 hour so that he can use one of the two hours for regrouping. If necessary, he is reminded that hours are counted in 60-minute groups, just as he did with his clock. The resulting computation looks like this:

	1 hour ~~2 hours~~	60 + 15 = 75 minutes
−		45 minutes
	1 hour	30 minutes

This activity should be followed by a situation that does not require renaming, so that students do not assume all subtraction of time problems, or any type, require renaming the digits.

Measurement activities: Renaming units in the customary system or "inch–pound" system is more complex than doing so in the metric system, which is built on the base-10 system. The former is structured so that feet are converted to inches using base 12, yards to feet in base 3, and pounds to ounces employing the base of 16. All exchanges use different bases to recall and compute. Activities that begin with direct measurement experience are essential to providing a conceptual foundation for skills and reasonable answers.

Colin works in a small group and is given a ruler or tape with which to measure items in the classroom. Students are to find and measure three objects in the classroom that are between 2 and 6 feet tall or wide. It is important to remind students that the end of the ruler and the end of the item must match at the "0" point to ensure accuracy. The following is an example:

The height or width of each is recorded in the chart below:

Item	Measurement
1. ______________	1. _____ feet _____ inches
2. ______________	2. _____ feet _____ inches
3. ______________	3. _____ feet _____ inches

Groups report their findings to the class so that it can be determined how much taller or wider one group's objects are than another. For instance, one group reports that their bookcase is 5 ft, 3 in. wide. Another group reports that the case they measured is 4 ft, 9 in. wide. The class determines how to find which is wider in this way:

5 feet	3 inches
−4 feet	9 inches

Because Colin already counted inches by 12s to measure the length of the object, he can regroup to exchange 12 in. for 1 ft. He records that trade as:

4 feet	12 + 3 = 15	inches
~~5 feet~~		
−4 feet	9	inches
	6	inches

Six inches was the result from counting. The computational result is confirmed from actual experience.

This type of measurement lesson/activity can be extended with situations involving the comparison of objects measured in pounds and ounces, because the base of 16 ounces is also confusing to children. Items can be weighed on classroom scales and then the difference in measurement is calculated, following the actual counting phase of the lesson. Students could bring labels to school to compare measurements and create many interesting, real-life problems for the class to solve. These activities can also be completed by a student working alone.

Conclusions: Instructional Strategies Summary

Conceptual understanding of place value is possible when lessons are designed in a developmental learning sequence as follows:

1. Materials and diagrams are used to express multidigit numerals.
2. Numeric symbols are connected to materials by writing the numerals that represent the quantity in the presence of manipulatives.
3. Number words are connected to numerals and materials that represent a quantity.

The trading aspect of learning about place value is essential to conceptual development. Students bundle objects, exchange place value blocks, and indicate the trades on place value charts. Last, results are recorded with numerals and words. Skills can be practiced and sustained by providing students with frequent and targeted instructional feedback. The cycle is interactive in that students are able to understand and express quantities with materials, numerals, and/or words within place value systems.

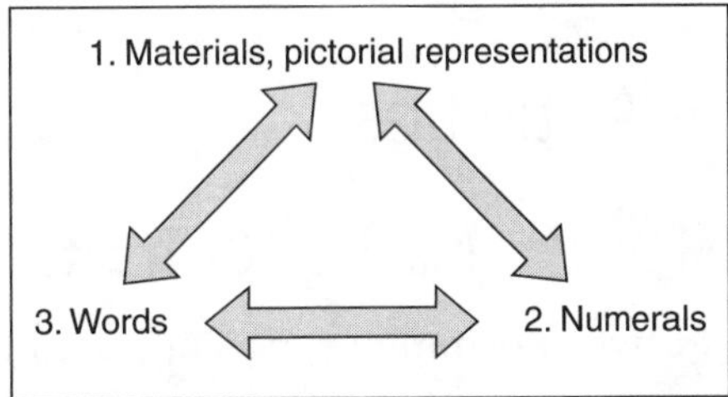

Understanding place value systems, whether base 10 or non-base 10, is fundamental to computing and number sense. Remediation should be based on determining whether students' errors are based upon conceptual or rule misunderstandings. If the former is true, students can be assisted by bundling objects in groups of 10, trading them, and recording the trades in diagrams and with numerals. Questions should be framed in real-world situations and inquiry to help students personally relate to the mathematics content. If students' errors are the results of forgetting rules, activities that focus on paper-and-pencil games can be very helpful. Examples of these useful instructional strategies are found in the following activities. Each activity is effective for work in a small group, with the whole class, or for one-on-one interaction.

Instructional Activities

ACTIVITY: Making 10s Treats

Objective: Forming groups of 10 and counting by 10s

Materials:

Small paper bags, each marked "Ten"

Pieces of cereal such as Cheerios or Fruit Loops

Play money dimes (optional)

Dice (regular or wooden cubes marked with numerals)

Directions: Tell the children that they are going to make bags of treats to sell. Taking turns, each rolls the dice and takes that number of cereal pieces. When a child has 10 pieces, they are put in a bag marked "Ten." Each bag of 10 may be exchanged with the storekeeper for a dime. After all the children have several turns, ask each of the students to tell, and write down, how many "cereal 10s" they made.

ACTIVITY: Order Game

Objective: Writing two- and three-digit numbers in order

Materials:

Two number cubes, each marked with the digits 0–5

Two number cubes, each marked with the digits 4–9

Playing chart

Directions:

1. Students use their own individual charts.
2. For a two-digit game, the student rolls any three of the cubes. For a three-digit game, the student rolls all four of the cubes.
3. Player selects any two numbers rolled to make a two-digit number or combines any three cubes to make a three-digit number. In either case, players must choose the lowest two- or three-digit number they see for their turn.
4. For each turn, the cubes are rolled again and the student forms a two- or three-digit number greater than the last number he or she wrote, if possible. The new number is written in the next space.
5. Once a player cannot make a greater two- or three-digit number, he or she loses.
6. The first player to fill in all the boxes is a winner.

Example

1. Start Box 42

2. 45

3. 57

4. 63

Variation: Five cubes could be rolled to play a four-digit Start game.

ACTIVITY: Right Place

Objective: Identify place values for large numbers

Materials:

Paper

Pencil

One set of index cards marked 1 to 9, with the word "ones" written on each one

One set of index cards marked 1 to 9, with the word "tens" written on each one

One set of index cards marked 1 to 9, with the word "hundreds" written on each one

One set of index cards marked 1 to 9, with the word "thousands" written on each one

Directions:

1. Students write any four-digit number they wish on their paper. If more places are to be practiced, the students could write any number digit.
2. Playing cards are shuffled.
3. Leader calls out the number and the place marked on the card. For example, the leader says, "8 in the hundreds place."
4. If a student has an 8 written in the hundreds place for the number written, the number is circled.
5. Numbers and places are called until a student has circled all the digits in the number written. That student calls out "Right Place!" and wins the game after the digits are checked against the cards drawn by the leader.
6. The game can continue until more players win, or the game can be restarted.

   Example:

   Student records 4876.

   Leader calls "Four in the thousands place."

   Student circles "4."

   When all numbers in each place are circled for his number, student wins.

Discussion Questions

1. Why are only 10 symbols needed to express any value in base-10 place value system?
2. The value of a number written in the base-10 place value system is based on the principle of multiplying each numeral by the base group. For example, 589 represents 5 hundreds, 8 tens, and 9 ones. Discuss and explain the next step one takes to find the total value of the numeral. What might be a real-world problem you could pose to help students understand the need to learn about place value?
3. Why are the bills and coins of U.S. currency not examples of proportional manipulatives? How might you help students understand their value using some type of hands-on teaching approach?
4. Provide two examples of proportional materials and two examples of non-proportional materials that help students model the base-10 positional system. Describe why you chose these manipulatives and how they can be effective in helping students build conceptual understanding of place value.
5. In a positional or place value system, why is it not necessary to notate 35 as 305? Explain your reasoning.
6. Why would a student make the mistake of renaming 8 feet 9 inches as 7 feet and 19 inches? Why would this error seem reasonable to a student?
7. Many errors are understandable. For example, students will count, ". . . twenty-nine, twenty-ten. . . ." What techniques from your reading of the chapter might help them understand and name the "bridge" numbers correctly?

References

Baroody, A. J. (1990). How and when should place value concepts and skills be taught? *Journal for Research in Mathematics Education, 21*(4), 281–286.

Bassarear, T. (1997). *Mathematics for elementary school teachers.* Boston, MA: Houghton Mifflin Company.

Charlesworth, R., & Lind, K. K. (2003). *Math and science for young children* (4th ed.). Thomson Clifton Park, New York, *Delmar Learning.*

Clausen-May, T. (2005). *Teaching math to pupils with different learning styles.* Paul Chapman Publishing A Sages publication company, Thousand Oaks, California, London, England, New Delhi, India.

Fuson, K. C. (1990). Conceptual structures of multiunit numbers: Implications for learning and teaching mulitdigit addition, subtraction, and place value. *Cognition and Instruction, 7*(4), 343–403.

Fuson K. C. (1990). Issues in place-value and multidigit additional and subtraction learning and teaching. *Journal for Research in Mathematics Education, 21,* 273–280.

Fuson K. C., & Briars, D. J. (1990). Using a base-ten blocks learning/teaching approach for the first- and second grade place-value and multidigit addition and subtraction. *Journal for Research in Mathematics Education, 21*, 180–206.

Hiebert, J., & Wearne, D. (1992). Links between teaching and learning place value with understanding in first grade. *Journal for Research in Mathematics Education, 23*(2), 98–122.

Kamii, C. K. (1986). Place value: An explanation of its difficulty and educational implications for the primary grade. *Journal of Research in Childhood Education, 1*, 75–86.

Kilpatrick, J., Swafford, J., & Findell, B. (Eds.). (2001). *Adding it up: Helping children learn mathematics*. Washington, DC: National Academy Press.

Ma, L. (1999). *Knowing and teaching elementary mathematics*. Mahwah, NJ: Lawrence Erlbaum Associates.

National Council of Teachers of Mathematics. (2000). *Principles and standards for school mathematics*. Reston, VA: Author.

Sherman, H. J. (1992). Reinforcing place value. *Arithmetic Teacher, 40*(2), 169–171.

Chapter 3

Addition of Whole Numbers

I like learning about plussing.

Adding is easy . . . just count on your fingers as fast as you can before the teacher sees you.

I know how to add. My big brother showed me and so I don't have to learn it.

If you see "more" in the problem, just add.

What Is Addition?

Addition of whole numbers is represented in the physical world by the union of sets. The cardinal numbers of the sets involved are represented by addends. The sets are disjoint in that they do not share any elements (objects) in common. For example, three apples and two hammers can be joined to form a set of five objects. The apples and the hammers are members of two separate sets. Students can model these combinations with real objects, draw pictures of the two sets, and then connect symbols to the drawings to build a conceptual, pictorial, and abstract understanding of addition:

Sets are represented with tallies or X marks:

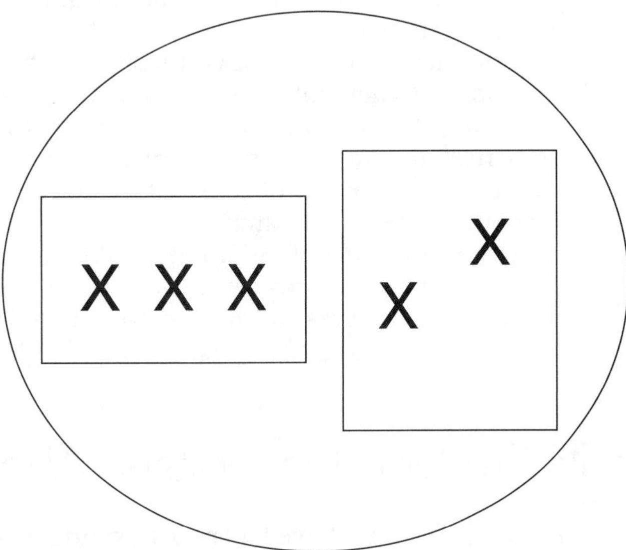

Symbols are then "attached" to sets:

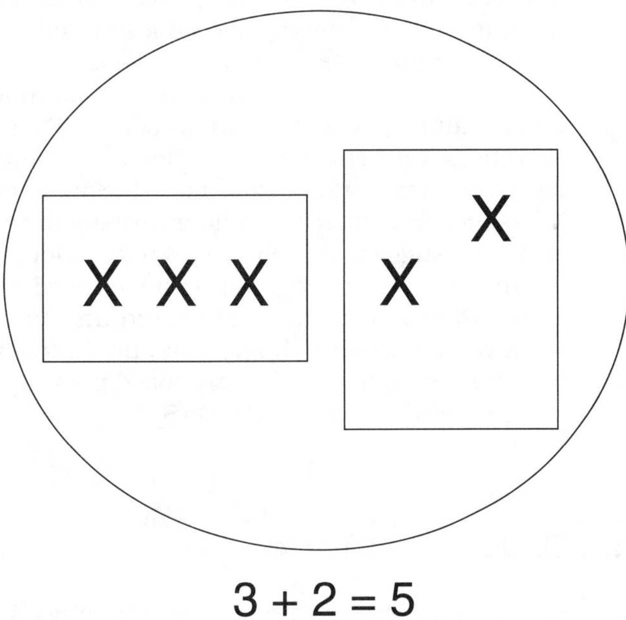

As children work to understand the addition concept, developmental work with understanding the algorithm for combinations of two or more addends is begun. Children learn algorithmic understandings of place value and procedures of "regrouping and renaming" by using the same developmental process that they use to learn the foundations of set unions to represent addition. First, learners combine sets of objects, such as base-10 blocks, to demonstrate ability to combine addends and determine the sum. Then learners' drawings are connected to the manipulative work of unioned sets, as illustrated with apples and hammers. Finally, the symbols that represent the drawings and objects are written and the regrouping is indicated with tally marks to aid in visualizing the regrouping process. This symbolic work is included in the third picture shown in the previous illustration.

Each time the concept is introduced, for both union of sets and then algorithmic work including place value, students should be presented with a situation that poses a "real-world" problem that must be solved by utilizing objects, drawings, and/or work with numerical symbols. The key to success is to make sure the sets used are disjoint sets. Remember, sets are disjoint if they share no elements (objects) in common.

Understanding of addition begins at the concrete level (working with manipulatives), progresses to working at the semiabstract level (working with pictures), and moves to working abstractly (with written symbols).

What Should Students Understand About Addition?

Although children have had many experiences with addition situations in grades K–2, Silver, Strutchens, and Zawojewski (NCTM, 2000, p. 143) report that 75 percent of fourth graders like mathematics, find it practical, and believe it is important to learn. Students typically have a good grasp of additive reasoning by the third grade. Teaching should foster and encourage conceptual understanding of addition processes rather than focusing on mimicking algorithmic processes. Focus should be on making sense of addition by using various modeling techniques and on engaging in intellectually stimulating discussions. Many researchers (Carpenter, Franke, Jacobs, Fennema, & Empson, 1997; Cox, 1975; Issacs & Carroll, 1999; Roseman, 1985; Selter, 2001; Sisul, 2002; Tucker, 1989; Villasenor & Kepner, 1993) have investigated aspects of teaching addition to children and suggest approaches that have formed the basis for this chapter.

In this section, you will be introduced to error analysis. This is one of the steps toward designing a DAS and an MIP for a student. A child's simulated work will be presented, and you should follow the directions in analyzing each of the three examples. The proposed prescription will direct your suggested MIP design based on the child's DAS.

About the Student: Ian

Ian is a fifth grader who is generally in good health. He has many strengths in the classroom and around the school building. He completes his assignments, likes to be near the teacher, enjoys working with his peers, and actively engages in cooperative learning activities. He likes manipulatives and enjoys giving simple answers and working at the board or at his laptop computer. He is a visual learner, uses manipulatives well, is good at using graphs, and does well with performing pencil-and-paper activities. Ian seems to function at grade level in math. He accepts teacher guidance and completes his assignments. His teacher reports that he loves social reinforcers, especially "atta-boy" type rewards. He is very proud of notes sent home by the teacher and will work hard to earn the right to move around the room.

Ian faces numerous tasks within the learning environment. He exhibits low self-control and poor social language usage in written communication. These problems worsen during large-group activities. Like many students, he has social management difficulties during large-group activities and especially during transition periods while working independently and/or when authority figures are not present. He has problems with independent reading and understanding oral multitask directions.

When he is expected to speak during large-group activities, deal with fast-paced situations, or carry out written assignments, he exhibits considerable resistive behavior. Staying in his seat and on task while completing written tasks or activity-based lessons seem to pose considerable challenges for him. He resists intangible reinforcers, hates going to the principal's office for any reason, and does not like to be by himself while in school. In addition, grades mean little to him.

Error Patterns: Diagnosis, Prescription, Remediation

The following simulations assume that Ian has taken an addition test, and in each situation a different error has emerged. Even though Ian "supplied" all three examples in this chapter, you should treat each sample error as if it is independent of the other two samples when designing the prescription and remediation suggestions. The task in each sample is to identify appropriate lessons based on the knowledge of the child and the knowledge of the exhibited math deficiency.

Addition Error Pattern I for Ian

The first sample test for Ian is a completed addition paper. You should follow the following four-step process:

1. Score the paper.
2. Begin with the first incorrect problem and attempt to determine the algorithm the child is using to obtain the answers.
3. Use the child's pattern and see if the second incorrect problem follows the pattern.
    a. If it does, go to step 4.
    b. If it does not, study the error in the second problem and revise your prediction of the algorithm used.
4. Confirm the pattern using the third incorrect problem.

Begin the four-step process now by scoring Ian's paper.

Diagnosing the Error: There often is not a patterned error in a student's work; however, for the practice of learning to identify patterned errors, each example of Ian's work does have a pattern. Once you have finished scoring the paper and identifying the proposed pattern of error, you should reflect on the strengths exhibited in Ian's addition work. Strengths to look for include knowledge of place value, facts (both easy and hard), work with zero in addition, and the

STUDENT WORK SAMPLE ERROR I FOR IAN

1) 16 + 7 = 113	2) 14 + 3 = 17	3) 35 + 81 = 116
4) 62 + 8 = 610	5) 407 + 63 = 4610	6) 569 + 724 = 12813
7) 78 + 16 = 814	8) 25 + 35 = 510	

ability to regroup and rename in addition—to mention just a few. Use the space below to record your observations.

Ian's Error Pattern(s):
Ian's Strengths:

Scoring sample I, you find that Ian got two of eight (25 percent) correct. It is obvious that this is a very poor performance. However, closer inspection of Ian's works shows that he has a number of strengths. He knows that multidigit addition involves working with columns, he just does not perform it correctly. He worked with zero, the additive identity, correctly in problem 5. Ian also knows:

1. easy addition facts involving sums less than 10
2. hard addition facts involving sums between 11 and 18
3. sums of 10, as in problems 4, 5, and 8

A completed DAS for Ian appears in Table 3.1.

Prescription: The child's difficulty seems to involve not knowing what to do when the sum is 10 or larger in one of the column additions. This could be a conceptual error in that the child does not understand the place value nature of writing the result of a sum larger than nine. Quite often, children are so focused on the task of performing the addition and on getting each addition fact correct that they do not think conceptually about the result of writing that fact or using number sense. They do not connect the addition result with its implication when written.

On the other hand, the child may forget to write the unit's digit and regroup the tens value to the next larger place (the column to the left). This often happens with children who are below average in mathematics; they remember parts of what to do but do not remember the complete addition algorithm.

Remediation: Based upon assessment of the elements in the DAS for Ian, an MIP (Table 3.2) is developed. This plan serves to help prepare for remediation of the exhibited addition errors. The MIP could then be used multiple times for Ian, throughout the academic year, with elements related to content or other elements altered as different types of errors are made and as mathematical topics change.

You should use a manipulative, such as popsicle sticks, when working with Ian. Guide him to bundle them in as many groups of 10 as possible and then place the singles nearby.

Begin with a problem Ian worked correctly, such as problem 2: 14 + 3. Have him set out 14 sticks. If he counts out 14 single sticks, work to bundle all the tens possible to have one group of 10 and 4 single sticks. It is acceptable to have Ian pick a bundle of 10 and 4 single sticks. Now have him simulate the addition by combining the 14 sticks with 3 more sticks (see Figure 3.1).

When he slides the sticks together and arrives at 17, provide positive feedback for correctly completing the problem. Then give him a new problem, such as problem 1: 16 + 7. Once again, let him gather a bundle of 10 and 6 singles. Then have him add seven by getting seven singles and finding out how many total sticks there are. Ian should report that there are 23 sticks. If he just counted up from 17, then encourage him to take the pile of 13 singles and see if there are any groups of 10. Once tens have been counted, bundle them with a rubber band so the answer now looks like 2 tens and 3 singles (see Figure 3.2).

Ask Ian to compare the answer of 23 to the answer on test question 1, where 113 had been recorded.

TABLE 3.1 Data Analysis Sheet

Student: Ian						
Team Members:						
Context	**Content Assessment**	**Process**		**Behavior**		**Reinforcement**
		Input	Output	Academic	Social	
+	+	+	+	+	+	+
• Close to teacher • Working with peers • Classroom paired with peers	***Learned Concepts I*** • Knowledge of 100 basic addition facts • Knowledge of proper alignment of digits in sum according to place value • Knowledge of identity property of addition ***Learned Concepts II*** • Sums less than 10 • Sums 11–18 • Sums of 10 • Three one-digit addends including a zero • Format (by column) ***Learned Concepts III*** • Sums less than 10 • Sums 11–18 • Sums of 10 • Additive identity • Three one-digit addends including a zero • Format (correct sums and recording in columns)	• Tactile materials • Visuals • Graphics • Pencil/paper	• Manipulatives • Single-word answers • Working at board or on laptop	• Turns in material upon request • Completes graphics or numerical tasks • Completes computational activities	• Positive response to praise • Turns in assignments • Accepts teacher guidance	• Sitting with peers • Social reinforcements • Good behavior notes to home • Group classroom activities • Movement within classroom
–	–	–	–	–	–	–
• Hallway • Study hall • Large student settings • Working independently • Distances away from authority figure	***Error Pattern I*** • Addition place value, renaming places from ones to tens and tens to hundreds • Directionality: may not begin addition algorithm by adding ones in the right hand column of problem ***Error Pattern II*** • Format (directionality problems) • Place value (more than a single digit recorded in a place) ***Error Pattern III*** • Correctly recognizing three one-digit addends problems	• Independent reading of directions • Oral directions that include more than one activity • Auditory aids	• Oral activities • Written assignments • Rapid-paced activities	• Staying in seat • Staying on task • Completion of written task	• Low social language during writen exercise • Low self-control during large-group activities	• Intangible reinforcers • Contact by principal • Contact by unknown persons • Quiet time away from peers

Note: The + symbols indicate strengths and the – symbols indicate areas of concern.

TABLE 3.2 Mathematics Improvement Plan I for Ian: Regrouping Sums of 10 or Larger

Time		15 minutes	20–30 minutes	15 minutes
Context		Close to teacher (+) In classroom (+) Large-group setting (−)	In classroom (+) With peer (+) Close to teacher (+)	Working independently (−) Close to teacher (+) In classroom (+)
Content		Play skill game "Add Around" with one or two children to practice basic addition facts (+)	Work with another child in rolling number cubes to determine number of popsicle sticks to group and then combine. Children check each other's work in bundling, combining, trading, and reporting sums. Included a zero addend to work with identity property using base-10 blocks (+)	Work with another child on algorithmic procedures to find sums of addition problems with regrouping involved. Problems include work with zero (+)
Process	Input	Pencil/paper (+) Oral instruction by teacher (−)	Tactile material (+) Pencil/paper (+)	Tactile materials supported by visuals and graphics (+)
	Output	Oral activities, student responds (−) Use written task (+)	Answers in single words (+) Working on laptop (+)	Oral activities (−) Laptop usage (+)
Behavior	Academic	Completing the assignment, hands in material, performs at acceptable competence level (+)	Turns in assignments (+) Accepts teacher directions (+)	Staying in seat (−) Turning in material upon request (+)
	Social	Follows teacher's directions (+) Controlling vocalization (−)	Positive response to peers and turns in the assignment upon request (+)	Monitoring for student use of self-control (−)
Reinforcement		Receives "good student" note from teacher (+)	Allowed movement in classroom (+) Gets "good student behavior" note to give to parent/guardian (+)	Group classroom activities (+) Sitting with peers (+)

Note: The + symbols indicate strengths and the − symbols indicate areas of concern.

FIGURE 3.1
14 + 3 = 17

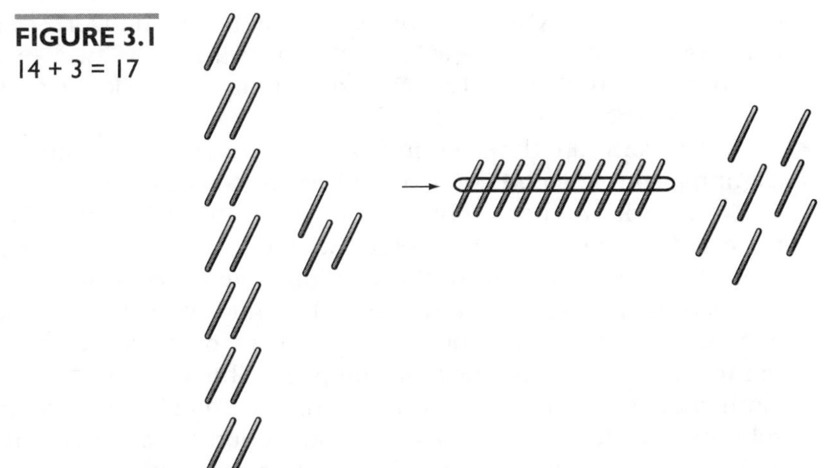

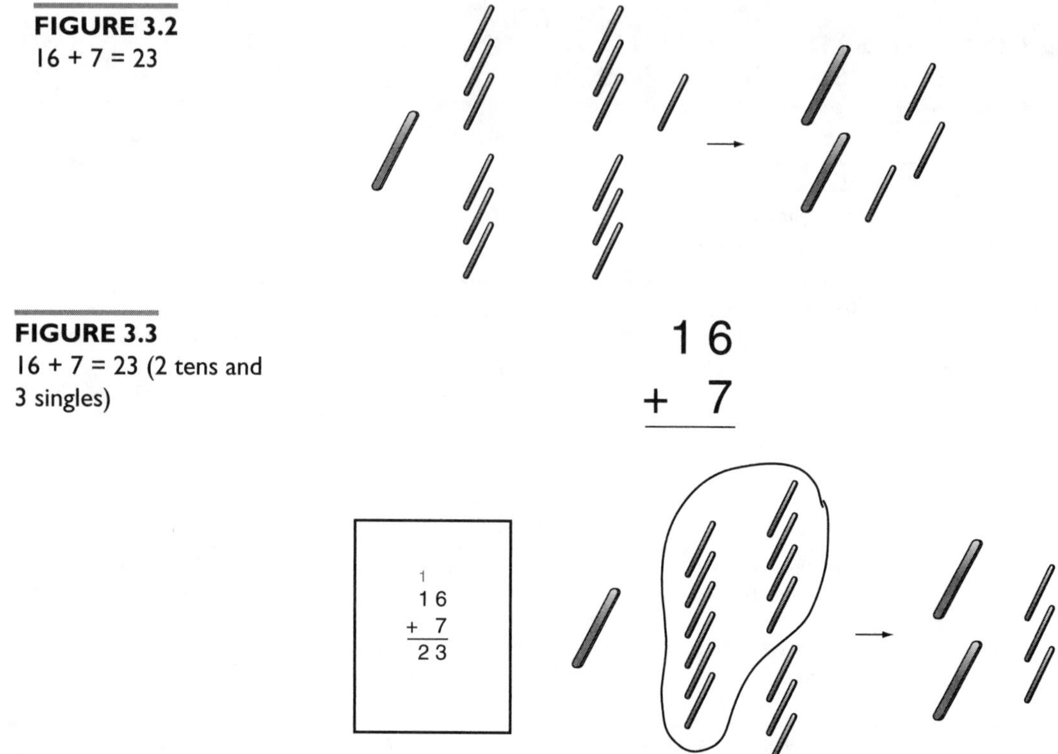

FIGURE 3.2
16 + 7 = 23

FIGURE 3.3
16 + 7 = 23 (2 tens and 3 singles)

Now is the time to rework the problem with Ian. Have him write the problem on a paper. Tell him that he will record as you work the problem with him. Begin by indicating that you noticed he started with 16 (you should get one bundle of 10 and 6 singles), then he added 7 by putting 7 more sticks on the workspace. Help Ian combine the 6 singles and 7 singles, count out a set of 10, and bundle them. Put the bundle in his hand. Note that 6 plus 7 is 13, which is 10 (show the bundle in his hand) and 3 (point to the three sticks remaining on the workspace). Have Ian record the 3 in the units place and mark a 1 over the 1 in 16 to record that there is one group of 10 to be regrouped to the tens column (see Figure 3.3). After having recorded the 1, the child places the bundle in his hand next to the one bundle of 10 on the workspace. Ask him how many bundles of 10 we now have. When he answers "two," point out that if we now add the numbers in the tens column on the worksheet, we do indeed have 2 tens. So, the answer is 23.

Ian's work on the test indicates that he is accustomed to working in columns, so this connection should not be too difficult.

Now work another problem, such as problem 7, but indicate that Ian is to perform the combining of sticks in the column, bundling for tens if possible, and recording the number of units remaining while recording the bundle to be regrouped in the next column. Have the child work 5 to 10 of these problems (recording as he goes) so he can connect the operation with the physical material to the recorded symbols on the page. This connection is key to success in mathematics, as many children can use the manipulatives and demonstrate a solution but do not recognize the connection between the manipulative work and the abstract number symbols used to record that work.

Addition Error Pattern II for Ian

The second sample is another addition paper. Follow the same four-step procedure you used on page 47 to diagnose Error Pattern I.

STUDENT WORK SAMPLE ERROR II FOR IAN

1) 16 + 7 = 113	2) 14 + 3 = 17	3) 35 + 81 = 17 (carry mark: 1)
4) 62 + 8 = 610	5) 407 + 63 = 4610	6) 569 + 724 = 1113 (carry marks: 2 0)
7) 78 + 16 = 814	8) 25 + 35 = 510	

Begin the four-step process and score Ian's paper.

Diagnosing the Error: After you have scored the paper, identify the proposed pattern of error and reflect on the strengths exhibited in the child's addition work. Strengths to look for include knowledge of place value, facts (both easy and hard), work with zero in addition, and the ability to regroup in addition. Use the space below to record your observations.

Ian's Error Pattern(s):
Ian's Strengths:

Ian scored worse than he did on the first test, getting just one of eight (12.5 percent) correct. This is a very poor performance. Yet, closer inspection of the child's work shows that Ian has a number of strengths. He knows that column addition involves adding in the columns, he just does not do it correctly. Ian also knows:

1. easy addition facts involving sums less than 10
2. hard addition facts involving sums between 11 and 18
3. sums of 10, as in problems 4, 5, and 8
4. three one-digit addends (including zeros)

Ian worked well with zero, the additive identity, in problem 5.

The first incorrect problem, problem 1, seems to exhibit the same error displayed in the first sample paper. To confirm this diagnosis, move to the second incorrect problem: problem 3. Ian added 3 + 8 to get a sum of 11. It is unclear whether he wrote the units digit of the sum and regrouped the other 1 to the units column or wrote the tens value and regrouped the ones value to the right.

Moving to the next two incorrect problems on Ian's paper yields no insight to the error. Problem 6 is the first incorrect problem that provides useful information. He began on the left and proceeded left to right. He began adding in the problem on the left, added the 5 + 7, and obtained 12. Then he recorded the tens value of the 12 (1) and regrouped the units value (2) to the tens column.

Prescription: This child appears to have a conceptual problem with place value and regrouping, and has a directional error (moving left to right). However, one must be cautioned not to conclude that every inappropriate computational operation is conceptual in nature. This error may simply be a procedural problem. The child's initial work with operations will exhibit Piaget's preoperational level of cognition. That is, the child will be very egocentric in approaching the operation in a mechanical way and not connecting the answers with their place value implications. In fact, students will not even consider the place value implications of each step involved in the computation until they are very experienced with the operation and/or are questioned by the teacher regarding a step in the process or the meaning of a part of the answer.

When questioned, the child's attention is refocused away from the mechanical process he has undertaken and onto the implication of the written symbols. This ability to refocus (without prompting by the teacher) and see the problem from a different perspective is indicative of a child who is functioning at Piaget's concrete operational level. Quite often, children with left-right reading disabilities exhibit this type of error. The error begins appearing in grade 2 or 3, just when the teacher is emphasizing the need to work from left to right in reading.

TABLE 3.3 Mathematics Improvement II for Ian: Working Right to Left in Addition Problems

Time		15–20 minutes	20 minutes	20 minutes
Context		Close to teacher (+) In classroom (+) Large-group setting (−)	In classroom (+) With peer (+) Close to teacher (+)	Working independently (−) Close to teacher (+) In classroom (+)
Content		Play the skill game "Make 100," with one or two children to practice basic addition facts (+)	Combine place value blocks to find sums indicated on a worksheet that is marked with arrows to indicate that addition algorithm work begins in the units column (+)	Work with examples on a worksheet that has some addition problems marked with an arrow over the units place to indicate where to start and some problems with no such support mark (+)
Process	Input	Pencil/paper (+) Oral instruction by teacher (−)	Tactile material (+) Independent reading (−) Pencil/paper (+)	Tactile materials supported by visuals and graphics (+)
	Output	Oral activities, student responds (−) Written task (+)	Answers in single words (+) Working on laptop (+)	Oral activities (−) Laptop usage (+)
Behavior	Academic	Completing the assignment, hands in material, performs at acceptable competence level (+)	Turns in assignments (+) Accepts teacher directions (+)	Staying in seat (−) Turning in material upon request (+)
	Social	Follows teacher's directions (+) Controlling vocalization (−)	Positive response to peers and turns in the assignment upon request (+)	Monitoring for student use of self-control (−)
Reinforcement		Receives "good student" note from teacher (+)	Allowed movement in classroom (+) Gets "good student behavior" note to give to parent/guardian (+)	Group classroom activities (+) Sitting with peers (+)

Note: The + symbols indicate strengths and the − symbols indicate areas of concern.

This emphasis on left-right in reading carries over into the child's mathematics work because the child is so cued to concentrate on the left-right nature of reading. This type of thinking may lead a child to make a procedural error.

Remediation: The MIP for Sample Error II appears in Table 3.3. Initial work with Ian should be the same as with the first error. Ian, using popsicle sticks and/or base-10 blocks, should complete numerous examples. Even if the error is procedural, teachers should use base-10 blocks or popsicle sticks to have the child generate a problem answer that is different from the one arrived at with pencil and paper. Most of the remediation for Sample Error I would also be appropriate for remediation purposes for Sample Error II.

Addition Error Pattern III for Ian

The third sample is another addition paper. Follow the same four-step procedure (page 47) you used to diagnose Error Patterns I and II.

Diagnosing the Error: Once you have finished scoring the paper and identifying the proposed pattern of error, you should reflect on the strengths exhibited in

STUDENT WORK SAMPLE ERROR III FOR IAN

1) 16 + 7 = 14

2) 14 + 3 = 8

3) 35 + 81 = 116

4) 62 + 8 = 16

5) 407 + 63 = 470 (carried 1)

6) 569 + 724 = 1293 (carried 1)

7) 78 + 16 = 94 (carried 1)

8) 25 + 35 = 60 (carried 1)

the child's addition work. Strengths to look for include knowledge of place value, facts (both easy and hard), work with zero in addition, and the ability to regroup in addition. Use the space below to record your observations.

Ian's Error Pattern(s):
Ian's Strengths:

Ian scored five of eight (62 percent) correct. This is not a very good performance. However, closer inspection of Ian's work shows a number of strengths. First, Ian knows the format in column addition, which involves adding in the columns. He also knows:

a. easy addition facts involving sums less than 10
b. hard addition facts involving sums between 11 and 18
c. sums of 10, as in problems 4, 5, and 8
d. three one-digit addends (including zeros)
e. some regrouping, as in problems 5, 6, 7, and 8
f. the additive identity, as in problem 5

Looking at the first incorrect problem reveals that Ian is adding all the digits of the two numbers to be added, that is, $1 + 6 + 7 = 14$. Checking the next incorrect problem, problem 2, confirms the error; $1 + 4 + 3 = 8$. To make sure of the diagnosis, we look at problem 4. As before, $6 + 2 + 8 = 16$.

Discussion with the classroom teacher revealed that, just days before this paper was completed, the class had reviewed three one-digit addends. The teacher had been adamant that when there are three numbers to be added, "you have to do them two at a time," which is the binary operation principle. Ian knows how to perform column addition, as evidenced by the correct work on much harder test problems when more than three digits are present. However, for some reason, when there were just three digits involved in the column addition problem, Ian made the connection between the recent lesson on three one-digit addends and the problem at hand.

Prescription: This error is a procedural error, as the child is obviously cueing in on the fact that three digits are present and is performing a "three one-digit addend" problem. Correctness on the other problems indicates that this is a careless error in thought. Had the teacher not confirmed the recent lesson involving three one-digit addends, this might be misunderstood as a lack of understanding of place value.

Remediation: The MIP for Error Pattern III appears in Table 3.4. This will not be a difficult remediation problem. Before giving Ian a problem like:

$$\begin{array}{r} 23 \\ +\ 5 \\ \hline \end{array}$$

you could give him a problem such as:

$$\begin{array}{r} 23 \\ +15 \\ \hline \end{array}$$

and ask the child to work the problem.

Next, review the work (it will probably be correct, as indicated by his test performance). As you review with him how he worked the problem, use a 3×5 card and slide it over the problem as shown in the accompanying figure.

As each column is revealed, discuss that the sum is correct and indicate that Ian is correct in his process. This sets the stage for the next step: presenting the first problem where he used an incorrect procedure. Write the problem on the page (out of sight of the child) and cover the problem with the card.

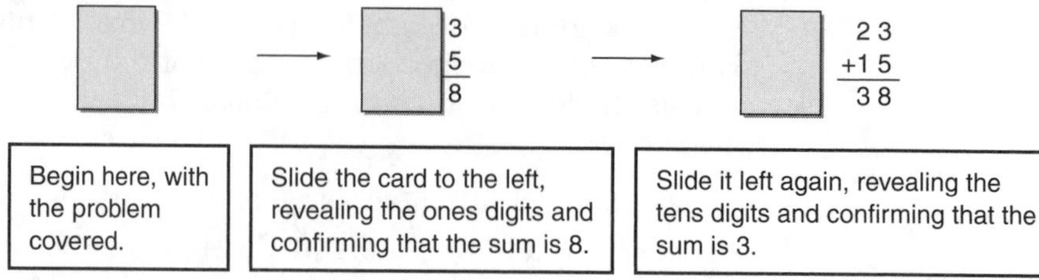

Proceed as before, revealing the units digit and having Ian write the correct sum on the page. Then move the card left to reveal the tens digit and have him write the sum.

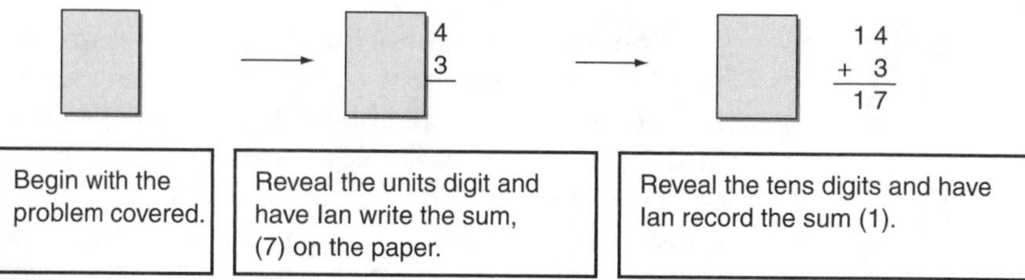

TABLE 3.4 Mathematics Improvement III Plan for Ian: Correcting Procedural Errors

Time		15 minutes	15–20 minutes	20 minutes
Context		Close to teacher (+) In classroom (+) Large-group setting (−)	In classroom (+) With peer (+) Close to teacher (+)	Working independently (−) Close to teacher (+) In classroom (+)
Content		Play the skill game "Who Can Tell" to practice basic addition facts with the type of examples that have some two-digit numbers added to one-digit numbers as well as two-digit plus two-digit numbers (+)	Work with 3 × 5 cards and two-digit plus two-digit numbers. Slide the card over to the tens place to reveal a single column at a time (+)	Work with a worksheet on mixed-type addition problems to help the child discriminate between procedures for two-digit plus two-digit and two-digit plus one-digit number addition problems (+)
Process	Input	Pencil and paper (+) Oral instruction by teacher (−)	Tactile material (+) Independent reading (−) Pencil and paper (+)	Tactile materials supported by visuals and graphics (+)
	Output	Oral activities, student responds (−) Written task (+)	Answers in single words (+) Working on laptop (+)	Oral activities (−) Laptop usage (+)
Behavior	Academic	Completing the assignment, hands in material, performs at acceptable competence level (+)	Turns in assignments (+) Accepts teacher directions (+)	Staying in seat (−) Turning in material upon request (+)
	Social	Follows teacher's directions (+) Controlling vocalization (−)	Positive response to peers and turns in the assignment upon request (+)	Monitoring for student use of self-control (−)
Reinforcement		Receives "good student" note from teacher (+)	Allowed movement in classroom (+) Gets "good student behavior" note to give to parent/guardian (+)	Group classroom activities (+) Sitting with peers (+)

Note: The + symbols indicate strengths and the − symbols indicate areas of concern.

Ian should now have 17 recorded as the answer. Have him compare that answer to the answer on problem 1 and discuss what the difference is. Ian quickly commented that he had used an incorrect approach on the problem because he had confused the problem with some they had been doing last week. This is not a very difficult error to help the child overcome. However, if he had not made the connection with a previous lesson but rather continued making an incorrect sum (of 8 in this case), then you would use some of the ideas from the place value chapter (Chapter 1) and work to help him conceptualize what he is doing incorrectly.

Conclusions: Instructional Strategies Summary

Throughout the remediation plan for all three samples, the following suggestions would be very helpful:

1. Have learners complete a few problems at a time. Once you are satisfied that they understand something, move on.
2. Pair a slow learner with an average learner. They can help each other. Combine older and younger peers.
3. Use simple numbers to explain a mathematical operation, then move to a more complex level.

Instructional Activities

Assessing whether children's addition errors are primarily results of a low level of conceptual understanding or a lack of ability to recall basic facts or work with algorithmic rules can be accomplished with various types of questions. Children's conceptual learning can be assessed and evaluated more readily by utilizing authentic, real-world situations in which learners must decide not only how to solve the problem but also whether the result is reasonable. The following is an example of such a question: The third and fourth graders at Mill Town Elementary School want to hold a bake sale to earn money for computers. If the third grade sells 14 cakes and the fourth grade sells 8 cakes, how many cakes have been sold?

The following two activities are examples of ways in which teachers can determine the level of students' skill abilities in terms of knowledge of basic facts and algorithmic procedures.

ACTIVITY: The Case of the Missing Numbers

Directions:
Fill in the blanks for the missing numbers.

$$\begin{array}{rrr} & 8 & \_ \\ + & \_ & 6 \\ \hline \_ & 8 & 3 \end{array}$$

ACTIVITY: Make 100

Play this game with a friend.

Objective: Addition of one-, two-, three-, and four-digit numbers

Materials: Two to four wooden cubes. Two are marked 0, 1, 2, 3, 4, 5 and the others show the numerals 5, 6, 7, 8, 9, and 0.

Directions:

1. Take turns being the first player.
2. For round 1, the first player rolls two cubes. One should be the cube with low digits and the other cube should be the one with higher numbers. She records the starting two-digit number, which must be greater than 25 and less than 75. These numbers, 25 and 75, are random and can be changed by the teacher. If the student rolls a 4 and a 5, she can record either 45 or 54.
3. For round two, the second player rolls the cubes and uses one or both of the cubes to make a one- or two-digit number. The second player adds the number he created to the starting number. If the sum is over 100, the second player automatically wins the round. If the sum is not 100 or more, play continues until one player reaches that goal. If the first combination recorded was 54 and the second student rolls a 6 and

a 3, the second student would add 63 to 54 (a sum of 117) and wins to get one point.

4. Play begins again, starting over or continuing, depending on the results of step 3.

Variation: Use three-digit numerals as well and make the target 1,000.

ACTIVITY: Add Around

Objective: Practice the skill of addition with one- and two-digit numbers.

Materials:

Objects for each player to move on chart

Number cube with the sides marked with: R (which means to move to the right); L (which means to move to the left); D (which means to move any way diagonally); N (which means to lose a turn); C (which means to move any direction); and U (which means to move up)

Directions: The game is played on one grid. The one pictured is an example and should be changed by the teacher to include numbers that need to be practiced.

7	6	10	21	37
12	8	4	63	29
9	18	Start	30	46
6	42	72	58	5
15	55	86	32	90

Each player puts an object to move on the square marked *Start*. The first player rolls the cube and moves in the direction indicated. The object is placed on that numeral and that is the first number the player has. The next player does the same. The first player rolls again and moves in the direction from where the object is to the next square. The player then adds the first number to the second and keeps the sum as her score. The next players do the same. As the objects are moved around the board, each player adds on the new number to the previous score. The first player with a sum that hits, but does not exceed, the target number, wins. If a player is at a square on the board that would not allow a move (if the player's object were at the top of the playing grid and the player rolled a "U"), the player loses that turn and the next player takes a turn.

For example, the target number could be 200. The first player rolls an "R" and lands on 30. His next roll is "U" and so the object is moved to 63. That player's score is now 93. The second player first rolls a "D" and moves to 42. Her next roll is an "L" and the object is moved to the 6 for a score of 48. Play continues until a player's sum is 200 (or is the closest to 200).

Discussion Questions

1. List the key steps a teacher would take when diagnosing a student's mathematical error from evidence in student work. Explain the purpose of each step in preparing for the prescription and remediation phase.
2. Identify five characteristics of a math activity that would be used with the described child, and identify two characteristics that should *not* be included in the activity.
3. What are some advantages of the diagnosis/prescription/remediation process versus the traditional evaluation strategy?
4. How do the advantages of the diagnosis/prescription/remediation process benefit both students and teachers?
5. Discuss your understanding of the distinction between a conceptual error and a procedural error. What are the reasons for your definitions of the categories?
6. The following worksheet shows Student Work Sample Error IV for Ian:

1) 16 + 7 = 13	2) 14 + 3 = 17	3) 35 + 81 = 116
4) 62 + 8 = 60	5) 407 + 63 = 460	6) 569 + 724 = 1283
7) 78 + 16 = 84	8) 25 + 35 = 50	

a. Score Student Work Sample Error IV for Ian. Identify his strengths and error patterns. Complete a DAS for Ian.

b. Complete an MIP.

7. The following worksheet shows Student Work Sample Error V for Ian:

1) 16 + 7 = 25

2) 14 + 3 = 17

3) 35 + 81 = 126

4) 62 + 8 = 70 (carried 1)

5) 407 + 63 = 470 (carried 1)

6) 569 + 724 = 1192 (carried 1)

7) 78 + 16 = 95 (carried 1)

8) 25 + 35 = 60 (carried 1)

a. Score Student Work Sample Error V for Ian. Identify his strengths and error patterns. Complete a DAS for Ian.

b. Complete an MIP.

8. Find or design a mathematics activity to use with this child (Ian) in addressing Error Pattern I.

9. Design a question that would focus on the conceptual understanding of addition regrouping. The question should help the teacher determine which students understood why regrouping would be necessary from place to place.

References

Ashlock, R. B. (1990). *Error patterns in computation: A semiprogrammed approach* (5th ed.). Upper Saddle River, NJ: Merrill/Prentice Hall.

Baroody, A. (2006). Why children have difficulties mastering the basic number combinations and how to help them. *Teaching Children Mathematics, 13*(1), 22–31.

Brown, J. S., & Burton, R. R. (1978). Diagnostic models for procedural bugs in basic mathematical skills. *Cognitive Science, 2*, 155–192.

Campbell, P. F., Rowan, T. E., & Suarez, A. R. (1998). What criteria for student-invented algorithms? In L. J. Morrow & M. J. Kenny (Eds.), *The teaching and learning of algorithms in school mathematics, 1998 Yearbook of the National Council of Teachers of Mathematics* (NCTM) (pp. 49–55). Reston, VA: NCTM.

Carey, D. A. (1991). Number sentences: Linking addition and subtraction word problems and symbols. *Journal for Research in Mathematics Education, 22*(4), 266–280.

Carpenter, T. P., Franke, M. L., Jacobs, V. R., Fennema, E., & Empson, S. B. (1997). A longitudinal study of invention and understanding in children's multidigit addition and subtraction. *Journal for Research in Mathematics Education, 29*(1), 3–20.

Chambers, D. L. (1996, October). Direct modeling and invented procedures: Building on children's informal strategies. *Teaching Children Mathematics, 3*, 92–95.

Clements, M. A. (1980). Analyzing children's errors on written mathematical tasks. *Educational Studies in Mathematics, 11*, 1–21.

Cox, L. S. (1975). Diagnosing and remediating systemic errors in addition and subtraction computations. *Arithmetic Teacher, 22*(2), 151–157.

Enright, B. (1989). *Basic mathematics: Detecting and correcting for special needs*. Boston: Allyn & Bacon.

Fuson, K. C. (1990). Issues in place value and multidigit addition and subtraction learning and teaching. *Journal for Research in Mathematics Education, 21*, 273–280.

Fuson, K. C., & Briars, D. J. (1990). Using a base-ten blocks learning/teaching approach for the first- and second-grade place-value and multidigit addition and subtraction. *Journal for Research in Mathematics Education, 21*, 180–206.

Fuson, K. C., Stigler, J. W., & Bartsch, K. (1988, November). Grade placement of addition and subtraction topics in Japan, Mainland China, the Soviet Union, Taiwan, and the United States. *Journal for Research in Mathematics Education, 19*, 449–456.

Groen, G., & Resnick, L. (1977). Can pre-school children invent addition algorithms? *Journal of Educational Psychology, 69*, 645–652.

Guberman, S. R. (2004). A comparative study of children's out-of-school activities and arithmetical achievements. *Journal for Research in Mathematics Education, 35*(2), 117–150.

Isaacs, A. C., & Carroll, W. M. (1999). Strategies for basic facts instruction. *Teaching Children Mathematics, 32*(6), 508–515.

Kamii, C., & Dominick, A. (1998). The harmful effects of algorithms in grades 1–4. In L. J. Morrow & M. J. Kenney (Eds.), *The teaching and learning of algorithms in school mathematics, 1998 Yearbook of the National Council of Teachers of Mathematics* (NCTM) (pp. 130–39). Reston, VA: NCTM.

Kamii, C., Lewis, B., & Livingston, S. (1993). Primary arithmetic: Children inventing their own procedures. *Arithmetic Teacher, 41*, 200–203.

Kenney, P. A., & Silver, E. A. (Eds.). (1997). *Results from the sixth mathematics assessment of the National Assessment of Educational Progress*. Reston, VA: National Council of Teachers of Mathematics. (ERIC Document Reproduction Service No. ED 409 172)

Leutzinger, L. P. (1999). Developing thinking strategies for addition facts. *Teaching Children Mathematics, 6*(1), 14–18.

Murata, A., & Fuson, K. (2006). Teaching as assisting individual constructive paths within an interdependent class learning zone: Japanese first graders learning to add using 10. *Journal for Research in Mathematics Education, 37*(5), 421–456.

National Council of Teachers of Mathematics. (2000). *Principles and standards for school mathematics*. Reston, VA: Author.

Radatz, H. (1979). Error analysis in mathematics education. *Journal for Research in Mathematics Education, 10*(3), 163–172.

Rathmell, E. C. (1978). Using thinking strategies to teach the basic facts. In M. N. Suydam & R. E. Reys (Eds.), *Developing computational skills, 1978 Yearbook of the National Council of Teachers of Mathematics* (NCTM) (pp. 13–38). Reston, VA: NCTM.

Roseman, L. (1985). Ten essential concepts for remediation in mathematics. *Mathematics Teacher, 78*(7), 502–507.

Sáenz-Ludlow, A. (2004). Metaphor and numerical diagrams in the arithmetical activity of a fourth-grade class. *Journal for Research in Mathematics Education, 35*(1), 34–56.

Selter, C. (2001). Addition and subtraction of three-digit numbers: German elementary children's success, methods, and strategies. *Educational Studies in Mathematics, 47*, 145–173.

Sisul, J. (2002). Fostering flexibility with numbers in the primary grades. *Teaching Children Mathematics, 9*(4), 202–204.

Skemp, R. (1976). Relational understanding and instrumental understanding. *Mathematics Teacher, 77*, 20–26.

Starkey, P., & Gelman, R. (1982). The development of addition and subtraction abilities prior to formal schooling in arithmetic. In T. Carpenter, J. M. Moser, & T. A. Romberg (Eds.), *Addition and subtraction: A cognitive perspective* (pp. 99–116). Hillsdale, NJ: Lawrence Erlbaum Associates.

Sun, W., & Zhang, J. Y. (2001). Teaching addition and subtraction facts: A Chinese perspective. *Teaching Children Mathematics, 8*(1), 28–31.

Thornton, C. A. (1978, May). Emphasizing thinking strategies in basic fact instruction. *Journal for Research in Mathematics Education, 9*, 214–227.

Thornton, C. A. (1990). Strategies for the basic facts. In J. N. Payne (Ed.), *Mathematics for the young child* (pp. 132–151). Reston, VA: National Council of Teachers of Mathematics.

Tucker, B. (1989). Seeing addition: A diagnostic-remediation case study. *The Arithmetic Teacher, 36*(5), 10–11.

Villasenor, A., & Kepner, H. S. (1993). Arithmetic from a problem-solving perspective: An urban implementation. *Journal for Research in Mathematics Education, 24*(1), 62–69.

Warren, E. (2007). Children's invented notations as insights into mathematical thinking: A review of mathematical development in young children: Exploring notations. *Journal for Research in Mathematics Education, 38*(3), 322–326.

Wood, T., Williams, G., & McNeal, B. (2006). Children's mathematical thinking in different classroom cultures. *Journal for Research in Mathematics Education, 37*(3), 222–255.

Zhou, Z., & Peverly, S. T. (2005). Teaching addition and subtraction to first graders: A Chinese perspective. *Psychology in the Schools, 42*(3), 259–272.

Chapter 4

Subtraction of Whole Numbers

Subtraction is much harder than addition because you have to think down.

If I can't take the bottom number from the top number, I just take the top number away from the bottom number.

Subtracting with 0s is easy since they don't mean anything.

I can't count backwards on my fingers as fast as forwards so subtracting is harder for me.

What Is Subtraction?

Subtraction of whole numbers is represented in the physical world by the complement of one set within a larger set. The cardinal numbers of the large set represents the minuend, one of the subsets is the subtrahend, and the cardinal number of the remaining set is the difference. There are at least two situations depicting subtraction. One involves "take away," where something is taken away; and the other involves "how many more," where two sets are compared to determine how many more are in the larger set. A situation such as: "Imir has five apples and eats two of them. How many apples does Imir have left?" is depicted in Figure 4.1 and involves something being "taken away."

The representation of $5 - 2 = 3$ involves a set of five apples, with two of the apples within a subset. The answer to the problem is the remaining set that is left (the complement set), or three apples.

The second subtraction situation is present in a problem such as: "Imir has five apples and Branca has two apples. How many more apples does Imir have?"

In this problem, the representation of $5 - 2 = 3$ involves two separate sets, as shown in Figure 4.2. The sets are compared and the answer is the number of apples in the large set minus the number of apples in the smaller set—that is, how many "more" apples Imir has in his set.

Children need to understand both subtraction situations well before beginning work on subtraction algorithms. After children understand the subtraction concept, developmental work with understanding the algorithm can begin.

FIGURE 4.1
Subtraction:
"How Many Left?"

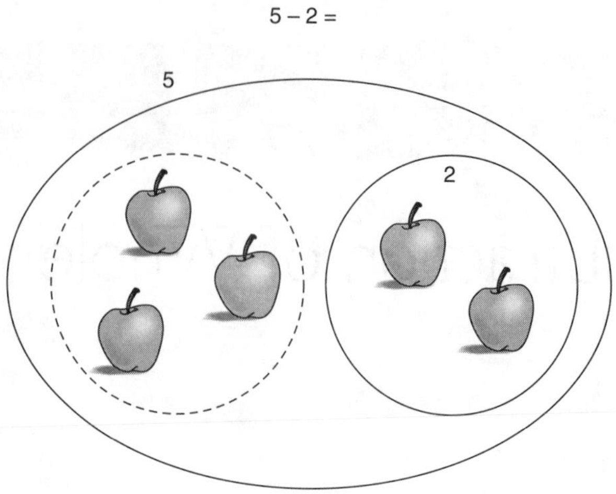

FIGURE 4.2
Subtraction:
"How Many More?"

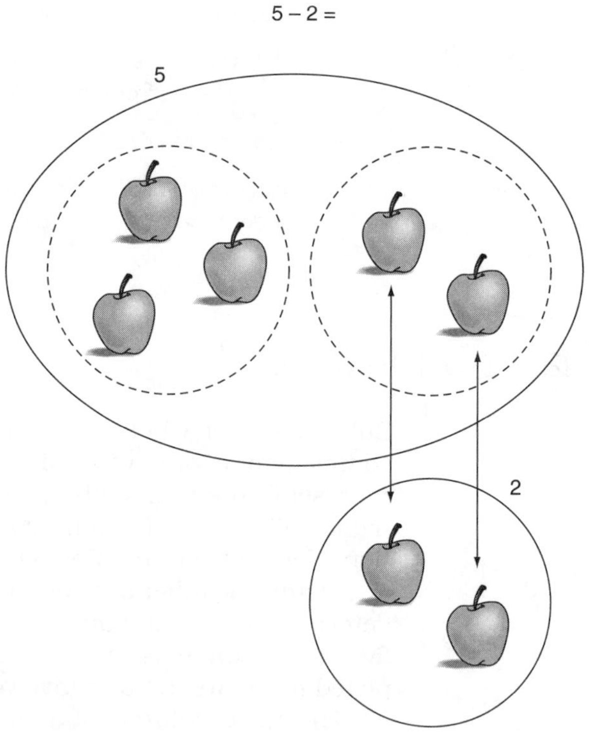

Algorithmic understandings of place value and procedures of regrouping or renaming are also learned. Learners break a set, such as base-10 blocks, apart into constituent subsets to demonstrate ability to identify minuends and subtrahends when determining a difference. Drawings are connected to the manipulative work. Each time the concept is introduced, for both set and algorithmic work including place value use of regrouping, students should be presented with a situation that poses a "real-world" problem that must be solved by utilizing objects and drawings and working with numerical symbols. The key process in all of the work is to make sure the child understands the subtraction concept before working with abstract symbols.

What Should Students Understand About Subtraction?

During primary grades K–2, children should develop an understanding of whole numbers and instructional attention should have been focused on strategies for computing with whole numbers (NCTM, 2000, p. 35). Operations of addition and subtraction should be understood by the beginning of grade 3, with instruction focusing on strategies for computing with whole numbers. Children should have developed methods for subtracting two-digit numbers by experiencing a variety of computational situations that require subtractive thinking; children should have shared and discussed their methods of solution. Efficiency of children's methods should be a part of the discussion of various strategies, according to Hiebert as well as Kamii, Lewis, and Livingston (as cited in NCTM, 2000, p. 35). They further indicate that children should have developed efficient, accurate methods supported by an understanding of subtraction operations.

The literature features many researchers (Fuson, 1990; Isaacs & Carroll, 1999; Lee, 1991; Leutzinger, 1999; Sun & Zhang, 2001; Whitenack, Knipping, Novinger, & Underwood, 2001) who have suggestions for approaches to subtraction. What they all share in common is that the subtraction situation must be conceptually understood in order for children to be successful with subtraction. Helping children understand subtraction within the context of the base-10 system is essential for computation success. Suggestions in this chapter will focus on engaging children in discussions that foster conceptual understanding.

In this section, you will continue an error analysis approach. This is one of the steps to be used in designing a DAS and an MIP for a student. Again, a child's paper will be presented and you should follow the directions for working through each of the three examples. The proposed prescription will direct your suggested MIP design based on the child's DAS.

About the Student: Caitlin

Caitlin is a 12-year-old fifth grader of average intelligence and ability. She is well liked by her peers and has a good attitude about school. She likes to study either by herself or in small groups. She also likes to be seated close to the front of the room and resists being separated from the teacher for a prolonged period of time. She generally avoids large-group activities and has been observed reacting to these settings by pushing her peers or calling them insulting names.

Caitlin responds well to having material explained by examples put on the board or the overhead projector. She seems to do well when material is put on tape, so she can listen and relisten to the directions at her leisure. She does not do well when the same material is given to her in written form and she is expected to read and understand without teacher assistance.

When she is expected to read or present her answers to the whole class, she either does not respond or becomes verbally aggressive to the teacher. She typically will respond positively when she can give her answers to a small group or to the teacher. She enjoys writing her answers out on paper and giving them to the teacher without any attention from classroom peers.

She enjoys tangible rewards from her teacher, especially written notes or stickers that can be taken home to her family for their observation. She seems to appreciate it when the teacher calls her mother and praises her class work. However, she does not like the teacher giving negative evaluations to her mother but will not object verbally or behaviorally when the teacher does so. She likes small-group competition and will ask to play academic games within the small group.

She does not like to be recognized by the teacher in front of the entire class, but does enjoy having her small group made aware of her successes. Being able to eat with the teacher or work as a helper to the teacher is reinforcing to her.

Caitlin has the ability to concentrate on a task for about 30 minutes. However, she has a tendency to become physically aggressive when transition activities include physical movement in the room. Any school activity that causes physical contact will often cause her to either withdraw from the activity or become aggressive. Therefore, she does not do well in physical education class or when movement occurs during class changes.

Error Patterns: Diagnosis, Prescription, Remediation

The following simulations assume Caitlin has taken a subtraction test. In each situation a different error has emerged. The task in each sample is to identify appropriate lessons based on knowledge of the child and knowledge of the exhibited math deficiency.

Subtraction Error Pattern I for Caitlin

The first sample for Caitlin is a completed, nine-problem subtraction paper. You should use the following four-step process:

1. Score the paper.
2. Begin with the first incorrect problem and attempt to determine the algorithm Caitlin is using to obtain the answers.
3. Use Caitlin's pattern and see if the second incorrect problem follows the pattern.
   a. If it does, go to step four.
   b. If it does not, study the error in the second problem and revise your prediction of the algorithm used.
4. Confirm the pattern using the third incorrect problem.

Complete the four-step process now, using the data shown.

Diagnosing the Error: Once you have finished scoring the paper and identifying the proposed pattern of error, you should reflect on the strengths exhibited in the child's subtraction work. Strengths to look for include knowledge of place

STUDENT WORK SAMPLE ERROR I FOR CAITLIN

1. 34	2. 86	3. 71
− 2	− 7	−69
32	81	18
4. 42	5. 56	6. 854
−27	−51	− 60
25	5	814
7. 305	8. 832	9. 420
−147	−807	−119
242	35	319

value, facts (both easy [minuends 10 or less] and hard [minuends 11 to 18]), work with zero in subtraction, and the ability to regroup in subtraction—to mention just a few. Use the space below to record your observations.

Caitlin's Error Pattern(s):
Caitlin's Strengths:

Scoring Work Sample Error I finds Caitlin getting two of nine (22 percent) correct. She has a number of strengths that should prove beneficial in any remediation. She knows the column format for subtraction. Caitlin also knows:

1. easy subtraction facts involving minuends less than 10 (she gets all of these differences correct)
2. subtraction when the subtrahend is a zero

It is not possible to determine whether she knows the hard subtraction facts because she never subtracts from a minuend of 10 or more. You would need to determine her knowledge of these facts through a follow-up discussion with her.

An example of a completed DAS for Caitlin is included in Table 4.1.

Prescription: Caitlin seems to be always subtracting the smaller value from the larger value, regardless of whether the smaller value is in the minuend or the subtrahend. This is not an uncommon problem as students move from subtraction fact work to working with column subtraction. Early work with column subtraction usually does not involve a need to regroup, so many students invent a method of working in the columns and then invoke that method when first encountering a need to regroup in column subtraction.

Caitlin seems to have a good grasp of subtraction facts, so this is probably a procedural error. If the student knows her hard subtraction facts, this probably is a case of not recognizing a need to regroup (a procedural error). It could be a conceptual error in place value, and if so, it will become apparent as you work with her in remediation. Should it prove to be a place value problem, then review Chapter 2 for suggestions.

Remediation: Begin working with Caitlin by using bundled sticks that represent tens and single sticks that represent ones. Start with a problem that she worked correctly on the test, such as problem 1, 34 – 2. Caitlin should get 3 tens and 4 ones. Have her take away two. Then record what she has just done as you describe and write (we suggest you do the writing, because Caitlin likes working with the teacher and it will allow her to focus on handling the manipulatives while watching how they are written). This also avoids the difficulty of her writing the information in an incorrect place and you having to either erase or correct what she had done. It helps to set up a win-win situation.

3 4	the student gets 3 tens and 4 ones
−2	she takes away 2 ones
3 2	this leaves 2 ones, which you record in the ones column, and 3 tens, which you record in the tens column.

Now present a problem such as problem 2 on the test:

$$\begin{array}{r} 86 \\ -7 \\ \hline \end{array}$$

Have Caitlin work out the problem with the manipulatives and see if she arrives at an answer of 79. If she does, have her compare this result with the answer she wrote on the test. Now she should recognize the disequilibrium between the answer she obtained by using her invented method and the answer she obtained with the manipulatives. Base-10 materials will work just as well if you have them available.

TABLE 4.1 Data Analysis Sheet

Student: Caitlin						
Team Members:						
Context	**Content Assessment**	**Process**		**Behavior**		**Reinforcement**
		Input	Output	Academic	Social	
+	+	+	+	+	+	+
• Seated in front of room, by herself or in small groups • Likes to be close to the teacher	***Learned Concepts I*** • Knows column format for subtraction • Knows easy facts and minuends less than 10 • Knows subtraction involving zero ***Learned Concepts II*** • Place value • Format for subtraction • Easy facts, minuend less than 10 • Hard facts, minuend greater than 10 • Borrowing across a zero • Subtrahends involving zero ***Learned Concepts III*** • Format for column subtraction • Easy facts, minuend less than 10 • Hard facts, minuend greater than 10 • Decision to borrow, zero in subtraction	• Small-group instruction • Likes the material to be presented on tape and can listen or relisten to it at her leisure	• Can stay on task for 30 minutes • Has good concentration when talking to the teacher	• One-on-one or study groups • Does better during classroom instruction	• Likes small groups • Enjoys one-on-one • Likes to be near the teacher	• Rewards from her teacher • Tangible and take-home rewards • Likes the teacher to call her mother • Likes to eat with the teacher and being the teacher's helper • Likes school and her teacher
–	–	–	–	–	–	–
• Large groups • Away from the teacher • Hallway • Recess • Physical education classes	***Error Pattern I*** • Does not regroup, no indication of order of subtraction ***Error Pattern II*** • Decision of when to borrow. ***Error Pattern III*** • Borrows from wrong place	• Written material • Read material without teacher assistance • Reading or speaking her answers to the class as a whole	• Speaking in an audience situation	• Large-group instruction • Speaking her answers to the large group during instruction	• Physically aggressive during transition periods • Stays away from large groups	• Negative calls from her teacher to the home • Recognition of herself to the class as a whole

Note: The + symbols indicate strengths and the – symbols indicate areas of concern.

Talk with Caitlin about how she arrived at 79. Have her rework the problem, and at some point, she will unbundle a group of 10 and combine those 10 sticks with the 6 singles, leaving a total of 16 singles. Have Caitlin record what she is doing with the materials in order to help her connect the manipulative work with the written symbols that record that work, beginning with the following:

8 6	the total sticks counted out as 8 tens and 6 ones
− 7	the number we wish to take away

As Caitlin unbundles the one group of 10 and combines it with the six singles, she should record what is being done as:

7 16	
~~8~~ ~~6~~	crossing out the 8 in the tens column and writing a 7 above, then crossing out the 6 in the ones column and writing a 16 above it
− 7	have Caitlin take away 7
9	record the 9 in the ones column and discuss with the student why this is written down at this time (the 9 records how many ones are left when 7 are taken away)

At this point, ask Caitlin how many she has left after taking away the seven singles. She should respond that she has 79 sticks. If she does, then have her record the 7 in the tens column on the paper, with a discussion that because there are not any 10s to be taken away, we record the number of 10s in the tens column. You should write a zero in the tens column of the subtrahend at this point if you think it will facilitate understanding. It would look something like this:

```
  7 16
  8  6   (8 and 6 crossed out)
 −0  7
 -----
  7  9
```

It is critical that you guide the student to make the connection between the action she is performing on the manipulative materials and the mathematical symbolism used to record that action. This connection of concrete materials with symbolism is often missing from classroom instruction.

It is critically important that you understand that we are not advocating directly teaching the student the algorithm. We are encouraging you to serve as a recorder for the student as she works the problem with the manipulatives. You must have her explain what she has done at each step of the problem, and you then record the information—explaining to her why you are writing the symbols where you are writing them. You serve as the recorder for the student while she does the actual work. In this way, you help the student connect what she has done with the manipulatives to the symbolism that records that result or action.

Have Caitlin work another problem, such as 34 – 6. Once again, record what is being done as the student works with the manipulatives.

It is now time to have Caitlin work a problem with the manipulatives and record, at each step, the result of what she is doing. After a few of these connecting problems, see if the student can work the problem using only the symbols. Then have her work the problem with manipulatives to see if she gets

TABLE 4.2 Mathematics Improvement Plan I for Caitlin: Correcting Procedural Errors in Subtraction

Time		15 minutes	10–15 minutes	10 minutes
Context		Close to teacher (+) In classroom (+) Use small-group setting (+)	In classroom (+) With peer (+) Close to teacher (+)	Working independently (–) Close to teacher (+) In classroom (+)
Content		Play skill game "What's the Difference" with another student to practice basic subtraction (+)	Work with another child with a subtraction fact card deck. Child models the fact using sticks to verify the answers to the fact (+)	Work with another child (or small group) using algorithmic procedures to find differences for subtraction problems that require regrouping (+)
Process	Input	Pencil and paper (+) Oral instruction by teacher (–)	Tactile material (+) Independent reading (–) Pencil and paper (+)	Tactile materials supported by visuals and graphics (+)
	Output	Oral activities, student responds (–) Written task (+)	Answers in single words (+) Working on laptop (+)	Oral activities (–) Laptop usage (+)
Behavior	Academic	Completing the assignment, hands in material, performs at acceptable competence level (+)	Turns in assignments (+) Accepts teacher directions (+)	Staying in seat (–) Turning in material upon request (+)
	Social	Follows teacher's directions (+) Controlling vocalization (–)	Positive response to peers and turns in assignments upon request (+)	Monitoring for student use of self-control (–)
Reinforcement		Receives "good student" note from teacher (+)	Allowed movement in classroom (+) Gets "good student behavior" note to give to parent or guardian (+)	Group classroom activities (+) Sitting with peers (+)

Note: The + symbols indicate strengths and the – symbols indicate areas of concern.

the same answer. Through this guided dialogue, you are developing a conceptual understanding for Caitlin of how to record the steps involved in performing subtraction. Once she feels that she can understand what is taking place in the subtraction situation (feels empowered), she should be encouraged to work the problems symbolically. Encourage her to use the manipulatives at any time she feels confused or wants to confirm what she has written. Table 4.2 contains an MIP for Caitlin.

Subtraction Error Pattern II for Caitlin

The second sample paper also involves nine subtraction problems. You should complete the four-step process outlined for Error Pattern I.

Diagnosing the Error: After you have scored the paper, identify the proposed pattern of error and reflect on the strengths exhibited in the child's subtraction work. Strengths to look for include knowledge of place value, subtraction facts

STUDENT WORK SAMPLE ERROR II FOR CAITLIN

	Problem	Student's regrouping marks	Student's answer
1.	34 − 2	2 1	212
2.	86 − 7	7 1	79
3.	71 − 69	6 1	2
4.	42 − 27	3 1	15
5.	56 − 51	4 1	115
6.	854 − 60	7 14 1	7814
7.	305 − 147	2 9 1	158
8.	832 − 807	7 12 1	1125
9.	420 − 119	3 11 1	2101

(both easy [minuends 10 or less] and hard [minuends 11 to 18]), work with zero in subtraction, and the ability to regroup in subtraction. Use the space below to record your observations.

Caitlin's Error Pattern(s):
Caitlin's Strengths:

Caitlin scores four correct of the nine problems. While this 44 percent performance seems quite low, Caitlin exhibits many strengths and should enjoy improved performance almost immediately. Caitlin knows:

1. the format for performing subtraction (an excellent knowledge of place value is involved when regrouping is apparent)
2. hard subtraction facts (many of the subtractions involved difficult processes such as those in problems 2, 5, 6, 8, and 9)
3. regrouping and renaming across a zero, such as in problem 7

She also works correctly with a zero subtrahend in problems 6 and 8.

The first incorrect problem, problem 1, seems to exhibit a regrouping when it is not needed. Going to the second incorrect problem, problem 5, shows the same pattern. Looking at the third incorrect problem, problem 6, confirms that the child is regrouping whether it is necessary or not.

Prescription: Caitlin appears to have a conceptual problem with subtraction. She is regrouping every time, whether she needs to or not. She isn't making a decision about whether she can perform a subtraction with the numbers given, but is blindly regrouping every time. Caitlin's major problem is making a decision for the need to regroup in order to work the problem. This first step is critical when working a subtraction problem.

Remediation: Table 4.3 contains the MIP. Initial work with Caitlin should be the same as with the previous error. Rather than repeat the remedial suggestion, you might reread the previous remediation suggestions. One cannot overemphasize the need to do the conceptual work with manipulatives and the following assumes that you have completed that work.

In our experience, this error will not require a difficult remediation. We have found that a mnemonic as simple as a 3 × 5 card can be used to focus Caitlin on the critical decision of whether the subtraction can be performed or whether she will need to regroup in order to perform the subtraction. A problem such as:

$$\begin{array}{r} 34 \\ -\ 2 \\ \hline \end{array}$$

can be used with the 3 × 5 card to make the decision. Caitlin should have already worked this problem with manipulatives to see that she gets an answer different from the 212 she recorded on her test paper. Given that, have the student get the 34 sticks (3 tens and 4 ones). You record the problem on paper. Cover the problem with the 3 × 5 card. Then slide the card from right to left to expose the ones column.

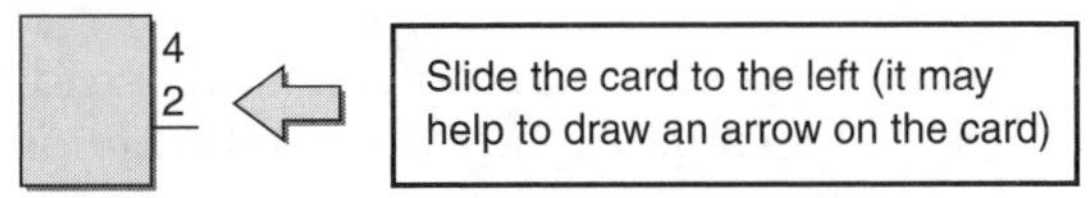

Once the ones column is exposed, ask Caitlin to make a decision about whether the subtraction can be performed. She should indicate that she can subtract, and should get 2 as an answer to this part of the problem. Have her record her answer to this part of the problem before going on. Then slide the

TABLE 4.3 Mathematics Improvement Plan II for Caitlin: Deciding Whether to Regroup

Time		**10–15 minutes**	**15 minutes**	**15–20 minutes**
Context		Close to teacher (+) In classroom (+) Large-group setting (–)	In classroom (+) With peer (+) Close to teacher (+)	Working independently (–) Close to teacher (+) In classroom (+)
Content		Play skill game "The Pot Thickens" with another child to practice subtraction facts (+)	Work with another child or small group using subtraction fact card deck. Child models the fact using sticks to verify the answer to the fact (+)	Work with another child or small group using algorithmic procedures to find differences for subtraction problems requiring regrouping (+) Teams of children play "Zero Wins" to practice subtraction (+)
Process	Input	Pencil/paper (+) Oral instruction by teacher (–)	Tactile material (+) Independent reading (–) Pencil/paper (+)	Tactile materials supported by visuals and graphics (+)
	Output	Written task (+)	Answers in single words (+) Working on laptop (+)	Oral activities (–) Laptop usage (+)
Behavior	Academic	Completing the assignment, hands in material, performs at acceptable competence level (+)	Turns in assignments (+) Accepts teacher directions (+)	Staying in seat (–) Turning in material upon request (+)
	Social	Follows teacher's directions (+) Controlling vocalization (–)	Positive response to peers and turns in the assignment upon request (+)	Encourage student use of self-control (+)
Reinforcement		Receives "good student" note from teacher (+)	Allowed movement in classroom (+) Gets "good student behavior" note to give to parent/guardian (+)	Group classroom activities (+) Sitting with peers (+)

Note: The + symbols indicate strengths and the – symbols indicate areas of concern.

card to the left again and expose the tens column. This will reveal the 3 in the tens column, which is then recorded as 3 tens.

$$\begin{array}{r} 34 \\ -\ \ 2 \\ \hline 32 \end{array}$$

(Card is slid to the left, revealing the problem)

This approach has helped many students to focus on the decision about the need to regroup as they work subtraction problems.

Subtraction Error Pattern III for Caitlin

The third sample paper appears on the following page. You should use the same four-step process you used to assess Sample Errors I and II for Caitlin.

STUDENT WORK SAMPLE ERROR III FOR CAITLIN

1. 34 − 2 = 32	2. 86 − 7 = 79 (8 crossed out to 7; 1 written beside the 6)	3. 71 − 69 = 2 (7 crossed out to 6; 1 written beside the 1)
4. 42 − 27 = 15 (4 crossed out to 3; 1 written beside the 2)	5. 56 − 51 = 5	6. 854 − 60 = 794 (8 crossed out to 7; 1 written beside the 5)
7. 305 − 147 = 68 (3 crossed out to 1; 1s written beside the 0 and the 5)	8. 832 − 807 = ~~35~~ 25 (8 crossed out to 7; 1 written beside the 2)	9. 420 − 119 = 211 (4 crossed out to 3; 1 written beside the 0)

Diagnosing the Error: Once you have finished scoring the paper and identifying the proposed pattern of error, you should reflect on the strengths exhibited in the child's subtraction work. Strengths to look for include knowledge of place value, facts (both easy [minuends 10 or less] and hard [minuends 11 to 18]), work with zero in subtraction, and the ability to regroup in subtraction. Use the space given on the following page to record your observations.

Caitlin's Error Pattern(s):
Caitlin's Strengths:

Caitlin got six of the nine problems correct (67 percent), which is a borderline performance. Closer inspection of Caitlin's work shows tremendous strength in subtraction. First, Caitlin knows the format in column subtraction. She also knows:

1. easy subtraction facts (those involving minuends less than 10)
2. hard subtraction facts involving minuends greater than 10
3. regrouping, as in problems 2, 3, 4, and 6
4. use of zero in subtraction, as in problem 6 and 8

Looking at the first incorrect problem reveals that Caitlin always regroups from the left-most column. In two-digit problems the error doesn't emerge; it surfaces only when there are three or more columns. Caitlin has invented an approach to subtraction that has worked successfully for at least one or two grade levels and has probably been internalized through multiyear practice with the method. This appears to be a procedural error rather than a conceptual error, as Caitlin is not reasoning when she performs with the symbols. She also does not seem to have a cognitive organizer for what she is regrouping and from where; rather, she seems to just be manipulating the symbols in the same way she manipulated two-digit problems. She seems to have a conceptual error involving place value as it relates to subtraction.

Depending upon the richness of the environment within which Caitlin has encountered subtraction, she may be transferring how her invented approach worked with two-digit problems to problems with three, four, or more digits. Given the strengths of this student, remediation of this difficulty should be rather easily achieved. The degree to which Caitlin has reinforced this incorrect thinking will dictate how hard this problem is to extinguish.

The displayed work in problem 8 seems to indicate that Caitlin changed strategies on this problem. When discussing this problem with her, she indicated that she got to the "7 take-away 8" and realized something was wrong, so she just reasoned that 800 take-away 800 was just going to leave 32 take-away 7, which was 25, so she just wrote it in. This was an excellent example that when a student is using a procedure and arrives at what appears to be a paradox, the student will shift strategies altogether and use a technique that does not seem to fit the pattern. The student will rarely, however, realize this has implications for how other problems have been worked. Instead, she will treat it as an isolated event that is unique to this particular problem. It also should reinforce the need for you to speak with students and have them explain what they were doing in order for you to correctly assess problems.

Prescription: We consider this error to be a procedural error. When regrouping is necessary, Caitlin is going to the farthest digit on the left and proceeding to regroup. All other aspects of the subtraction are performed correctly. However,

TABLE 4.4 Mathematics Improvement Plan III for Caitlin: Procedural Errors Involving Regrouping

Time		10 minutes	20 minutes	10–15 minutes
Context		Close to teacher (+) In classroom (+) Large-group setting (–)	In classroom (+) With peer (+) Close to teacher (+)	Working independently (–) Close to teacher (+) In classroom (+)
Content		Play skill game "What's the Difference" with another child to practice subtraction (+)	Work in teams of children with the game "Zero Wins." The team works the problem together (+)	Works with another child or small group using algorithmic procedures to find differences for subtraction problems requiring regrouping (+)
Process	Input	Pencil and paper (+) Oral instruction by teacher (–)	Tactile material (+) Independent reading (–) Pencil and paper (+)	Tactile materials supported by visuals and graphics (+)
	Output	Oral activities, student responds (–) Written task (+)	Answers in single words (+) Working on laptop (+)	Oral activities (–) Laptop usage (+)
	Academic	Completing the assignment, hands in material, performs at acceptable competence level (+)	Positive response to peers and turns in the assignment upon request (+)	Monitoring for student use of self-control (–)
Behavior	Social	Follows teacher's directions (+) Work on controlling vocalization (–)	Turns in assignments (+) Accepts teacher directions (+)	Work on staying in seat (+) Turning in material upon request (+)
Reinforcement		Receives "good student" note from teacher (+)	Allowed movement in classroom (–) Gets "good student behavior" note to give to parent/guardian (+)	Group classroom activities (+) Sitting with peers (+)

Note: The + symbols indicate strengths and the – symbols indicate areas of concern.

when working with Caitlin it may become apparent that this error is rooted in a misunderstanding of place value. In that case, the remedial suggestions for place value should be undertaken. We will treat this as a procedural error due to her strengths. Table 4.4 contains the MIP for Caitlin.

Remediation: Use base-10 blocks to work with Caitlin because after working a couple of preliminary two-digit problems, the base-10 blocks will be the most efficient manipulative for modeling three-digit minuends. The flats (100s), longs (10s), and units will make modeling big numbers feasible.

The first problem to have Caitlin work should be a problem such as:

$$\begin{array}{r} 63 \\ -18 \\ \hline \end{array}$$

She will (probably without prompting) take 6 longs and 3 units to model the 63 (see illustration, p. 82).

Now ask her to take away 18. At this point, the approach each student takes will vary with the method she has invented for performing subtraction.

Because of the way she has performed the subtraction on the test, Caitlin will probably begin by trading in one of the longs for 10 units. Assuming this is

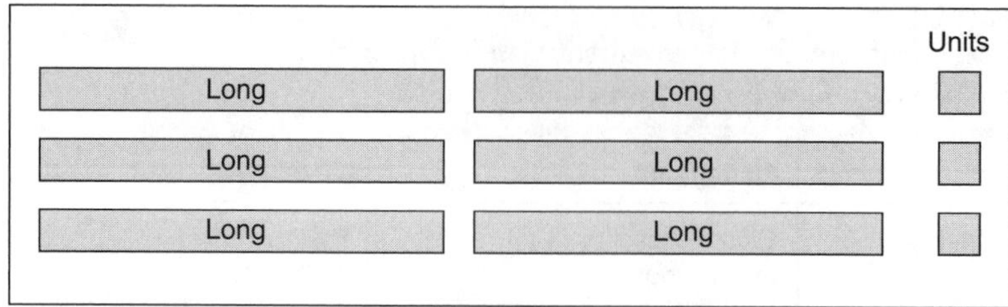

the approach taken, ask her to show you, on paper, how she would record what she has just done. What you are looking for is:

```
   5 13
   6̸ 3̸    crossing out the 6 and recording 5,
          crossing out the 3 and recording 13
 − 1 8
 ─────
```

Discuss with Caitlin that she has traded the long for 10 ones, so she reduced the longs by 1 and made the units 13. Point out to her how she has written this action. Now encourage her to complete the subtraction. She should complete the problem as she did on test problems 2, 3, and 4, recording 45 for the answer. Working a couple of problems of this type will establish correct use of the manipulatives before moving to the focus of the remedial instruction with three-digit minuends.

Now present the problem 251–14 by writing it out in vertical form. Ask Caitlin to get 251 using the manipulatives.

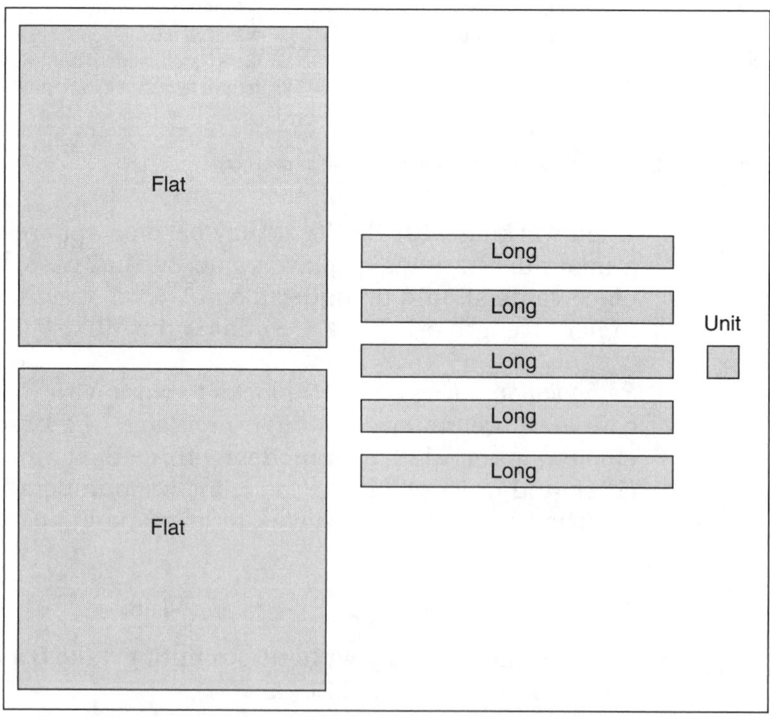

Ask her to subtract the 14. Caitlin will probably trade 1 long for 10 ones. After this is done, ask her to record on the sheet what she has just done. She should cross out the 5 and record a 4, then cross out the 1 and record 11.

```
 4 11   cross out the 5 and record a 4,
2 5 1   cross out the 1 and record an 11
 -1 4
```

Now direct Caitlin to complete the subtraction. She should arrive at an answer of 237.

```
 4 11
2 5 1
 -1 4
-----
2 3 7
```

Work a few three-digit subtraction problems, recording the result from use of the manipulatives, and writing it as she goes through the problem. Focus Caitlin on the idea that when she needs to subtract and cannot, she should go to the next column (the next larger place), regroup one group from that column, and rename it when bringing it to the digit on the right by adding 10. Once she is comfortable with expressing what she is doing, have her work a problem by using just the written problem as a guide. Then have her check her work with the manipulatives to confirm she has done the problem correctly. This should help Caitlin connect the concept of appropriately regrouping to the physical action taking place with the manipulatives. This should enhance conceptual understanding of the procedure.

Conclusions: Instructional Strategies Summary

Throughout the remediation plan for all three samples, the following suggestions would be very helpful:

1. Have learners complete a few problems at a time. Once you are satisfied that they understand something, move on.
2. Pair a slow learner with an average learner. They can help each other. Combine older and younger peers.
3. Use the simplest possible numbers to explain a mathematical operation, then move to a more complex level.

Instructional Activities

Assessing whether children's subtraction errors are primarily a result of a low level of conceptual understanding or a lack of ability to recall basic facts or work with algorithmic rules can be accomplished with various types of questions. Children's conceptual learning can be assessed and evaluated more readily by utilizing authentic, real-world situations in which learners must decide not only how to solve the problem but also whether the result is reasonable. The following are activities that can be used to reinforce subtraction knowledge.

ACTIVITY: Zero Wins

This activity is for two or more students who have knowledge of basic subtraction facts and have grasped the concept of subtraction with regrouping.

Objective: Practice subtraction with regrouping and strategic thinking

Materials:

Pen

Paper

Directions: Divide the students into two teams. Explain that each team will start with 100 points and the first team to get exactly to zero wins. Have the teams choose which one goes first by any method you wish. The team that begins the game may subtract up to 10 points on its first move. Play then goes to the next team, which may subtract up to 10 points more than the amount subtracted by the first team on its first move, or any amount of points below that number. For example, if Team A had just subtracted 8, Team B could subtract 18 points (8 + 10) or fewer. Alternate calling on different members of each team to give numbers. Encourage the students to develop game strategies—for example, while a high number might be subtracted, it gives the opposing team the opportunity to subtract an even higher number on their turn. For example:

Team A	Team B
100	100
−1	−11
99	89
−21	−3
78	86
−13	−23
65	63
−33	−10
32	53
−20	−30
12	23
−12	
0—Winner	

ACTIVITY: What's the Difference?

This game is for two students who have mastered the concept of subtraction.

Objective: Practice subtraction facts

Materials:

3 sets of 0–18 cards

Equal number of counters for each player

Directions: Place the deck face down. Each player draws a card. Whoever has the largest number gets the difference between the numbers in counters from the opponent. Play continues until the deck is used up. Player with the most counters is the winner.

ACTIVITY: The Pot Thickens

This is a developmental activity for two players.

Objective: Subtraction fact practice

Materials:

Cards numbered 1–10

Counters

Directions:

1. Deal the cards to two players.
2. Players turn cards up at the same time.
3. Player who has the low card for the round gives the other player a number of counters equal to the difference between the two cards shown.
4. If the cards are the same, take another turn. The winner is the one who has the most counters.

Discussion Questions

1. List the key steps a teacher would take when diagnosing a student's subtraction error from evidence of student work. Explain the purpose of each step in preparing for the prescription and remediation phase.
2. The following worksheet shows Student Work Sample Error IV for Caitlin:

1. 34 − 2 = 12	2. 86 − 7 = 9 (8 crossed out, 7 written above; 1 written before 6)	3. 71 − 69 = 2 (7 crossed out, 6 written above; 1 written before 1)
4. 42 − 27 = 15 (4 crossed out, 3 written above; 1 written before 2)	5. 56 − 51 = 5	6. 854 − 60 = 194 (8 crossed out, 7 written above; 1 written before 5)
7. 305 − 147 = 158 (3 and 0 crossed out, 2 and 9 written above; 1 written before 5)	8. 832 − 807 = 25 (3 crossed out, 2 written above; 1 written before 2)	9. 420 − 119 = 301 (2 crossed out, 1 written above; 1 written before 0)

   a. Score Student Work Sample Error IV for Caitlin. Identify her strengths and error patterns. Complete the DAS for Caitlin.

   b. Complete an MIP.

3. The following worksheet shows Student Work Sample Error V for Caitlin:

1. 34 − 2 2	2. 7 1 ~~8~~ 6 − 7 79	3. 6 1 ~~7~~ 1 − 69 2
4. 1 4 2 − 27 25	5. 56 − 51 5	6. 7 1 ~~8~~ 5 4 − 60 794
7. 2 1 1 ~~3~~ 0 5 − 147 168	8. 1 8 3 2 − 807 35	9. 1 4 2 0 − 119 311

a. Score Student Work Sample Error V for Caitlin. Identify her strengths and error patterns. Complete the DAS for Caitlin.

b. Complete an MIP.

4. Identify three key characteristics of a mathematics activity that would be used to address Error Pattern II for a child with the described profile.

5. Find or design an activity that you would use with students to address Error Pattern III.

6. Design a skill activity to provide practice for subtraction and fact recall. Make the activity suitable for short periods of practice for two to three students.
7. Design a question that would focus on the conceptual understanding of subtraction involving regrouping. The question should help the teacher know whether students understood why regrouping would be necessary from place to place.

References

Ashlock, R. B. (1990). *Error patterns in computation: A semiprogrammed approach* (5th ed.). Upper Saddle River, NJ: Merrill/Prentice Hall.

Baroody, A. (2006). Why children have difficulties mastering the basic number combinations and how to help them. *Teaching Children Mathematics, 13*(1), 22.

Behrend, J. L. (2001). Are rules interfering with children's mathematical understanding? *Teaching Children Mathematics, 8*(1), 36–40.

Brown, J. S., & Burton, R. R. (1978). Diagnostic models for procedural bugs in basic mathematical skills. *Cognitive Science, 2*, 155–192.

Brownell, W. A., & Moser, H. E. (1949). *Meaningful vs. mechanical learning: A study in grade III subtraction.* Durham, NC: Duke University Press.

Campbell, P. F., Rowan, T. E., & Suarez, A. R. (1998). What criteria for student invented algorithms? In J. Morrow & M. J. Kenny (Eds.), *The teaching and learning of algorithms in school mathematics, 1998 Yearbook of the National Council of Teachers of Mathematics* (NCTM) (pp. 49–55). Reston, VA: NCTM.

Carey, D. A. (1991). Number sentences: Linking addition and subtraction word problems and symbols. *Journal for Research in Mathematics Education, 22*(4), 266–280.

Carpenter, T. P., & Moser, J. M. (1982). The development of addition and subtraction problem-solving skills. In T. P. Carpenter, J. M. Moser, & T. A. Romberg (Eds.), *Addition and subtraction: A cognitive perspective* (pp. 9–24). Hillsdale, NJ: Lawrence Erlbaum Associates.

Carpenter, T. P., & Moser, J. M. (May, 1984). The acquisition of addition and subtraction concepts in grades one through three. *Journal for Research in Mathematics Education, 15*, 179–202.

Cobb, P. (1993). *Children's construction of arithmetical algorithms in social context.* Final report to the National Science Foundation. Available from author, Vanderbilt University.

Drucker, H., McBride, S., & Wilbur, C. (1987). Using a computer-based error analysis approach to improve basic subtraction skills in the third grade. *The Journal of Educational Research, 80*(6), 363–365.

Engelhardt, J. M. (1977). Analysis of children's computational errors: A qualitative approach. *British Journal of Educational Psychology, 47*, 149–154.

Flowers, J., Kline, K., & Rubenstein, R. N. (2003). Developing computational examples in subtraction. *Teaching Children Mathematics, 9*(6), 330–334.

Fuson, K. C. (1990). Issues in place-value and multidigit addition and subtraction learning and teaching. *Journal for Research in Mathematics Education, 21*, 273–280.

Fuson, K. C., & Briars, D. J. (1990). Using a base-ten blocks learning/teaching approach for the first- and second-grade place-value and multidigit and addition and subtraction. *Journal for Research in Mathematics Education, 21*, 180–206.

Fuson, K. C., Stigler, J. W., & Bartsch, K. (1988, November). Grade placement of addition and subtraction topics in Japan, Mainland China, the Soviet Union, Taiwan, and the United States. *Journal for Research in Mathematics Education, 19*, 449–456.

Guberman, S. R. (2004). A comparative study of children's out-of-school activities and arithmatical achievements. *Journal for Research in Mathematics Education, 35*(2), 117–150.

Huinker, D., Freckman, J. L., & Steinmeyer, M. (2003). Subtraction strategies from children's thinking: Moving toward fluency with greater numbers. *Teaching Children Mathematics, 9*(6), 347–353.

Isaacs, A. C., & Carroll, W. M. (1999). Strategies for basic facts instruction. *Teaching Children Mathematics, 32*(6), 508–515.

Kamii, C. (1994). *Young children continue to reinvent arithmetic: 3rd grade*. New York: Teachers College Press.

Kamii, C., & Dominick, A. (1998). The harmful effects of algorithms in grades 1–4. In L. J. Morrow & M. J. Kenny (Eds.), *The teaching and learning of algorithms in school mathematics, 1998 Yearbook of the National Council of Teachers of Mathematics* (NCTM) (pp. 130–139). Reston, VA: NCTM.

Lee, K. S. (1991). Left-to-right computations and estimation. *School Science & Mathematics, 91*, 199–202.

Leutzinger, L. P. (1999). Developing thinking strategies for addition facts. *Teaching Children Mathematics, 6*, 14–18.

National Council of Teachers of Mathematics. (2000). *Principles and standards for school mathematics*. Reston, VA: Author.

Osburn, W. J. (1927). How shall we subtract? *Journal of Educational Research, 16*, 237–246.

Postlewait, K. B., Adams, M. R., & Shih, J. C. (2003). Promoting meaningful mastery of addition & subtraction. *Teaching Children Mathematics, 9*(6), 354–357.

Radatz, H. (1979). Error analysis in mathematics education. *Journal for Research in Mathematics Education, 10*(3), 163–172.

Rathmell, E. C. (1978). Using thinking strategies to teach the basic facts. In M. N. Suydam & R. E. Reys (Eds.), *Developing computational skills, 1978 Yearbook of the National Council of Teachers of Mathematics* (NCTM) (pp. 13–38). Reston, VA: NCTM.

Skrtic, T. M., Kvam, N. E., & Beals, V. L. (1983). Identifying and remediating the subtraction errors of learning disabled adolescents. *The Pointer, 27*(2), 32–38.

Sun, W., & Zhang, J. Y. (2001). Teaching addition and subtraction facts: A Chinese perspective. *Teaching Children Mathematics, 8*(1), 28–31.

Thompson, C. S., & Van de Walle, J. (1984, October). Let's do it: Modeling subtraction situations. *Arithmetic Teacher, 32*, 8–12.

Thornton, C. A. (1989, April). Look ahead: Activities spark success in addition and subtraction number-fact learning. *Arithmetic Teacher*, 8–11.

Thornton, C. A. (1990). Strategies for the basic facts. In J. N. Payne (Ed.), *Mathematics for the young child* (pp. 132–151). Reston, VA: National Council of Teachers of Mathematics.

Thornton, C. A., & Smith, P. J. (1988, April). Action research: Strategies for learning subtraction facts. *Arithmetic Teacher, 35*, 8–12.

Van Houten, R. (1993). Rote vs. rules: A comparison of two teaching and correction strategies for teaching basic subtraction facts. *Education and Treatment of Children, 16*(2), 147–159.

Whitenack, J. W., Knipping, N., Novinger, S., & Underwood, G. (2001). Second graders circumvent addition and subtraction difficulties. *Teaching Children Mathematics, 8*(4), 228–233.

Zhou, Z., & Peverly, S. T. (2005). Teaching addition and subtraction to first graders: A Chinese perspective. *Psychology in the Schools, 42*(3), 259–272.

Chapter 5

Multiplication

Multiplying by 9s has lots of tricks but I get them mixed up.

We're learning times . . . I can't remember the answers all the time but it's ok because I got a calculator.

We're supposed to move the numbers over when we multiply by lots of numbers but I don't know why . . . I just do it because the teacher said to and it works.

If you multiply 3 apples by 4 apples, you get 12 apples.

Multiplying is hard for me because I have to make all the little marks and sometimes there are so many I get mixed up.

What Is Multiplication?

Multiplication of whole numbers is represented in the physical world by unioning multiple sets of equal cardinality. An example is a drawing of three sets of two objects:

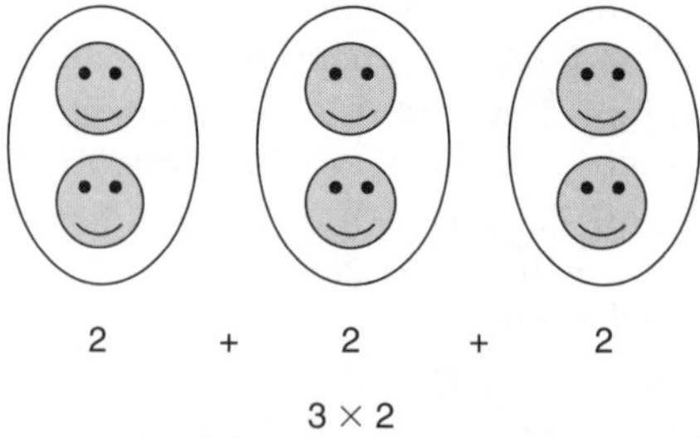

The representation of the arithmetical operation for expressing this unioning process is multiple addition. Thus, two plus two plus two is written as three 2s, using the notation 3×2. Early work with multiplication should mainly be devoted to the conceptual understanding that multiplication is a shorthand notation for denoting multiple addition. Multiplication situations should be presented to children, and they should then use materials (beans, counters, etc.) to demonstrate the problem given and to generate an answer (a product).

Do not be concerned with habituating the facts too early. It is essential that children understand that the multiplication problem expresses a relationship between the numbers involved and that they own the meaning of the symbolism—that the first factor in the problem denotes the number of sets and the second factor denotes the number of objects contained in each set. The product is then the total number of objects when the sets are joined (unioned). For example, consider the following problem: Two children each have four hearts on Valentine's day. How many hearts are there altogether? This problem is then expressed using materials, by constructing two sets with four hearts in each set. The shorthand way of writing this is 2 × 4, which results in 4 plus 4, or 8 hearts altogether.

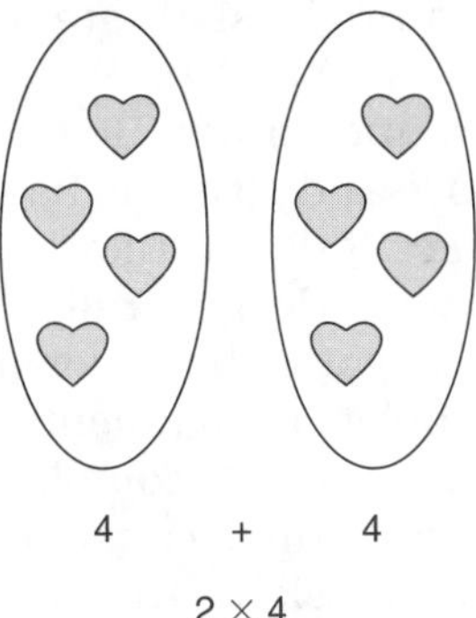

As children progress in conceptualizing the meaning of multiplication and can express what the multiplication situation means, it is time to begin habituating the facts. We do not like the word "memorizing" because it communicates that the fact is a paired association, of 2 with 4 in the above example, but the student could be devoid of an understanding of what the multiplication symbol means. Instead, after much work with material objects, the association of 2 with 4 is habituated so the child can develop speed and accuracy in recalling the fact. Habituation does not contribute to understanding; it presumes that understanding precedes the habituation, and the fact is habituated in order for the child to gain speed in working with multiplication situations.

What Should Students Understand About Multiplication?

In grades 3–5, a central focus should be directed at helping children develop the conceptual meaning for whole number multiplication and division (NCTM, 2000). Multiplication and division can begin to have meaning in earlier grades by engaging children in problem situations that utilize multiplication concepts for solution. Further, developing fluency involves a connection and a balance between conceptual understanding and computational proficiency. Understanding without fluency can inhibit children's problem-solving abilities (Thornton, 1990). When discussing computational strategies by developing, recording, and discussing each other's strategies, important kinds of learning can occur (NCTM, 2000). The NCTM Standards also point out that children must become fluent in computation and must have efficient, accurate methods supported by an understanding of numbers and operations. On the other hand, overpracticed computational procedures that are devoid of conceptual understanding are an undesirable classroom practice (NCTM, 2000, p. 35).

In this chapter you will continue an error analysis approach. This is one of the steps to be used in designing a DAS and an MIP for a student. A simulated child's paper will be presented and you should follow the directions in working through each of the three examples. The prescription proposed will direct the instructional design suggested in the MIP.

About the Student: Alberto

Alberto is a bright sixth grader who likes school. He enjoys learning activities and the social aspect of school. He is open and friendly with peers but is more reticent around adults. He has a very strong sense of fairness and is well liked by both boys and girls. He has excellent coordination and prefers an active life, which makes it difficult for him to sit still for long periods and stay focused on routine tasks. He generally follows school and classroom rules and rarely receives a negative behavior mark. He does not like to make mistakes and is slow to complete assignments because he tries to get everything done perfectly. Rather than turn in incomplete work, he will put it in his desk. Alberto does not like to ask for help because he does not want to look "stupid."

His reading skills are appropriate for sixth grade; however, Alberto dislikes reading and delays tasks involving reading. When avoidance tactics are unsuccessful, he reads quickly and with little attention to nuances and detail. Consequently, he misses important information. Alberto's reading style causes him to misinterpret directions. His reading style also causes him to think he has read one thing when that is not what was written, resulting in his answers being incorrect. He then becomes frustrated and angry with himself but does not acknowledge the connection between his approach to reading and the resulting errors in his work in math.

Alberto quickly memorizes math facts. He knows addition, subtraction, multiplication, and division facts and is learning a division algorithm. He is concrete in his thinking, which slows his understanding of abstract concepts. Once he has grasped a concept, he retains the information. Alberto's rapid reading and skimming of details causes problems for him in math. He may not attend to all the steps in a multistep problem, which results in a poor grade. When solving word problems, Alberto's reading creates numerous problems for him. When confronted with his errors he becomes frustrated, which results in self-deprecating comments.

Alberto enjoys helping his peers but especially enjoys helping adults. He likes to feel useful but quickly sees through "made up" jobs. He likes to earn free time, which he usually spends drawing or playing games with friends. Alberto does not respond to tangible reinforcers, such as stickers or points, unless the points lead to free time or helping time.

Alberto prefers learning tasks that require active participation or a hands-on approach. He enjoys class discussion and is an active participant in group work. He gets upset if he perceives a group member is not doing their share of the work or is "goofing off." Alberto is able to put his ideas in written form, although he has difficulty getting started. Once he gets the first sentence down, he usually has little difficulty completing the task. He especially likes giving reports and does not mind being in front of the group.

Error Patterns: Diagnosis, Prescription, Remediation

Each of the following simulations assumes that Alberto has taken a test, and in each situation, a different error has emerged. The task is to identify appropriate lessons based on the background of the child and your knowledge of the exhibited math deficiency.

Multiplication Error Pattern I for Alberto

The first sample paper is a completed, nine-problem multiplication paper. You should use the following four-step process:

1. Score the paper.
2. Begin with the first incorrect problem and attempt to determine the algorithm Alberto is using to obtain the answers.
3. Use Alberto's pattern and see if the second incorrect problem follows the pattern.
   a. If it does, go to step four.
   b. If it does not, study the error in the second problem and revise your prediction of the algorithm used.
4. Confirm the pattern using the third incorrect problem.

Complete the four-step process now, using the data shown.

Diagnosing the Error: Once you have finished scoring the paper and identifying the proposed pattern of error, you should reflect on the strengths exhibited in the child's multiplication work. Strengths to look for include knowledge of place value, facts (both easy [products involving 2, 5, 3, and 4] and hard [products involving 6, 7, 8, and 9]), work with zero in multiplication, and the ability to regroup in multiplication—to mention just a few. Use the space below to record your observations.

Alberto's Error Pattern(s):
Alberto's Strengths:

Scoring Work Sample Error I for Alberto finds him getting four of nine (44 percent) correct. While he has a failing score, he has a number of strengths that should prove beneficial in any remediation. He knows the column format for multiplication and he knows that he should begin multiplying by the ones digit of the multiplier. Alberto also knows:

1. easy multiplication facts involving 2s, 5s, 3s, and 4s (he gets all of these products correct)
2. multiplication involving hard facts (6s, 7s, 8s, and 9s)
3. multiplication when zero or one are involved

STUDENT WORK SAMPLE ERROR I FOR ALBERTO

```
   3                         1
1.  17        2.  40     3.  23
  × 5           × 8        × 4
   85           320         92

              3           4
4.  27        5.  54     6. 56
  ×31           ×19        × 28
    27           486        448
   81            84        142
   837          1326       1868

     1          2 1       1
7. 405        8. 143     9. 930
  × 63          ×806       ×884
   1215          858        3720
  2410         1034        7340
  25315        11198      7340
                          811120
```

4. he shifts to the tens column when multiplying by the tens digit in the multiplier, and so on.

He seems to add the partial products obtained from each subpart of the multiplier. Not a single product is incorrect in the use of his multiplication facts to obtain the partial products. This child is really quite strong in multiplication and surely feels frustrated getting incorrect answers when doing so much correct.

Prescription: On each problem, this student seems to perform the first part of the multiplication correctly when multiplying by the units digit of the multiplier. He regroups correctly and writes the digit to be regrouped in the correct place throughout the first iteration.

It is when he begins to multiply by the tens digit (as in problem 5) that the error begins to occur. He has not erased or marked out the previous multiplications. So when he multiplies the 1 by the 5, he adds in the digit from the previous multiplication, thus getting 1×5 plus 3, yielding the 8. His error seems to be that he is reusing values from previous multiplications. Look at the next incorrect problem to see if this is the case.

Problem 6 reveals that when he begins to multiply by the 2 in the tens column of the multiplier, he obtains 2 times 6 equals 12. He records the 2 in the tens column but does not change the regrouped 4 from the previous product to the new 1 in the 2×6 result. Then he multiplies 2 times 5, which is 10, and adds on the 4 from the previous multiplication sequence. This yields the 14, which he records on the second line of the partial product.

Checking problem 7 confirms the error diagnosis. When multiplying by the 6 in the tens digit, he multiplies 6 times 5 and records the 0 in the 30. Instead of regrouping the 3 from the 30, he multiplies the 6 times 0 and adds the 1 from the previous partial product. He then records the 1 in the partial product and moves on to multiply the 6 times 4 and records the 24.

A complication occurs in problem 8. When multiplying by the 0 in the tens digit of the multiplier, he fails to record the zero product, thus causing the multiplication by the 8 in the multiplier to be recorded in the wrong columns. This will require some special attention, but is independent of the primary error exhibited throughout the test. A completed DAS for Alberto is included (see Table 5.1).

Remediation: Alberto's first MIP appears in Table 5.2. Begin working with this child by working a problem like the following:

$$\begin{array}{r} 16 \\ \underline{\times 12} \end{array}$$

Have the child work the problem with pencil and paper. The child should obtain an answer of 292 if he uses the incorrect procedure exhibited on his test. Then have the child work the problem using base-10 blocks or popsicle sticks.

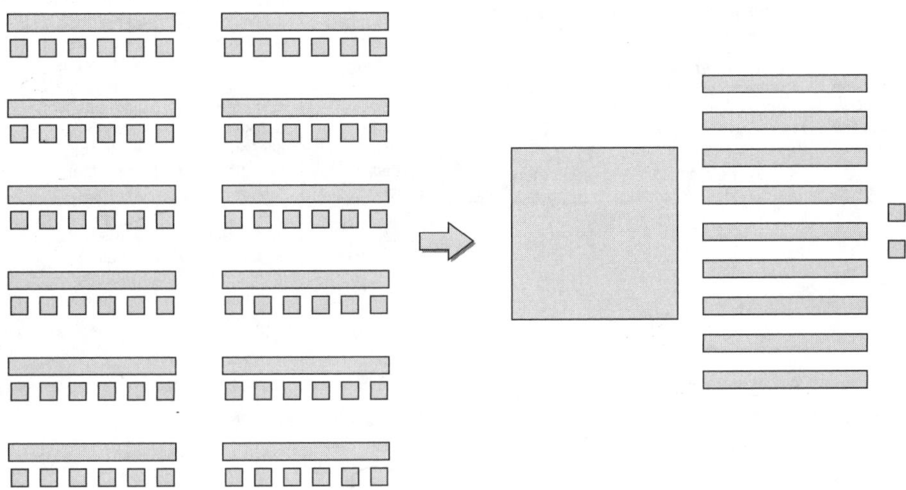

Alberto should arrive at 192 using the base-10 blocks. At this point, ask why the two answers are different. Listen carefully to the explanation, because it will

TABLE 5.1 Data Analysis Sheet

Student: Alberto						
Team Members:						
Context	**Content Assessment**	**Process**		**Behavior**		**Reinforcement**
		Input	Output	Academic	Social	
+	+	+	+	+	+	+
• Likes school • Open and friendly with peers • Likes to be clustered with his peers • Enjoys all cooperative learning activities • Enjoys any and all group participatory activities • Likes being in front of class	***Learned Concepts I*** • Knows easy facts involving 2s, 5s, 3s, and 4s • Knows hard facts involving 6s, 7s, 8s, and 9s • Multiplies correctly when zero or one is a factor • Correctly uses place value format in multiplication ***Learned Concepts II*** • Knows easy facts involving 2s, 5s, 3s, and 4s • Knows hard facts involving 6s, 7s, 8s, and 9s • Multiplies correctly when zero or one is a factor • Works well with zero as a multiplicand ***Learned Concepts III*** • Knows easy facts involving 2s, 5s, 3s, and 4s • Knows hard facts involving 6s, 7s, 8s, and 9s • Multiplies correctly when zero or one is a factor • Correctly marks out previously regrouped digits when performing partial products	• Reading skills are grade appropriate • Memorizes quickly • Concrete thinker • Understands abstract concepts	• Excellent coordination • Prefers an active lifestyle • Retains information learned • Enjoys group work • Is good at putting ideas into written form • Once he gets started he rarely fails to complete his work • Likes giving oral reports	• Enjoys learning activities • Likes concrete activities • Wants to complete his activities • Good at math	• Enjoys social aspects of school • Strong sense of fairness • Well liked by boys and girls • Follows school rules	• Likes being with peers • Enjoys helping adults • Likes to feel useful • Free time is important to him • Likes drawing and playing games with his friends • Points help if they lead him to free time or helping time • Likes being in front of class
–	–	–	–	–	–	–
• Reticent around adults • Can't sit for a long period of time • Doesn't like to work with his teacher on a one-on-one basis • Doesn't like to work alone • Doesn't like to be isolated in the classroom	***Error Pattern I*** • When multiplying by tens or hundreds digit, reuses previously renamed values • Fails to record zero product when zero is one of the factors ***Error Pattern II*** • Fails to record regrouped digit in partial products ***Error Pattern III*** • When regrouped digits are involved in a partial product, adds the regrouped digit to the factor before multiplying by the multiplier • Adds before multiplying rather than multiplying then adding the regrouped digit	• Does not like to ask for help • Does not like reading • Misinterprets directions • Thinks he has read something when he hasn't • Doesn't do well with multitask assignments	• Slow to complete assignments; rather than turn in incomplete assignments he will put his work in his desk uncompleted • He reads quickly with little attention to material • Misses important information • Has trouble with word problems (reading related)	• Slow to complete assignments; rather than turn in incomplete assignments he will put his work in his desk uncompleted • He reads quickly with little attention to material • Misses important information • Has trouble with word problems (reading related)	• Rarely breaks school rules • Becomes frustrated and angry when he makes errors • Becomes upset when he believes a group member is not doing his share	• Does not like made-up work, nor does he like tangible reinforcers such as stickers and candy • Avoids indepen-dent reading • Doesn't like being with teacher one-on-one

Note: The + symbols indicate strengths and the – symbols indicate areas of concern.

TABLE 5.2 Mathematics Improvement Plan I for Alberto: Correctly Multiplying by the Tens Digit

Time		15 minutes	20–30 minutes	20 minutes
Context		Classroom activities of a cooperative type, he is in a group activity (+)	Independent seatwork (–)	He will work on this activity in the classroom with a classmate whom he likes (+)
Content		Group works multiplication problems (one-digit multiplier) using manipulatives (+)	Works and records exercises like those on test, uses base-10 blocks to check results, practices multidigit products requiring regrouping (–)	Group of four children plays Rollette activity (+)
Process	Input	Teacher gives multiple instructions for the task at hand (–)	The work has visual and written examples of the task at hand (+)	The written directions are at grade level and have a singular task (+)
	Output	Group is engaged in manipulative activities that requires a concrete outcome (+)	Student is expected to write his results and read them to the entire class (–)	The words in the word problem are at a challenging level (–)
Behavior	Academic	Group produces a single written project with all having input (+)	Student completes his work even though it has many errors (–)	He consistently has to ask questions of the teacher to complete the task (–)
	Social	Group works well together and all students have a sense of their responsibility (+)	Student becomes easily frustrated and does poorly at the beginning of his work (–)	His classmate is one whom he likes and he trusts (–)
Reinforcement		If the group does well they will get free time to play games with their partners (+)	For every problem he gets right he will get to help the teacher at a needed task (+)	Teacher gives all the students a smiley face as a reward for their work (–)

Note: The + symbols indicate strengths and the – symbols indicate areas of concern.

give clues to how you will discuss correcting the error. Probably, Alberto will think he has done something wrong but will not be sure which of the procedures has the error. We would suggest that you rework the problem with Alberto, with you recording information as the child performs the multiplication with the base-10 blocks:

$$\begin{array}{r} 16 \\ \underline{\times 12} \end{array} \quad \textit{means} \quad \begin{array}{r} 16 \\ \underline{\times 10} \end{array} \quad + \quad \begin{array}{r} 16 \\ \underline{\times 2} \end{array}$$

Using the base-10 blocks, point out to Alberto that 16 times 12 is 16 times 10 plus 16 times 2. Begin with the 2 and move 2 groups of 16 apart from the other 10 groups. Ask him to determine the answer to 2 times 16 using the base-10 blocks. The child should give 32 as the answer. Now you record the value:

$$\begin{array}{r} 16 \\ \underline{\times 12} \\ 32 \end{array} \quad \begin{array}{c} \textit{means} \\ \\ \leftarrow \end{array} \quad \begin{array}{r} 16 \\ \times 10 \\ \textit{(you write this)} \end{array} \quad + \quad \begin{array}{r} 16 \\ \underline{\times 2} \\ \end{array}$$

Now have Alberto determine what 10 times 16 is, using the base-10 blocks. He should answer 160. Record the value:

$$\begin{array}{r} 16 \\ \times 12 \\ \hline 32 \\ 160 \\ \hline \end{array} \quad \textit{means} \quad \begin{array}{r} 16 \\ \times 10 \\ \hline \end{array} \quad + \quad \begin{array}{r} 16 \\ \times 2 \\ \hline \end{array}$$

$$\leftarrow \quad \textit{(you write this)}$$

Have Alberto sum the two partial products to find the total. He will probably arrive at 192. Then it should be apparent that the answer obtained using the base-10 blocks is the correct one. At this point, Alberto should be ready to compare the way he worked the problem with pencil and paper with the answer just obtained. Encourage him to explain how he worked the problem, comparing the result to what was just obtained:

$$\begin{array}{r} 16 \\ \times 12 \\ \hline 32 \\ 160 \\ \hline 192 \end{array} \qquad \begin{array}{r} {}^{1}60 \\ \times 12 \\ \hline 32 \\ 26 \\ \hline 292 \end{array}$$

Alberto should arrive at the same first partial product of 32. However, on the second partial product, his invented algorithm will lead to 26 instead of 16. At this point, ask why he is using the regrouped 1 in this product. Alberto is very bright, and will realize immediately that the 1 has no place in this product—and will also realize that this mistake is leading to his error. Discuss with him what he thinks is the best way to not reuse the digit from the first product. In our experience, he will either say "mark it out" or "erase it." We would encourage you to suggest that it is best to mark it out. The reason is that when children write a problem, and then try to erase part of the work, they invariably smudge the problem and have trouble in further work with the problem. Marking it out will accomplish the same thing and will not lead to complications in further work with the problem.

This child has so many strengths that he will be quite relieved to finally determine why he is getting so many problems wrong when he thinks he is doing the problem correctly. You should work another problem that he got incorrect on the test and let him determine where he made the error. When you are working with a child, give extra credit for finding the errors if it makes him more interested in his math work.

Multiplication Error Pattern II for Alberto

Alberto's second paper is also a nine-problem multiplication paper. You should complete the four-step process outlined for Error Pattern II (see page 94).

Diagnosing the Error: Once you have finished scoring the paper and identifying the proposed pattern of error, you should reflect on the strengths exhibited in Alberto's multiplication work. Strengths to look for include knowledge of place value, facts (both easy [products involving 2, 5, 3, and 4] and hard [products involving 6, 7, 8, and 9]), work with zero in multiplication, and the ability to regroup in multiplication. Use the space in the chart on the next page to record your observations.

STUDENT WORK SAMPLE ERROR II FOR ALBERTO

1. 17 × 5	2. 40 × 8	3. 23 × 4
55	320	82

4. 27 × 31	5. 54 × 19	6. 56 × 28
27	456	408
61	54	102
637	996	1428

7. 405 × 63	8. 143 × 806	9. 930 × 884
1205	848	3620
2400	000	7240
	824	7240
25205	83248	800020

Alberto's Error Pattern(s):
Alberto's Strengths:

Alberto scored one correct of the nine problems (11 percent). While this performance seems quite low, he exhibits tremendous strength in multiplication and should improve his performance immediately. Alberto knows:

1. easy multiplication facts involving 2s, 5s, 3s, and 4s (he gets all of these products correct)
2. multiplication involving hard facts (6s, 7s, 8s, and 9s)
3. multiplication when zero or one are involved—he especially does well with zero in problem 8
4. he shifts to the tens column when multiplying by the tens digit in the multiplier, and so on
5. he works well with zero when it appears in the multiplicand, as in problems 2, 7, and 9

In the first incorrect problem, problem 1, the error stems from not regrouping when the product results in a value larger than 10. Alberto seems to drop the regrouped digit and just writes the units value of the product. Looking at the next error, problem 3, reveals the same error—but maybe it is because the digit to be regrouped is a 1. Investigating the third incorrect problem, problem 4, discloses that in the second partial product, he does not record the 2 that is regrouped from the 3×7 product. Thus, he is just not recording the regrouped digit—regardless of its value.

Prescription: Alberto needs to record the regrouped digit in all partial products.

Remediation: Alberto's second MIP appears in Table 5.3. Begin by asking Alberto to work problem 1 using base-10 materials. He should get 5 groups of 1 long (10) and 7 units. Now have him determine the total. He should get 85. Have him compare that with his answer on the test. This should put him in a state of disequilibrium according to Piaget, and he is at a point where he is ready to determine where the discrepancy is.

There are a number of ways to proceed at this point; you could have Alberto complete the problem while you record what is obtained. Have him gather his 5 groups of 17 and begin the problem solution again. You write the problem out so you can record as he works the problem.

Ask him to accumulate the 5 groups of 7 units. He will determine that it is 35, and will be able to show you. Encourage him to trade the units in for longs so he has 3 longs and 5 units at the end. You record this as:

$$\begin{array}{r} 17 \\ \underline{\times 5} \\ 35 \end{array} \quad \leftarrow \quad \textit{(you record this)}$$

Now have him accumulate the longs (10s) and tell you that the value is 50. You record this as:

$$\begin{array}{r} 17 \\ \underline{\times 5} \\ 35 \\ \underline{50} \\ 85 \end{array} \quad \leftarrow \quad \textit{(you record this)}$$

TABLE 5.3 Mathematics Improvement Plan II for Alberto: Recording the Regrouped Digit in all Partial Products

Time		15 minutes	20 minutes	20 minutes
Context		Classroom activities of a cooperative type, he is in a group activity (+)	Independent seatwork (–)	He will work on this activity in the classroom with a classmate whom he likes (+)
Content		Group generates multiplication problems and records process (problems should require regrouping on some problems) (+)	He works problems like on the test. He generates the problem with base-10 blocks, then draws a picture of the problem. He constructs his "my multiplication" book (–)	He and classmate will play "200 to Win" (+)
Process	Input	Teacher gives multiple instructions for the task at hand (–)	The work has visual and written examples of the task at hand (+)	The written directions are at grade level and have a singular task (+)
	Output	Group is engaged in manipulative activities that require a concrete outcome (+)	Is expected to write his results and read them to the entire class (–)	The problems in the activity are at a challenging level (–)
Behavior	Academic	Group produces a single written project, with all students having input (+)	Completes his work even though it has many errors (–)	He consistently has to ask questions of the teacher to complete the task (–)
	Social	Group works well together and all students have a sense of their responsibility (+)	Becomes easily frustrated and does poorly at the beginning of his work (–)	His classmate is one whom he likes and he trusts (+)
Reinforcement		If the group does well, they will get free time to play games with their partners (+)	For every problem he gets right he will get to help the teacher at a needed task (+)	Teacher gives all the students a smiley face as a reward for their work (–)

Note: The + symbols indicate strengths and the – symbols indicate areas of concern.

At this point, ask Alberto what happened to the 3 longs. He should indicate that he left them out. Point out to him why we write the regrouped value up to the left of the tens digit in the multiplicand. Now have him rework the problem while you write what the values are. In the first product, 35, record the 5 and write the regrouped digit above and to the left of the 1 in the 17, as follows:

$$\begin{array}{r} {}^{3}17 \\ \times\ 5 \\ \hline 85 \end{array}$$

Have Alberto rework problem 3. Encourage him to talk it out as he does it. Be sure to reinforce writing the regrouped digit when the product of 3×4 is stated. He should write the 2 as before, and then write the regrouped 1 above and to the left of the 2 in 23.

The tremendous strength exhibited by Alberto in multiplication knowledge should make this a rather easy error to correct. Point out to him how much he has done correctly on the test, and how writing the regrouped digits will result in his getting all the problems correct in the future. Have him rework the problems on the test and discover his errors. Give him free choice time for correcting all the errors, as his DAS indicates this is a meaningful reward for him.

Multiplication Error Pattern III for Alberto

The third paper is similar to the first two. You should complete the same four-step process used for Error Patterns I and II (see page 94).

STUDENT WORK SAMPLE ERROR III FOR ALBERTO

```
     3                              1
1.  17          2.  40          3.  23
   × 5             × 8             × 4
   205             320             122

     2               3             1
                                   4
4.  27          5.  54          6. 56
   ×31             ×19             × 28
    27             726              728
   121             54              122
   1237           1266             1948

     3              4 2             2
    1 1             3 1             1
7.  405         8.  143         9.  930
   × 63            ×806            ×884
   1235            2408            4020
   3080            000             8840
   32035          4084             8840
                  410808           976420
```

Diagnosing the Error: Once you have finished scoring the paper and identifying the proposed pattern of error, you should reflect on the strengths exhibited in the child's multiplication work. Strengths to look for include knowledge of place value, facts (both easy [products involving 2, 5, 3, and 4] and hard [products involving 6, 7, 8, and 9]), work with zero in multiplication, and the ability to regroup in multiplication. Use the space below to record your observations.

Alberto's Error Pattern(s):
Alberto's Strengths:

Alberto scores just one of nine (11 percent) correct, which is a failing performance. Yet, his work reveals numerous strengths in multiplication. First, he knows the format in multiplication. He also knows:

1. easy multiplication facts involving 2s, 5s, 3s, and 4s (all of these products are correct)
2. multiplication involving hard facts (6s, 7s, 8s, and 9s)
3. multiplication when zero or one are involved (he does well with zero, as evidenced in problem 8)
4. when multiplying by the tens digit in the multiplier, he records in the tens column, and so on
5. When needing to regroup a partial product, he crosses out the previous digit and records the new value to be used

The first incorrect problem, problem 1, reveals that Alberto adds the 3 and the 1 to get 4, then multiplies that result by 5, resulting in a value of 20. Looking at the next incorrect problem, problem 3, he again appears to add the 1 and the 2 to get 3, then multiplies by 4 to obtain the 12 recorded in his answer. Looking at problem 4 confirms that during the second partial product, 3 is multiplied by 7 to obtain 21, the 1 is recorded, the 2 tens are regrouped, and the 2 is written just above the 2 in the multiplicand. Then 2 is added to 2 to obtain 4, which is multiplied by the 3 to obtain 12. The 12 is recorded in the second partial product.

Prescription: Alberto's error appears to be a procedural error in which he regroups part of a product, then adds the regrouped digit before multiplying, rather than multiplying the values before adding the regrouped number. It appears that he is applying a process and not thinking about the conceptual implications of the process applied. Because he exhibits so many strengths (such as place value in partial products, work with zero in the multiplier and the multiplicand, and working with regrouped values in problems 7 and 8), we believe correcting this error will not prove difficult.

This is a case in which a discussion with the child will prove invaluable in assessing the extent to which the child is cognitively deficient or procedurally incorrect. We will assume that the difficulty is procedural for the discussion.

Remediation: Alberto's third MIP appears in Table 5.4. The remedial process would begin with work on a problem like problem 1. Have Alberto get 5 groups

TABLE 5.4 Mathematics Improvement Plan III for Alberto: Correcting Procedural Errors when Regrouping

Time		15 minutes	20 minutes	30 minutes
Context		Classroom activities of a cooperative type, he is in a group activity (+)	Independent seatwork (–)	He will work on this activity in the classroom with a classmate whom he likes (+)
Content		Group plays "Next Move," where each child provides the next step in working a problem—they say the step then the group does it (+)	Works problems similar to those on the test, practices order of procedure in multiplication with regrouping (–)	Group plays either "Zero Wins" or "200 Wins"
Process	Input	Teacher gives multiple instructions for the task at hand (–)	The work has visual and written examples of the task at hand (+)	The written directions are at grade level and have a singular task (+)
	Output	Group is engaged in manipulative activities that require a concrete outcome (+)	Student is expected to write his results and read them to the entire class at some point (–)	The words in the problem are at a challenging level (–)
Behavior	Academic	Group produces a single written project with all students having input (+)	Student completes his work even though it has many errors (–)	He consistently has to ask questions of the teacher to complete the task (–)
	Social	Group works well together and all students have a sense of their responsibility (+)	Student becomes easily frustrated and does poorly at the beginning of his work (–)	His classmate is one whom he likes and trusts (+)
Reinforcement		If the group does well, they will get free time to play games with their partners (+)	For every problem he gets right he will get to help the teacher at a needed task (+)	Teacher gives all the students a smiley face as a reward for their work (–)

Note: The + symbols indicate strengths and the – symbols indicate areas of concern.

of 17, using the base-10 blocks. Ask him to determine how many there are altogether. He should be able to arrive at 85. Ask him to compare that answer to the answer on his test. This should provide you with the opportunity to suggest reworking the problem with the base-10 blocks and comparing the situation to what was done with pencil and paper.

Once again, get the 5 groups of 1 long and 7 units. In the meantime, you might write the problem on a side sheet so that you and he can record his work. We would use something like:

	f	l	u	*
		1	7	
×			5	

*f = flats
l = longs
u = units

Ask Alberto what the first thing he did on the pencil-and-paper work was. He should tell you that he multiplied the 5 by the 7. Suggest that he multiply 5 times 7 by combining the 5 groups of 7 units. Let him exchange until he gets the 35 as 3 longs and 5 units. Now ask what he wrote on the pencil-and-paper work. He should indicate that he wrote the 5 to represent the 5 units and regrouped the 3 tens and wrote that above the 1 in the longs column. You should record that now.

	f	l	u
		^{3}1	7
×			5
			5

Have him set the 3 longs off to the side to represent regrouping the 30 units as 3 longs. Continue by asking him to find out how many longs are in the 5 groups. He should answer that there are 5 longs, plus the 3 from the regrouping, for a total of 8 longs.

Then ask him to compare what was just done with the work on his pencil-and-paper test. Can he tell you how the two are different? He will probably recognize that he added the 3 to the 1 before multiplying by the 5. Bright students (such as this student) will recognize, almost immediately, they have used an incorrect procedure. Quite often you will see this sort of need to refresh the algorithmic procedure if it has been a long period of time since they last used the procedure. Have him rework a problem like problem 3 and see if he can discover what he did incorrectly. It is very reinforcing for students who cannot determine why they are getting incorrect answers (when they feel they know multiplication so well) to determine exactly where they have gone astray when working problems. Have Alberto recheck his work on the other problems on the pencil-and-paper test and reward him with free choice time for finding the errors and correcting them.

We believe that children do not get wrong answers to frustrate you. It happens because they just do not know how to get correct answers. It will be so gratifying to these students to realize what they are doing incorrectly. With sustained practice, the correct procedure will become second nature to them.

Conclusions: Instructional Strategies Summary

Throughout the remediation plan for all three samples, the following suggestions would be very helpful:

1. Have learners complete a few problems at a time. Once you are satisfied that they understand something, move on.
2. Once an error has been corrected by the learner, have her practice ample examples to extinguish the incorrect procedure.
3. You might pair a slow learner with an average learner. They can help each other and both will profit from working together. Combine older and younger peers if appropriate.
4. Use the simplest possible numbers to explain a mathematical operation, then move to the more complex level. Always begin with simple examples before moving to complex examples.

Instructional Activities

Assessing whether children's multiplication errors are primarily results of a low level of conceptual understanding or a lack of ability to recall basic facts or work with algorithmic rules can be accomplished with various types of questions. As the teacher, you will develop a sense of what to ask and how to ask it in order to gain insight into a child's thinking. Children's conceptual learning can be assessed and evaluated more readily utilizing authentic, real-world situations in which learners must decide not only how to solve the problem but also whether the result is reasonable.

The following are examples of activities that can help in work with multiplication. Each is described with any special consideration you, as the teacher, need to know in order to optimize the activity's use with children.

ACTIVITY: Rollette (0 to 30)

Students should know how to generate facts by using materials and should be ready to practice habituating facts.

Objective: Habituate multiplication facts involving 0, 2, and 5

Materials:

- Pencil
- Sheet displayed in Figure 5.1
- Two number cubes (one cube with the numbers 0, 2, and 5 and one cube with numbers 1–6)

FIGURE 5.1

0	0	30	20	15	10	10	10	6	0	0	0
0	0	25	20	15	12	10	8	4	2	0	0
0	2									25	30
6	4									20	20
10	8									15	15
10	10									12	10
10	12									10	10
15	15									8	10
20	20									4	6
30	25									2	0
0	0	2	4	8	10	12	15	20	25	0	0
0	0	0	6	10	10	10	15	20	30	0	0

Directions: Four children play, and each child is responsible for his side of the board. The player throws the two cubes and says the fact. That player then marks out that number on his side of the board. Play then passes to the player on the left. The first person to mark out all facts on his side of the board is the winner.

ACTIVITY: Rollette (0 to 30)

Students should know how to generate facts by using materials and should be ready to practice habituating facts.

Objective: Habituate facts involving products to 30

Materials:

Pencil

Sheet as displayed in Figure 5.2

Two number cubes (one cube with numbers 0–5; one cube with numbers 1–6)

Directions: Four children play, and each child is responsible for her side of the board. The player throws the two cubes and says the fact. That player then marks out that number on her side of the board. Play then passes to the player on the left. The first person to mark out all facts on her side of the board is the winner.

ACTIVITY: Rollette (3 to 48)

Students should have generated facts using materials and should be ready to practice habituating facts.

FIGURE 5.2

1	0	30	24	18	15	12	9	6	4	2	1
2	0	25	24	16	12	10	8	5	3	0	0
4	3	MULTIPLICATION								25	30
6	5									18	24
9	8									16	24
12	10									12	15
15	12									10	12
18	16									8	9
24	24									5	6
30	25									3	4
0	0	3	5	8	10	12	16	24	25	0	2
1	2	4	6	9	12	15	18	24	30	0	1

0 1 2 3 4 5

1 2 3 4 5 6

FIGURE 5.3

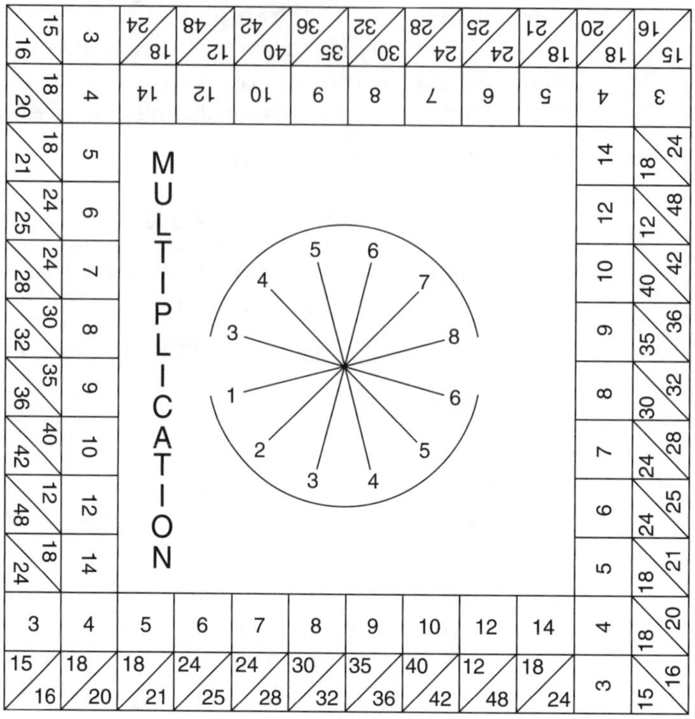

Objective: Habituate facts

Materials:

Pencil

Sheet as displayed in Figure 5.3

Two number cubes (one cube with numbers 3–8; one cube with numbers 1–6)

Directions: Four children play, and each child is responsible for his side of the board. The player throws the two cubes and says the fact. That player then marks out that number on his side of the board. Play then passes to the player on the left. The first person to mark out all facts on his side of the board is the winner.

ACTIVITY: 200 Wins

Students should have generated facts using materials and should be ready to practice facts.

Objective: Practice multiplication facts and maintain column addition skills

Materials:

Pencil

Sheet as displayed in Figure 5.4

Two number cubes (one cube with the numbers 1–6; one cube with numbers 0, 1, 2, 7, 8, and 9)

Directions: Four children play, and each child is responsible for one column on her sheet. The names of the players are written on the top of each player's sheet. All players begin with zero points, or with some specified value. The first player

FIGURE 5.4

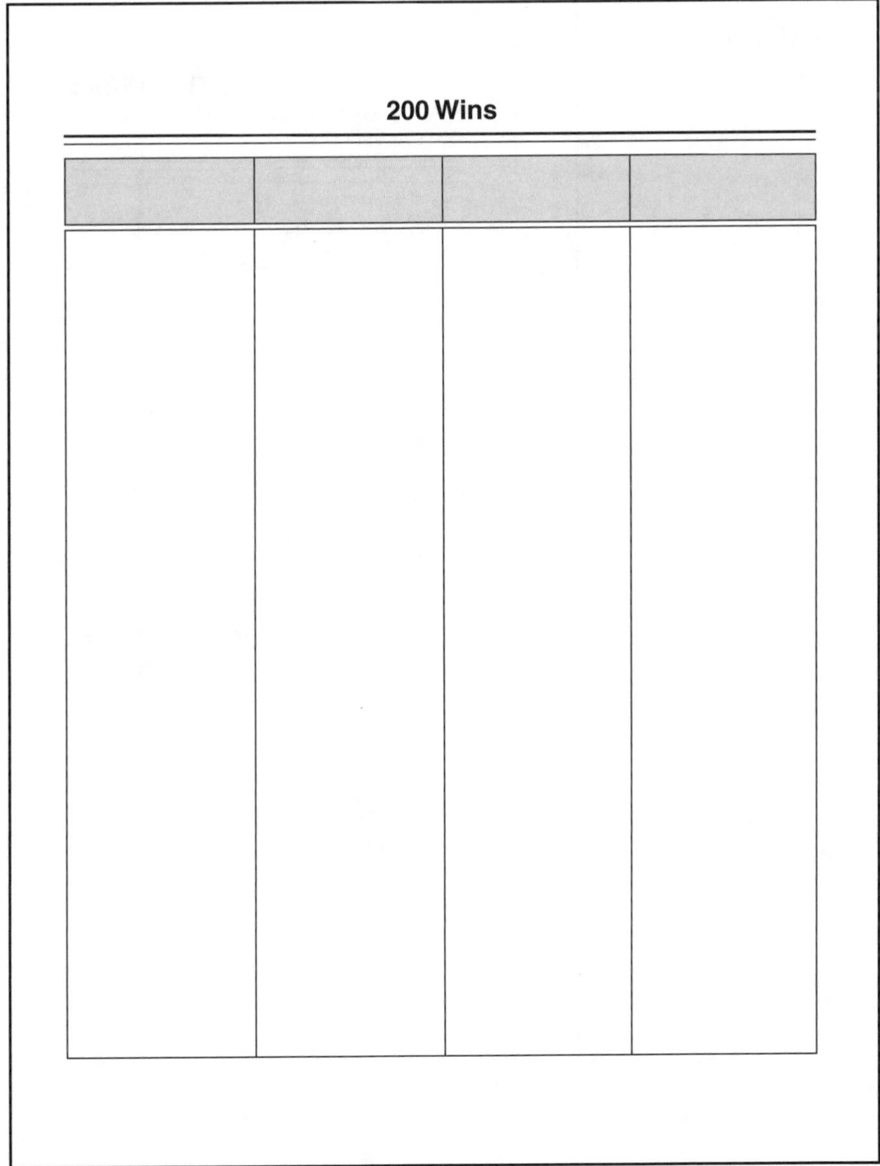

throws and *must say* the product. All players add the number to that player's score on their sheet. The next player then throws, and play continues. If a child thinks the player's product is wrong, she can challenge. If the product was correct, the player receives 10 more points. If the product was incorrect, the players receive no points added to their score. The child who challenged receives 5 points if the challenge is correct. The first player to get 200 wins.

ACTIVITY: Zero Wins

This activity is the same as "200 Wins," except that each player starts with 199 points. Each player obtains a multiplication value as before, then subtracts the value from his score. The first person to zero wins! See Figure 5.5.

Objective: Practice multiplication facts and maintain column subtraction skills

FIGURE 5.5

ZERO WINS

Rule: Throw the number cubes and multiply the numbers. Subtract the product from your score. First to zero wins.

299	299	299	299

Discussion Questions

1. Discuss your understanding of the distinction between conceptual errors and procedural errors in multiplication.
2. The following worksheet shows Student Work Sample Error IV for Alberto:

   a. Score Student Work Sample Error IV for Alberto. Identify his strengths and error patterns. Complete a DAS for Alberto.

   b. Complete an MIP.

---

1. $\begin{array}{r} {}^{3}\\ 17 \\ \times\ 5 \\ \hline 85 \end{array}$

2. $\begin{array}{r} 40 \\ \times\ 8 \\ \hline 320 \end{array}$

3. $\begin{array}{r} {}^{1}\\ 23 \\ \times\ 4 \\ \hline 92 \end{array}$

4. $\begin{array}{r} 27 \\ \times 31 \\ \hline 67 \end{array}$

5. $\begin{array}{r} 54 \\ \times 19 \\ \hline 36 \\ 5 \\ \hline 86 \end{array}$

6. $\begin{array}{r} 56 \\ \times\ 28 \\ \hline 48 \\ 10 \\ \hline 148 \end{array}$

7. $\begin{array}{r} 405 \\ \times\ 63 \\ \hline 15 \\ 240 \\ \hline 2415 \end{array}$

8. $\begin{array}{r} 143 \\ \times 806 \\ \hline 18 \\ 0 \\ 8 \\ \hline 818 \end{array}$

9. $\begin{array}{r} 930 \\ \times 884 \\ \hline 4 \\ 24 \\ 72 \\ \hline 7444 \end{array}$

3. The following worksheet shows Student Work Sample Error V for Alberto:

1. 17 × 5 = 12, 5 → 62	2. 40 × 8 = 328	3. 23 × 4 = 87
4. 27 × 31 = 8, 81 → 818	5. 54 × 19 = 13, 54 → 553	6. 56 × 28 = 14, 112 → 1134
7. 405 (carry 3) × 63 = 8, 2430 → 24308	8. 143 (carry 2) × 806 = 9, 0, 1144 → 114409	9. 930 × 884 = 4, 7440, 7440 → 818404

a. Score Student Work Sample Error V for Alberto. Identify his strengths and error patterns. Complete a DAS for Alberto.

b. Complete an MIP.

4. Design a multiplication activity to provide practice in multiplication facts. Make the activity suitable for a short period of practice for a group of four children.

5. Design a question that would focus on the conceptual understanding of multiplication. The question should help you know if the student understands why multiplication by the tens digit results in all the partial products being groups of tens.
6. Identify the characteristics of a mathematics activity you would use with a child with this behavioral profile (also include the characteristics that you would *not* want present in the activity).

References

Baroody, A. (2006). Why children have difficulties mastering the basic number combinations and how to help them. *Teaching Children Mathematics, 13*(1), 22.

Brown, J. S., & Burton, R. R. (1978). Diagnostic models for procedural bugs in basic mathematical skills. *Cognitive Science, 2*, 155–192.

Caliandro, C. K. (2000). Children's inventions for multidigit multiplication and division. *Teaching Children Mathematics, 6*(6), 420–426.

Cawley, J. F. (2002). Mathematics interventions and students with high-incidence disabilities. *Remedial and Special Education, 23*(1), 2–6.

Greer, B. (1994). Extending the meaning of multiplication and division. In G. Harel & J. Confrey (Eds.), *The development of multiplicative reasoning in the learning of mathematics* (pp. 61–85). Albany, NY: SUNY Press.

Monroe, E. E., & Orme, M. P. (2002). Developing mathematical vocabulary. *Preventing School Failure, 46*(3), 139–142.

Mulligan, J. T., & Mitchelmore, M. C. (1997). Young children's intuitive models of multiplication and division. *Journal for Research in Mathematics Education, 28*(3), 309–330.

National Council of Teachers of Mathematics. (2000). *Principles and standards for school mathematics*. Reston, VA: Author.

Sáenz-Ludlow, A. (2004). Metaphor and numerical diagrams in the arithmetical activity of a fourth-grade class. *Journal for Research in Mathematics Education, 35*(1), 34–56.

Sherin, B., & Fuson, K. (2005). Multiplication strategies and the appropriation of computational resources. *Journal for Research in Mathematics Education, 36*(4), 347–395.

Steffe, L. P. (1994). Children's multiplying schemes. In G. Harel & J. Confrey (Eds.), *The development of multiplicative reasoning in the learning of mathematics* (pp. 3–39). Albany: State University of New York.

Thornton, C. A. (1990). Strategies for the basic facts. In J. N. Payne (ed.), *Mathematics for the Young Child* (pp. 132–151). Reston, VA: National Council of Teachers of Mathematics.

Wood, D. K., & Frank, A. R. (2000). Using memory-enhancing strategies to learn multiplication facts. *Teaching Exceptional Children, 32*(5), 78–82.

Wood, T., Williams, G., & McNeal, B. (2006). Children's mathematical thinking in different classroom cultures. *Journal for Research in Mathematics Education, 37*(3), 222–255.

Chapter 6

Division

Dividing is the hardest one . . . you have to know where to put the answer.

If I divide into a number with a "0" it's easy, because there's nothing to do.

The remainder is hard to figure out so I just leave any numbers at the bottom when I'm done.

I can never remember which number goes in the little house if the teacher doesn't write the problem for me.

How am I supposed to know what number to start with?

I hate long division, it's too many steps that get all mixed up.

Division hurts my head!

What Is Division?

Division of whole numbers is represented in the physical world by partitioning and by measurement. Each of these conceptualizations can be represented in the physical world with real-world examples. The concept of measurement in division occurs in the following way: There are 6 pieces of candy. Each person is to get 2 pieces. How may people can get candy?

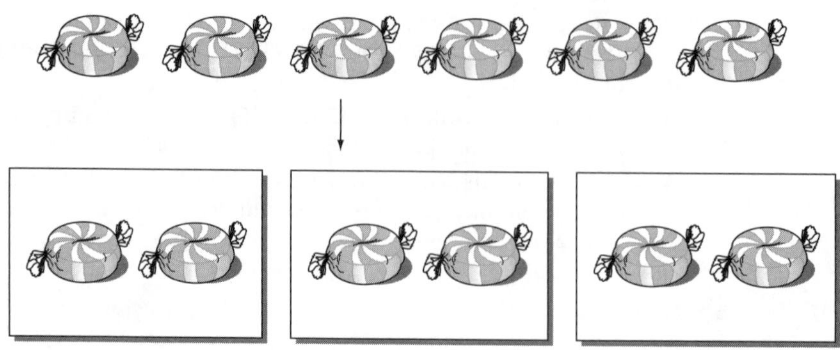

Answer: 3 people get candy.

Partitioning in division can be represented in the real world with the following example: There are 6 pieces of candy. If two children share the candy equally, how many pieces does each child get?

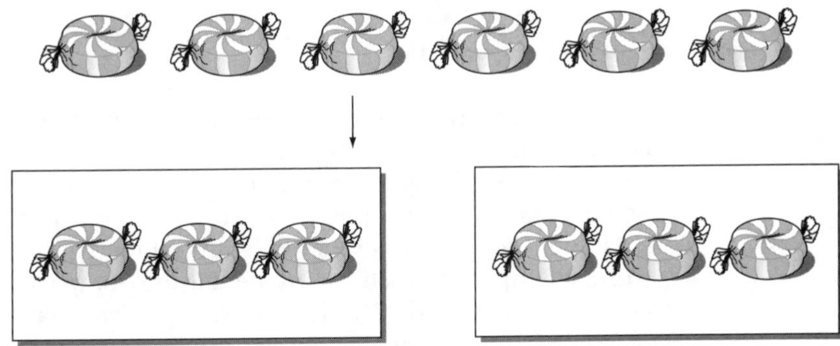

Answer: Each child gets 3 pieces of candy.

Beginning work with division should involve situations that require both conceptual notions of division. It is important that children conceptualize that division involves breaking a set into constituent parts—either by partitioning the set or by measuring the set. In the former case the answer to the division situation is the number of constituent sets, but in the latter case the answer is the number in each subset.

As children progress in conceptualizing division, work should focus more on the partitioning notion. Partitioning is the basis for understanding the traditional algorithm. Partitioning also forms the readiness foundation for later understanding of equations such as $3x = 14$. While many invented algorithms may allow children to perform division, the traditional algorithm is the most precise and efficient method, which is why it has evolved over the centuries as the preferred algorithm. The NCTM Standards (2000) allude to this by indicating that though the efficiency of various strategies can and should be discussed, it is important that children become fluent in arithmetical computation by using accurate, efficient methods that are supported by conceptual understanding of numbers and operations.

What Should Students Understand About Division?

For children in grades 3 through 5, a central focus should be the conceptual understanding of division (and multiplication) as well as the exploration of algorithmic strategies that are invented, recorded, and discussed. You, as the teacher, have the opportunity to provide a foundation for children to develop and understand efficient, accurate algorithms. The foundation of such algorithm conversations should be conceptual understanding of the operation (NCTM, 2000). A word of caution is that early, overpracticed computational algorithms that are absent of conceptual understanding are often forgotten or remembered incorrectly. Thus, overpracticing should be avoided.

In this section, you will continue an error analysis approach. This is one of the steps to be used in designing a DAS and an MIP for a student. A simulated child's paper will be presented and you should follow the directions in working through each of the three examples. The prescription proposed will direct the instructional design suggested in the DAS.

About the Student: Marie

Marie is a 12-year-old sixth grader who likes to work in groups. She likes her classroom and especially likes her seatmate. Her openness causes her to gravitate to groups of any kind. She enjoys school clubs and will join as many as possible. She wants people to talk to her and she clearly is an auditory child. She is quick to pick up on conversational ideas and can apply them.

She will apply herself to any pencil-and-paper work as long as she has had good oral instruction. She has a strong vocabulary and her word usage and meaning is three grades above her current placement. Her writing is clear and concise, and she excels when engaged in group written projects. She has a strong sense of social responsibility about her assignments. She completes all her assignments, even when the work is full of errors. Her work is clear, easily readable, and neat.

She will do anything to be around her peers and her desire for peer contact is as strong in the classroom as it is during recess. She loves to have her peers recognize her for her good deeds and is ready to reinforce her peers for their good behavior.

Marie is proud of her grades and feels good about the teacher letting her parents know she is doing well at school. Good grades, support from her peers, being assigned to groups, having positive notes sent home, and schoolwide recognition all reinforce her.

The chance to talk to her teacher on a one-on-one basis is a highlight of her day. Tokens do nothing for her and she does not like smiley faces or "happy grams." She does not believe she should get food in the classroom and feels insulted when it is offered to her. She believes such things belong at home. She does not like to work alone. Quiet time is difficult for her to manage.

None of her friends ride the bus and she has problems on the bus because she does not easily accept nonfriends. Unorganized times are especially hard for her, such as hallway, recess, lunchtime, and physical education class.

Written directions are difficult for her to follow. Teacher-directed written work is hard, and text material confuses her greatly. Written symbols seem to challenge her. She also does not like to get her direction on a one-on-one basis because she feels she is being singled out from the rest of the class. Graphs, maps, and charts cause her great frustration. She does not do well with workbooks or work charts.

When called on to speak independently, she will withdraw and often will become hostile. Her sense of well-being is challenged when she is singled out, which causes her to withdraw or become aggressive. Any pencil-and-paper work that requires independent activity will frustrate her. She rushes through her written assignments and seeks little help from the teacher when she is left alone. She verbalizes her desire to succeed but she misses many questions during independent work.

Her self-confidence is weak when she is required to be alone. Her tolerance levels have great swings, depending upon with whom she is working. She may withdraw and cry or lash out and be verbally abusive if she must work alone.

If she feels she is being isolated from her peers intentionally, she will exhibit off-task and verbally aggressive behavior. She finds it difficult to explain her aggressive behavior to her teacher and her mother. These episodes will often end in crying and screaming situations.

Error Patterns: Diagnosis, Prescription, Remediation

Each of the following simulations assumes that Marie has taken a test, and in each situation, a different error has emerged. The task is to identify appropriate lessons based on the knowledge of the child and your knowledge of the exhibited math deficiency.

Division Error Pattern I for Marie

The first sample paper is a completed, nine-problem division paper. You should use the following four-step process:

1. Score the paper.
2. Begin with the first incorrect problem and attempt to determine the algorithm Marie is using to obtain the answers.
3. Use Marie's pattern and see if the second incorrect problem follows the pattern.
   a. If it does, go to step four.
   b. If it does not, study the error in the second problem and revise your prediction of the algorithm used.
4. Confirm the pattern using the third incorrect problem.

Complete the four-step process now, using the data shown.

Diagnosing the Error: After you have scored the paper, identify the proposed pattern of error and reflect on the strengths exhibited in Marie's division work. Strengths to look for include knowledge of place value, knowledge of division facts, work with the number one in division, and understanding the format for division—to mention just a few. Use the space below to record your observations.

Marie's Error Pattern(s):
Marie's Strengths:

Scoring Student Work Sample Error I for Marie finds her getting just one of eight (13 percent) correct. She has a number of strengths, which should prove beneficial in any remediation. She knows the basic format for division, that is, beginning on the left, getting trial divisors, multiplying, subtracting, and regrouping. She also knows:

1. division facts, including how to divide by multidigit numbers
2. how to deal with zero in the quotient (she does make an error in problem 4, where she does not record the zero, but this is viewed as a careless error because she performs correctly in problems 5 and 8)
3. the format for performing division efficiently

The first problem Marie does incorrectly is problem 1. It appears she divides the 2 into the 8 and obtains 4, then proceeds to record the 4 above the units

STUDENT WORK SAMPLE ERROR I FOR MARIE

1. 2)86 — quotient 34
   8
   6
   6

2. 4)20 — quotient 5
   20

3. 7)133 — quotient 91
   7
   63
   63

4. 3)619 — quotient 62
   6
   19
   18
   1

5. 8)816 — quotient 201
   8
   16
   16

6. 6)678 — quotient 311
   6
   7
   6
   18
   18

7. 21)7309 — quotient 843
   63
   100
   84
   169
   168
   1

8. 86)8935 — quotient 301
   86
   335
   258
   77

column of the dividend. She then multiplies, records the 8 under the 8, subtracts, and brings down the 6. At this point she divides 2 into 6, yielding 3, and records the 3 in the tens column of the quotient.

The next incorrect problem is problem 3. She seems to divide the 7 into the 13, yielding 1, records the 1 above the units digit, multiplies the trial divisor (1) by 7, and records it under the 13. She subtracts, leaving 6. Now she regroups by bringing down the 3 to obtain 63, and divides the 7 into the 63 to obtain 9. The 9 is then recorded in the tens column of the quotient.

Skip incorrect problem 4—because it seems to have additional complications—and move to incorrect problem 5. The child appears to divide the 8 into 8, yielding 1, and records the 1 above the units column. Then she divides the 8 into the 1 and writes the 0 above the 1 in the tens column. Next, she regroups the 6, obtaining 16, and divides by the 8, yielding 2. She records the 2 in the hundreds column. She is very methodical in performing the division, but reverses the digits of the quotient because she incorrectly records the partial quotients.

Prescription: This student seems to be recording her quotient from right to left. This may be an artifact of the idea that one moves from right to left in addition, subtraction, and multiplication, but reverses this direction in division. However, it may be that the error is conceptual as the child is not reasoning why digits are recorded where they are recorded. Her error is that she reverses the digits in the quotient. A DAS for Marie is shown in Table 6.1.

Remediation: Marie's first MIP appears in Table 6.2. Begin working with Marie by presenting the following problem: If 2 people are to share 86 blocks, how many does each person get?

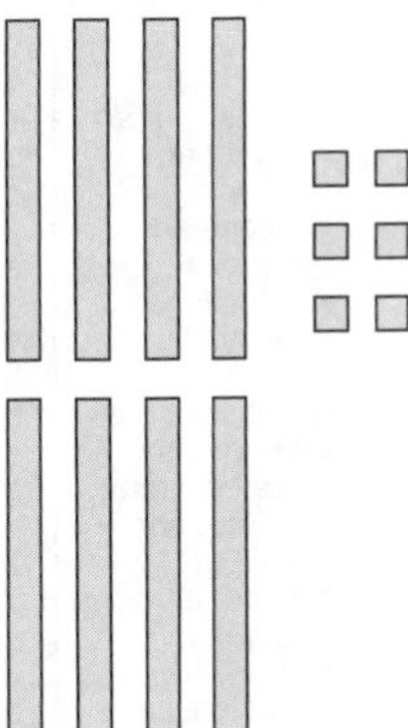

She will probably begin separating the 86 into two groups. Be very observant of her method, as you may be able to capitalize on her procedure in your next dialogue. If she first separates the longs and gives each set 4 longs, then separates the units, giving each set 3 units, then you will easily be able to talk with her about the procedure. However, if the units are separated first, then the longs, you will have to adjust your instructional dialogue to help her conceptualize why the algorithm works the way it does. In either event, she should arrive at an answer of 4 longs and 3 units, or 43. Have her compare that to the answer she recorded on her test. Ask why there is a discrepancy in her answers. Listen very carefully to her explanation, as it should provide clues about whether the error is conceptual or procedural. In all likelihood, given Marie's strengths in division

TABLE 6.1 Data Analysis Sheet

Student: Marie						
Team Members:						
Context	**Content Assessment**	**Process**		**Behavior**		**Reinforcement**
		Input	Output	Academic	Social	
+	+	+	+	+	+	+
• Enjoys working in groups. Likes her classroom and especially likes her seatmate • Her openness causes her to gravitate to groups of any kind • She enjoys school clubs and will join as many as possible	***Learned Concepts I*** • Knows division facts, including division by multidigit numbers • Knows format for performing division ***Learned Concepts II*** • Knows division facts, both easy and hard • Uses multidigit divisors well • Efficiently performs division • Records quotients correctly ***Learned Concepts III*** • Knows and uses efficient division algorithm • Knows all division facts • Works well with zero in quotients	• She wants people to talk to her, she clearly is an auditory child and is quick to pick up on conversational ideas and can apply them • She will apply herself to any pencil-and-paper task as long as she has good oral instruction • Written symbols seem to be a challenge, but she manages okay	• She has a strong vocabulary and her word usage and understanding is above her current placement • Her writing is clear and concise and she excels when engaged in group written projects	• She has a strong social responsibility about her assignments • She completes all her assignments, even when the work is full of errors • Her work is clear and easily readable, and papers are always neat	• She will do anything to be around her peers. Her desire for peer contact is as strong in the classroom as during recess • Seeks peer recognition; reinforces peers for their good behavior • She is proud of her good grades and pleased when the teacher lets her parents know she is doing well at school	• Good grades • Support from her peers • Assigned to groups • Positive notes sent home • Class- or school-wide recognition • The chance to talk to her teacher on a one-on-one basis
–	–	–	–	–	–	–
• She does not like to work alone • Quiet time is difficult for her to manage • None of her friends ride the bus so she has problems on the way to and from school • Unorganized times are especially hard for her, such as hallway, recess, lunch, and physical education class	***Error Pattern I*** • Records quotient in reverse order ***Error Pattern II*** • Difficulty with zero in quotients ***Error Pattern III*** • Does not record remainders in procedure or in quotient	• Written directions are difficult for her to follow • Teacher-directed written work is hard, but text material confuses her greatly • She also does not like to get her directions on a one-on-one basis because she feels she is being singled out • Graphs, maps, and charts cause her great frustration	• She does not do well with workbooks or work charts • When called on to speak independently, she will withdraw and often will become hostile • Her sense of well-being is challenged when she is singled out and she will withdraw or become aggressive • Any pencil-and-paper work that requires independent activity will frustrate her	• She rushes through her written assignments and seeks little help from the teacher when she is left alone • She verbalizes her desire to succeed but she misses many questions during independent work	• Self-confidence is weak when required to be alone • Tolerance levels have great swings, depending upon whom she is working with or if working alone • She may withdraw, cry, or lash out and be verbally abusive • If she feels she is being isolated from her peers intentionally, she will exhibit off-task and verbally aggressive behavior • She finds it difficult to explain her aggressive behavior to others	• Tokens do nothing for her and she does not like smiley faces or "happy grams" • She does not believe she should get food in the classroom and feels insulted when it is offered to her • Toys and games as rewards are ineffective, she believes such things belong at home

Note: The + symbols indicate strengths and the – symbols indicate areas of concern.

TABLE 6.2 Mathematics Improvement Plan I for Marie: Recording Digits in the Quotient in the Correct Order

Time		15 minutes	30 minutes	15–20 minutes
Context		She is assigned to her study group of three other students (+)	She is expected to complete this assignment on her own and at her desk (–)	Assigned to study group to complete the assigned task (+)
Content		Work assignment sheet of division problems using manipulative materials (+)	Completes three problems by drawing and recording each step of solution (–)	Complete an activity such as "100 and Out" or "20's Plenty" (+)
Process	Input	The teacher talks the class through the assignment and each group gets to talk it over before they begin their work (+)	The teacher writes the directions for this assignment, she is expected to read and follow the directions without prompts (–)	Work tasks are assigned to the group in written format (–)
	Output	She is expected to complete her assignment in her workbook after her group discusses the assignment (–)	She will write the assignment and turn it in to the teacher (+)	Her group is expected to give an oral presentation on their activity, they may pick a spokesperson to talk about the task outcomes (+)
Behavior	Academic	She fails to check her assignment and does not seek help from the teacher (–)	She completes this assignment in a written format and checks it with a classmate (+)	She and the group work through the activity as a team and check each other's work (+)
	Social	She stays with her assignment and discusses the assignment results with her peers (+)	The nature of this assignment isolates her from her peers (–)	She is expected to work effectively within her group (+)
Reinforcement		The teacher talks to each group concerning their outcomes and she gets to talk to the teacher about her problems (+)	The rewards are happy face stickers placed on her assignment (–)	She gets an A grade and the teacher talks to each student individually (+)

Note: The + symbols indicate strengths and the – symbols indicate areas of concern.

knowledge, she will express that she just wrote the numbers in the wrong places. Should this be the case, then we would suggest that you use a diagram to talk through the division procedure that optimizes performance.

Suggest to the child that you rework the problem together, while recording what is happening in the division. We would suggest you write the problem as pictured. As you are writing the problem, discuss that you are drawing the vertical line because you are working with tens and ones:

$$2\overline{)8\,|\,6}$$

Now ask Marie to divide the longs into two sets. As she puts the four longs in each set, you should write what has just happened:

$$\begin{array}{r|l} 4 & \\ 2\overline{)8} & 6 \end{array}$$

Discuss why the 4 is written over the 8 (because it tells us how many longs [10s] each person gets). Marie should be able to tell you what to do next, as she did it correctly in every problem on the test, so you might ask her. Then perform the multiplication:

$$\begin{array}{r|c|c} & 4 & \\ \hline 2 & 8 & 6 \\ & 8 & \\ \hline \end{array}$$

Now ask Marie what is done next. The 6 is "brought down" to show that there are 6 units left to divide:

$$\begin{array}{r|c|c} & 4 & \\ \hline 2 & 8 & 6 \\ & 8 & \\ \hline & & 6 \end{array}$$

It is essential that this dialogue take place so she conceptualizes why the numbers are written where they are written. It helps her organize why the numbers go where they go. This will help her see that, even though the 6 is brought down, it represents the 6 units left to distribute. We feel that through this process, she will eventually conceptualize a heuristic that guides her through the solution of the division once the materials are no longer in use.

Now ask Marie to divide the 6 units between the two sets. She should be able to distribute the 6 units between the two sets, arriving at 3 in each set. At this point, you should record how many units each set has in the units place of the quotient:

$$\begin{array}{r|c|c} & 4 & 3 \\ \hline 2 & 8 & 6 \\ & 8 & \\ \hline & & 6 \\ & & 6 \\ \hline \end{array}$$

After writing the 3 in the units position of the quotient, ask her what is to be done next. She should tell you to multiply the 3 by the 2 and record the value, 6, under the 6. She did this correctly in all the problems, so we anticipate no difficulty on her part in doing this.

At this point, ask Marie if there are any questions about what you and she have just done. If there are questions, you will need to examine them and provide explanations as required. Once there are no more questions, have the child work another problem, such as: Three people are to share 36 pieces of gum. How many pieces does each person get?

Be sure the chosen problem does not require any regrouping to complete, because that type of problem is more complex, and you should not confound her ability to acquire the mechanics of the process to be completed.

Have Marie work a few more problems until you are confident that she understands the process well. Then suggest that she rework the test. Provide some incentive to do this. Marie exhibited many strengths in division, and remediation of this error will probably be an easy process. We feel that she will probably be relieved, because she is frustrated that she is getting so many problems incorrect even though she understands division. She will be relieved to acquire an algorithm that works correctly, because the one she has invented doesn't work.

Division Error Pattern II for Marie

The second paper is similar to the first. You should use the same four-step process you used for Error Pattern I:

1. Score the paper.
2. Begin with the first incorrect problem and attempt to determine the algorithm the child is using to obtain the answers.

STUDENT WORK SAMPLE ERROR II FOR MARIE

```
        43              5              19
1.  2)86        2.  4)20       3.  7)133
      8                20              7
      --               --             ---
       6                               63
       6                               63
      --                               --

       26              12              113
4.  3)619       5.  8)816      6.  6)678
      6               8              6
      ---             ---            ---
       19              16             7
       18              16             6
       --              --             --
        1                             18
                                      18
                                      --

          348                  13
7.  21)7309         8.  86)8935
       63                  86
       ---                 ---
       100                 335
        84                 258
       ---                 ---
       169                  77
       168
       ---
         1
```

3. Use the child's pattern and see if the second incorrect problem follows the pattern.
    a. if yes, go to step 4.
    b. if no, then study the error in the second problem and revise your prediction of the algorithm used.
4. Confirm the pattern using the third incorrect problem.

Now, score the paper for Marie.

Diagnosing the Error: After you have scored the paper, identify the proposed pattern of error and reflect on the strengths exhibited in Marie's division work. Strengths to look for include knowledge of place value, knowledge of division facts, work with the number one in division, and understanding the format for division. Use the space below to record your observances.

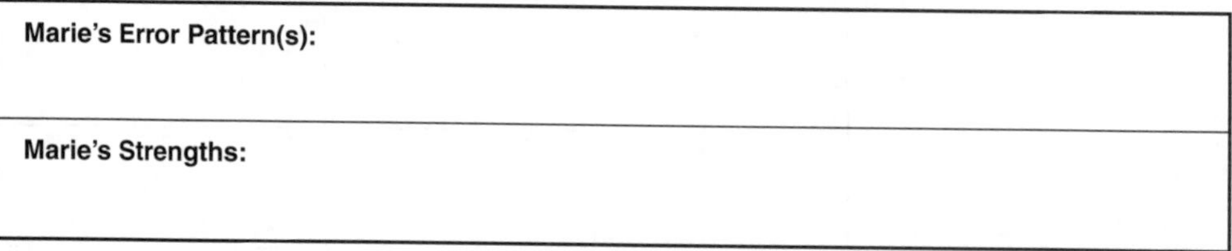
Marie's Error Pattern(s):

Marie's Strengths:

Marie gets just five correct of the eight problems (63 percent). While this performance is not a passing grade, Marie does exhibit strengths that are very encouraging for improved performance. She knows:

1. division facts (both easy and hard)
2. how to use multidigit divisors effectively
3. how to use an efficient format for performing division
4. how to record division quotients correctly

Generally speaking, Marie is quite competent in performing division but is showing a low performance because of the algorithm she has invented for herself.

The first incorrect problem, problem 4, reveals the omission of a zero in the quotient. All other aspects of the problem are performed effectively. The next incorrect problem reveals the same error and the last incorrect problem, problem 8, again reveals that the zero in the quotient has been omitted. Therefore, Marie does not record the zero in the quotient when dividing. We believe that when this error occurs, you should treat it as a conceptual error because she is not reasoning that (as in problem 4) 3 divided into 619 will be much more than 26. She seems to be blindly performing her algorithm without regard to the reasonableness of the answers obtained.

Prescription: Conceptual work with manipulatives (base-10 blocks, colored markers for place value, or some other device) should be used to help the child conceptualize the division. Initial work should be with problems that do not have a zero in the quotient, then move to problems that do have a zero present. In this way, Marie gains experience in simple situations before encountering problems that address her specific difficulty.

Remediation: Marie's second MIP appears in Table 6.3. Initial work with Marie should involve a couple of children working on a problem such as: Two children have 246 pieces of candy from trick-or-treating at Halloween. How much candy does each child get if they divide the candy equally?

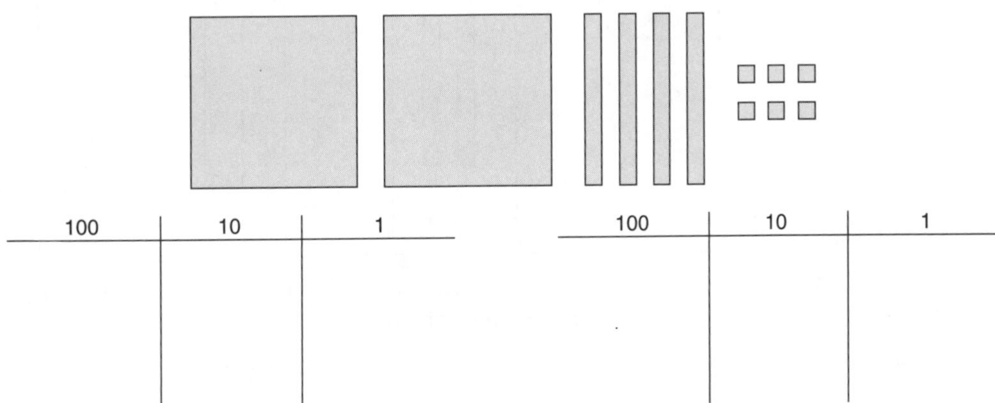

TABLE 6.3 Mathematics Improvement Plan II for Marie: Working with a Zero in the Quotient

Time		15 minutes	30 minutes	20 minutes
Context		She is assigned to her study group of three other students (+)	She is expected to complete this assignment on her own and at her desk (–)	Assigned to group to complete the assigned task (+)
Content		Complete assignment sheet of division problems using base-10 materials (+)	Completes similar problems using manipulatives, then records by drawing each step of solution (–)	Complete a group activity game that reinforces division (+)
Process	Input	The teacher talks the class through the assignment and each group gets to talk it over before they begin their work (+)	The teacher writes the directions for this assignment. She is expected to read and follow the directions without prompts (–)	Work tasks are assigned to the group in written format (–)
	Output	She is expected to complete her assignment in her workbook after her group discusses the assignment (–)	She will write the assignment and turn it in to the teacher (+)	Her group is expected to give an oral presentation on their activity, they may pick a spokesperson to talk about the task outcomes (–)
Behavior	Academic	She fails to check her assignment and does not seek help from the teacher (–)	She completes this assignment in a written format and turns it in to the teacher (–)	She and the group work through the activity and check each other's work (+)
	Social	She stays with her assignment and discusses the assignment results with her peers (+)	The nature of this assignment isolates her from her peers (–)	She is expected to work effectively within her group (+)
Reinforcement		The teacher talks to each group concerning their outcomes and she gets to talk to the teacher about her problems (+)	Use rewards other than happy face stickers placed on her assignment (+)	She gets an A grade and the teacher discusses the activity with the group (+)

Note: The + symbols indicate strengths and the – symbols indicate areas of concern.

Have Marie divide the 246. Each child should have 1 flat, 2 longs, and 3 units after dividing.

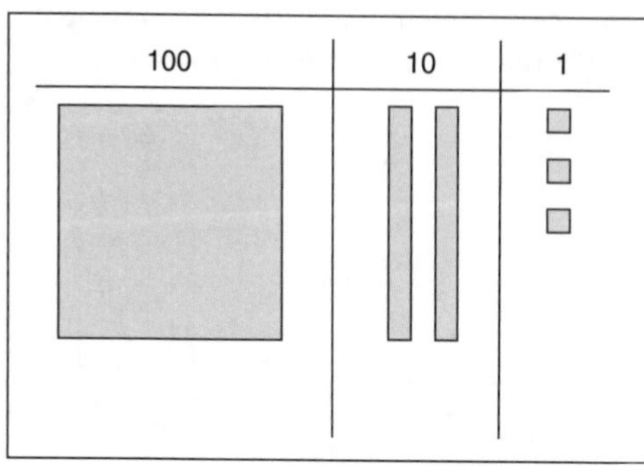

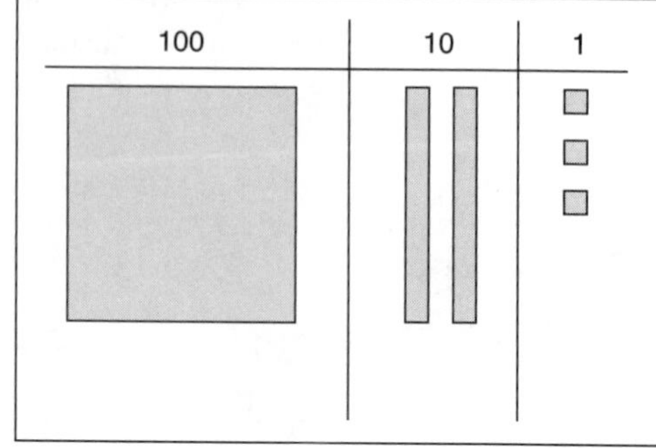

Discuss the answer that was obtained. Practice writing it. Be sure to express the problem in the division form:

$$2\overline{)2\,4\,6}\quad 1\,2\,3$$

In this way, Marie gets the idea of what the answer is expressing.

Work another problem, such as 428 divided by 2, using the base-10 blocks. Again, be sure to express the quotient in the form:

$$2\overline{)4\,2\,8}\quad 2\,1\,4$$

After you are certain that Marie understands the format for using the base-10 blocks and the recording of the answer (together with being able to discuss what the answer means in terms of place value), introduce a problem such as: Two children have 214 markers. How many would each person have if they shared equally?

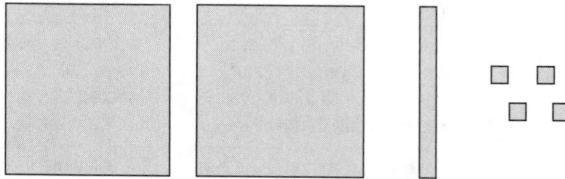

Use the base-10 blocks to get 214. Then have Marie divide them equally. At some point they will have:

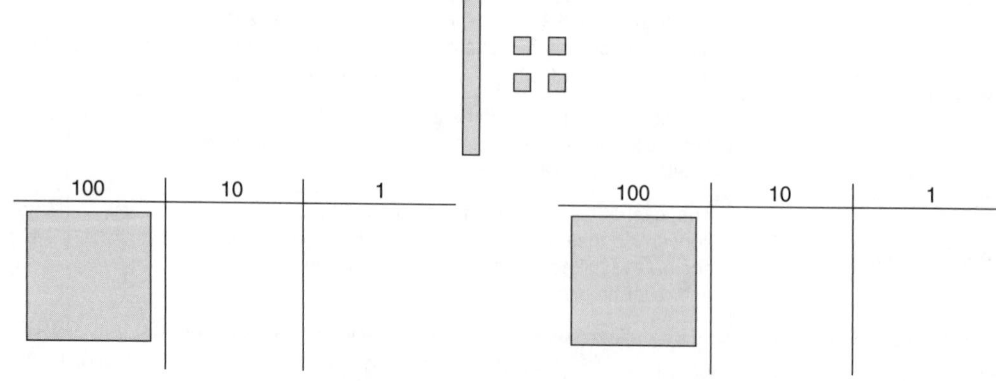

At this point, she will have to exchange the long for 10 ones. Her work will then look like:

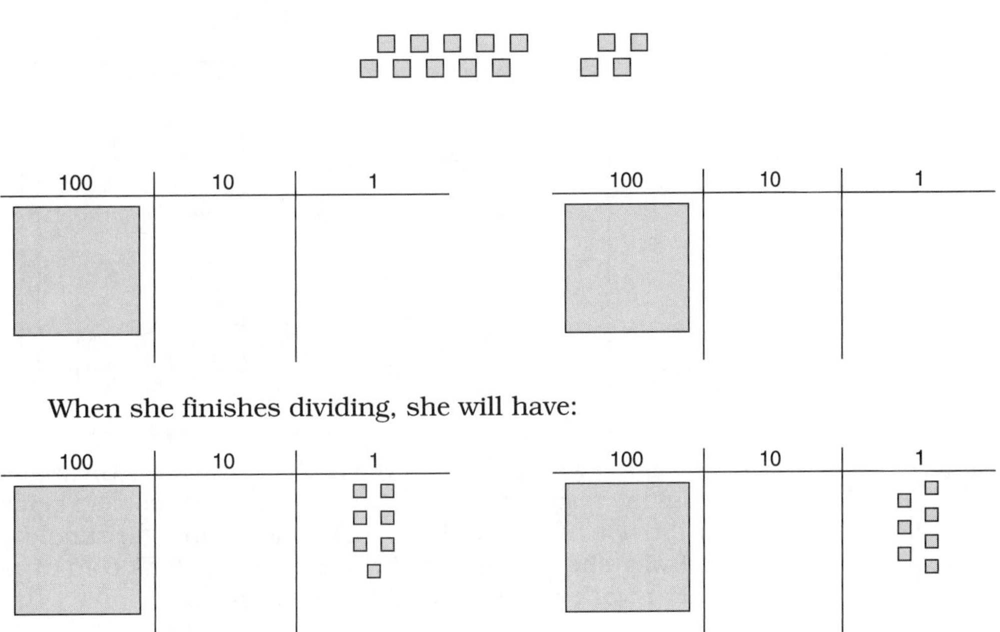

When she finishes dividing, she will have:

Now have them write out the solution in the form:

$$2\overline{)214}\quad\text{quotient } 107$$

It is now time to discuss the solution. It seems that the answer is 107. There are zero tens. Discuss that when the 2 hundreds were divided between the 2 children, each got 1 of the hundreds. Then there were not enough tens for each person to get one, so each person got zero tens, which is recorded with the zero. This tells how many tens each person got. The 1 ten is then regrouped with the 4 ones for a total of 14 ones. Each of the two children then gets 7, using all 14.

Make sure this is discussed thoroughly with Marie, and make sure she understands completely why the numbers are written where they are. It is most important that she conceptually owns this knowledge before going on. You may even have to rework the problem with her, if necessary. This checking for understanding is essential.

Now have Marie rework problem 4. She should get 619 using the base-10 blocks. Have her perform the division by dividing the blocks into three sets. Once she has obtained her answer of 206, have her write the problem solution in the following form:

$$3\overline{)619}\quad\text{quotient } 206\text{ R }1$$

Talk with Marie about the solution, and be sure she can explain exactly what the answer means (including the explanation of what the remainder means).

We suggest, at this point, that you encourage her to rework the problem and record what she is doing at each step of the problem solution. Use a form like:

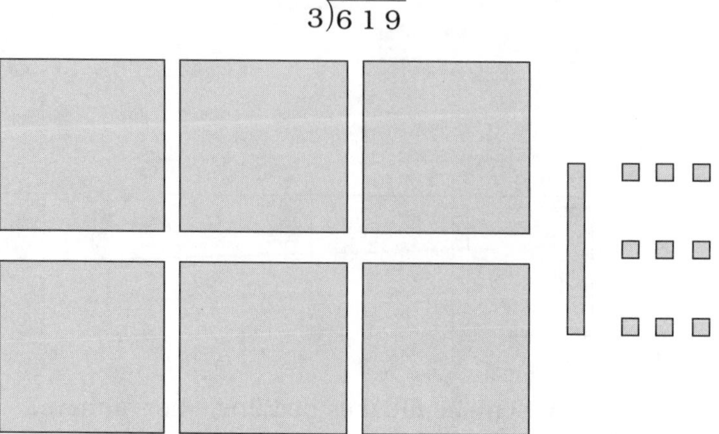

As Marie works through the problem, dividing the materials, encourage her to write the result of each step on the division problem before progressing to the next division of materials. At the conclusion, she should conceptually understand why she has recorded the zero in the tens column of the division problem. Her work should resemble something like:

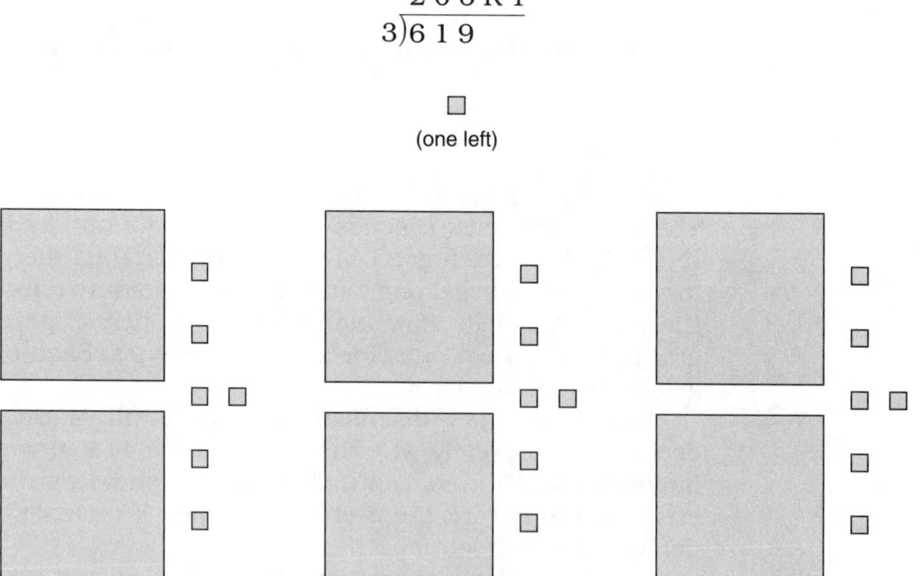

Continue practicing this process until you are certain that Marie owns the concept. Then encourage her to rework the other problems on the test. Provide some tangible reinforcement for performing this work.

Division Error Pattern III for Marie

The third sample paper is similar to the first two. You should use the same four-step process you used to assess Sample Errors I and II for Marie.

STUDENT WORK SAMPLE ERROR III FOR MARIE

1. $2\overline{)86}$ — answer 43; work: 8, 6, 6

2. $4\overline{)20}$ — answer 5; work: 20

3. $7\overline{)133}$ — answer 19; work: 7, 63, 63

4. $3\overline{)619}$ — answer 206; work: 6, 19, 18

5. $8\overline{)816}$ — answer 102; work: 8, 16, 16

6. $6\overline{)678}$ — answer 113; work: 6, 7, 6, 18, 18

7. $21\overline{)7309}$ — answer 348; work: 63, 100, 84, 169, 168

8. $86\overline{)8935}$ — answer 103; work: 86, 335, 258

Diagnosing the Error: After you have scored the paper, identify the proposed pattern of error and reflect on the strengths exhibited in Marie's division work. Strengths to look for include knowledge of place value, knowledge of division facts, work with the number one in division, and understanding of the format for division. Record your comments in the space below.

Marie's Error Pattern(s):
Marie's Strengths:

Marie scores five of eight (63 percent) correct. This is a rather low score, yet, upon closer inspection of her work, Marie shows numerous strengths in division. First, Marie knows the format of division. She also has the following strengths:

1. knows and uses a very efficient algorithm for division
2. knows all the division facts
3. performs with two-digit divisors excellently
4. works with zero in the quotient competently
5. multiplies, subtracts, and regroups correctly on every problem

Looking at the first incorrect problem reveals that Marie did not write the remainder on the last step of problem 4. Problems 7 and 8 have the same error. Aside from this, all work is correct. Although we do not agree with the practice, some teachers will mark a child's problem wrong if the quotient does not contain an "R" with the remainder written beside the quotient, such as 619 ÷ 3 = 206 R1.

TABLE 6.4 Mathematics Improvement Plan III for Marie: Remembering to Write Remainders

Time		15 minutes	30–40 minutes	10–15 minutes
Context		She is assigned to her study group of three other students (+)	She is expected to complete this assignment on her own and at her desk (–)	Assigned to study group to complete the assigned task (+)
Content		Complete assignment sheet of division problems using base-10 materials—focus is on finding remainders (+)	Completes similar problems using manipulatives, then records by drawing solutions and showing remainders (–)	Complete a group activity game that reinforces division remainders, such as "20's Plenty" (+)
Process	Input	The teacher talks the class through the assignment and each group gets to talk it over before they begin their work (+)	The teacher writes the directions for this assignment. Marie is expected to read and follow the directions without prompts (–)	Work tasks are assigned to the group in written format (–)
	Output	She is expected to complete her assignment in her workbook after her group discusses the assignment (–)	She will write the assignment and turn it in to the teacher (+)	Her group is expected to give an oral presentation on their activity, with a spokesperson talking about the task outcomes (+)
Behavior	Academic	She fails to check her assignment and does not seek help from the teacher (–)	She completes this assignment in a written format and turns it in to the teacher (–)	She and the group work through the activity as a team and check each other's work (+)
	Social	She stays with her assignment and discusses the assignment results with her peers (+)	The nature of this assignment isolates her from her peers (–)	She is expected to work effectively within her group (+)
Reinforcement		The teacher talks to each group concerning their outcomes and she gets to talk to the teacher about her problems (+)	Use rewards other than happy face stickers placed on her assignment (+)	She gets an A grade and the teacher talks to each student individually (+)

Note: The + symbols indicate strengths and the – symbols indicate areas of concern.

This practice seems too rigid, especially when the remainder is obvious at the end of the problem. However, when the remainder does not appear, the problem is incorrect. Thus the child should actually perform the last subtraction and should be encouraged to write the value, along with the quotient, using the "R" notation.

Prescription: This error is a procedural error because of the nature of the error in the face of all the correct problems. Marie should complete the division by writing the remainders on the work.

Remediation: Marie's third MIP appears in Table 6.4. Discuss problem 4 with Marie. Ask her to check the division by performing the multiplication of the answer with the divisor (206 × 3). The result of the multiplication is 618. Ask why the product is different from the number being divided (619). Marie will probably tell you that the 1 is the remainder. You should indicate that she needs to complete the subtraction of 18 from 19 and write the 1. Then encourage her to write the R1 by the answer to confirm that there is a remainder of 1.

Have Marie complete the other problems she missed and write the remainders correctly. This should not be a difficult remediation, because she exhibits many strengths, and this error is more procedural than conceptual.

Conclusions: Instructional Strategies Summary

Throughout the remediation plan for all three samples, the following suggestions would be very helpful:

1. Have learners complete a few problems at a time. Choose the problems carefully so they move from simple problems to complex problems. Once you are satisfied that they understand the concepts, move on.
2. Pair a slow learner with an average learner. They can usually help each other. Combining older students with younger students is another strategy you might try, given Marie's DAS.
3. Use the simplest possible numbers to explain a mathematical operation, then move to the more complex level. Plan ahead of time which problems you will use, so you do not accidentally choose special cases during the instruction.

Assessment of Children's Work: Assessing whether children's division errors are primarily results of a low level of conceptual understanding or a lack of ability to recall basic facts or work with algorithmic rules can be accomplished with various types of questions. Children's conceptual learning can be assessed and evaluated more readily by utilizing authentic, real-world situations in which learners must decide not only how to solve the problem but also whether the result is reasonable. Be sure to carry on a discourse with children as they work through a problem, having them explain to you what they are doing and why. From this dialogue, you will be able to determine when they are unclear in what they are doing.

Some activities are provided in the following section: You may use them when practicing division once conceptual understanding has been attained.

Instructional Activities

ACTIVITY: 100 and Out

Students should have a grasp of division facts and an invented knowledge of the division algorithm. The activity is for two or more students.

Objective: Practice division

Materials:

Pencil and paper

3 × 5 cards with division problems (problems like 26 ÷ 2, 69 ÷ 3, etc.)

Directions: Place the division deck face down in the center of the group. Taking turns, a player turns over a card, performs the division, and gets to add the quotient to her score. Then play passes to the next player. The first player to 100 wins.

ACTIVITY: 20's Plenty

Students should know division facts and should have an invented knowledge of the division algorithm. The activity is for two or more students.

Objective: Practice division problems with remainders

Materials:

Pencil and paper

3 × 5 card deck with division propblems that result in remainders (do include some problems without remainders to make the game fun)

Directions: Place the division deck face down in the center of the group. Taking turns, a player turns over a card, performs the division, and gets to add the remainder to the player's score. If the remainder is zero, then zero is added to the player's score. Then play passes to the next player. The first player to 20 has "plenty" and wins the game. (Children are to record their problems and answers as they go.)

Discussion Questions

1. Discuss your understanding of the distinction between "conceptual" errors and "procedural" errors in division.
2. The following worksheet shows Student Work Sample Error IV for Marie:

```
        43               5                19
1. 2)86          2. 4)20          3. 7)133
     8                20               7
     --               --               --
      6                                63
      6                                63
      --                               --

       238             102             113
4. 3)619         5. 8)816         6. 6)678
     5               8                6
     --              --               --
     11               16               7
      9               16               6
     --               --               --
      29                               18
      27                               18
      --                               --
       2

           3493                 1918
7. 21)7309           8. 86)8935
      63                   86
      ---                  ---
      100                  833
       84                  774
      ---                  ---
       269                 157
       189                  86
       ---                 ---
        80                 715
        63                 648
        --                 ---
        17                  77
```

a. Score Student Work Sample Error IV for Marie. Identify her strengths and error patterns. Complete a DAS for Marie.

b. Complete an MIP.

3. The following worksheet shows Student Work Sample Error V for Marie:

```
        43
1.  2)86
      40    20
      46
      40    20
       6
       6   3/43

        5
2.  4)20
      20  5/5

         19
3.  7)133
       70   10
       63
       63   9/19

        209
4.  3)619
       600   200
        19
        15     5
         4

        102
5.  8)816
       800   100
        16
        16     2

        113
6.  6)678
       600   100
        78
        60    10
        18     3
        18

          349
7.  21)7309
         4200  200
         3109
         2100  100
         1009
          630   30
          379
          210   10
          169
          105    5
           64
           63    3
            1

          180
8.  86)8935
         8600  100
          335
          [illegible, crossed out]
          258    3
           77
```

a. Score Student Work Sample Error V for Marie. Identify her strengths and error patterns. Complete a DAS for Marie.
b. Complete an MIP.

4. Design a division activity to provide practice with division facts. Make the activity suitable for a short period of practice for a group of four children.

5. Design a question that would focus on the conceptual understanding of division. The question should help the teacher know if the student understands why remainders are written with the "R" notation.

6. Identify three characteristics of a mathematics activity you would use with a child with this behavioral profile. Justify your answer.
7. Identify two characteristics that you would *not* want the activity developed in question 6 to utilize. Justify your answer.
8. Using library or Internet resources, find and/or modify an activity that you would utilize with a child exhibiting Error Pattern III. Identify specific reasons for your choice.

References

Ball, D. L. (1990). Prospective elementary and secondary teachers' understanding of division. *Journal of Research in Mathematics Education, 21*(2), 132–144.

Baroody, A. (2006). Why children have difficulties mastering the basic number combinations and how to help them. *Teaching Children Mathematics, 13*(1), 22.

Bates, T., & Rousseau, L. (1986). Will the real division algorithm please stand up? *Arithmetic Teacher, 33*(7), 42–46.

Caliandro, C. K. (2000). Children's inventions for multidigit multiplication and division. *Teaching Children Mathematics, 6*(6), 420–426.

Cawley, J. F. (2002). Mathematics interventions and students with high-incidence disabilities. *Remedial and Special Education, 23*(1), 2–6.

Cheek, H. N., & Olson, M. (1986). A den of thieves investigates division. *Arithmetic Teacher, 33*(9), 34–35.

Guberman, S. R. (2004). A comparative study of children's out-of-school activities and arithmetical achievements. *Journal for Research in Mathematics Education, 35*(2), 117–150.

Monroe, E. E., & Orme, M. P. (2002). Developing mathematical vocabulary. *Preventing School Failure, 46*(3), 139–142.

Mulligan, J. T., & Mitchelmore, M. C. (1997). Young children's intuitive models of multiplication and division. *Journal for Research in Mathematics Education 28*(3), 309–330.

National Council of Teachers of Mathematics. (2000). *Principles and standards for school mathematics*. Reston, VA: Author.

Sáenz-Ludlow, A. (2004). Metaphor and numerical diagrams in the arithmetical activity of a fourth-grade class. *Journal for Research in Mathematics Education, 35*(1), 34–56.

Sowder, J. T., & Wheeler, M. M. (1989). The development of concepts and strategies used in computational estimation. *Journal of Research in Mathematics Education, 20*(2), 130–146.

van Putten, C. M., van den Brom-Snijders, P. A., & Beishuizen, M. (2005). Progressive mathematization of long division strategies in Dutch primary schools. *Journal for Research in Mathematics Education, 36*(1), 44–73.

Chapter 7

Rational Numbers

> Fractions aren't really numbers.... they are parts of things and that's different.
>
> 1/2 is the same as 3/4 because the top number in each fraction is one away from the bottom numbers.
>
> I hate fractions.... I could never do them and that's when I knew I would never be good at math.

Perhaps as a teacher or parent, you have heard similar comments from learners studying rational numbers. Rational numbers are sometimes quite difficult for students who were successful with whole numbers in early grades. Understanding and becoming proficient in learning about numbers that represent parts, that have an infinite number of names, and that do not follow whole numbers patterns can be daunting. Although most students do eventually succeed in learning to use specific algorithms, general conceptual knowledge is often deficient. In their recommendations for curriculum reform in the area of rational numbers, Post, Cramer, Behr, Lesh, and Harel (1993) suggested that curriculum developers' attention should be directed away from the attainment of individual tasks and toward the development of more global cognitive processes. A similar point was made by Sowder (1995) and by Markovits and Sowder (1991), who suggested that children need to learn how to move among the various possible representations of rational numbers in a flexible manner. Because they retain a concern for deep conceptual understanding, contemporary analysts clearly urge instructors to create curricula that will help children develop overall conceptions of the rational number system as a whole and the way its various components fit together.

This chapter will highlight common errors that students make when learning to understand and operate on rational numbers. Alternative approaches to instruction will be presented for remediation of the most frequent types of mistakes.

What Are Rational Numbers?

Rational numbers are "abstract mathematical ideas" (NCTM, 2000, p. 10), as are counting numbers. They can be made to correspond to points on a number line: Fractions, also termed rational numbers, can be expressed as "$a \div b = c$," if and only if $a = bc$ (Crouch & Baldwin, 1964). That is, $12 \div 3 = 4$ because

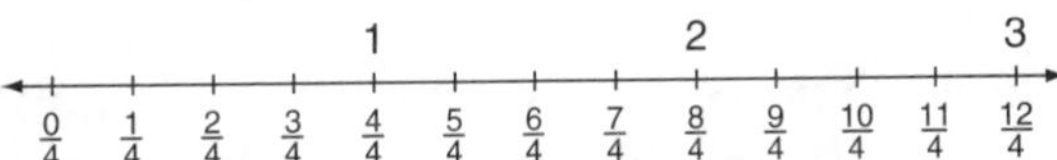

$4 \times 3 = 12$. The fraction 12/3 represents 12 divided by 3. Likewise, 4 divided by 6, is written as $4/6 = 2/3$ because $6 \times 2/3 = 4$. The bottom number of each fraction, the denominator, represents the total number of units in which the whole is subdivided. For 12/3 and 4/6, the denominators are 3 and 6, respectively. The numerator, or, the top number (12 and 4 above), indicates the number of sections used.

Three fundamental part–whole interpretations of rational numbers are of particular relevance to the elementary curriculum. In one case, regions, fractions can represent a relationship between a whole unit and its equal sized and shaped parts. For instance, three fourths represents three pieces of the whole unit, such as three pieces of a pizza that is cut into four sections. The denominator is "4" because there are 4 units in the pizza. The numerator is "3" because 3 pieces of the pizza were eaten. The diagrams below illustrate the region meaning for 3/4, 2/6, and 1/2.

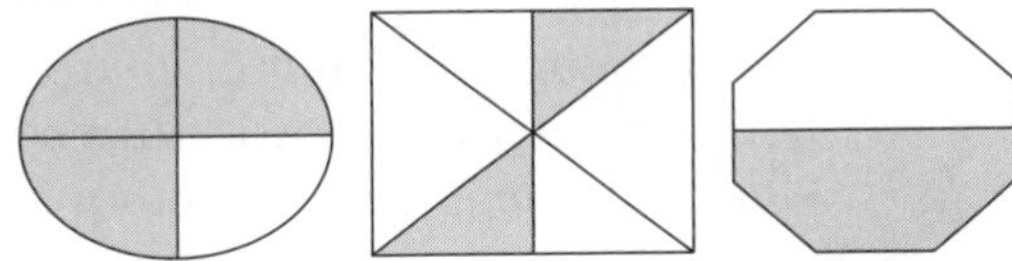

Fractions can also represent the number of objects in a set of discrete or separate items. In this situation, the fraction three fourths would indicate that three of four children are reading a book or three of four boxes of strawberries are filled. The children and the boxes are separate items that may or may not be the same size and shape and that make up a set, in contrast to the unit of pizza. The set diagram below shows that 3/4 would symbolize that 3 of 4 cookies were eaten.

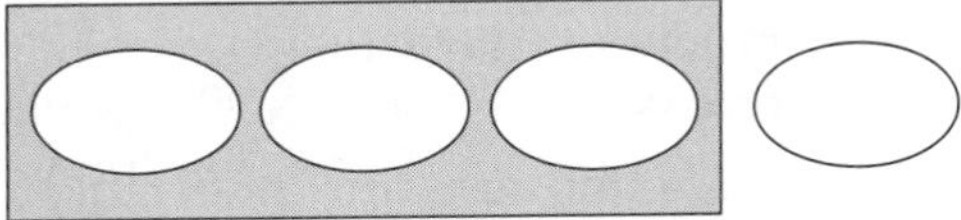

The linear interpretation of rational numbers involves partitioning a unit of length into fractional parts. A line can be subdivided into equal-length segments. For example, consider the number line:

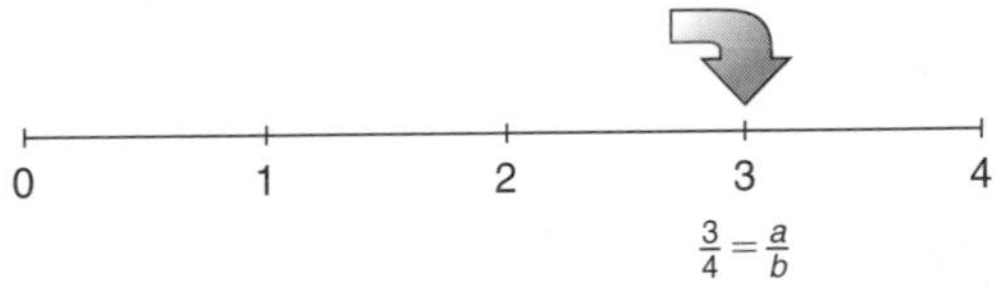

The denominator, *b*, represents the number 4 because there are four intervals on the number line and the numerator, 3, represents the number of intervals chosen to be marked off.

Any rational number can be renamed by multiplying both the numerator and the denominator by the same number. In effect, the original fraction is being multiplied by one, the identity element. Multiplying any rational number by the same numerator and denominator will not change the value of the original rational number. An example of renaming is:

$$\frac{3}{4} \times \frac{2}{2} = \frac{6}{8}$$

Why Do Students Struggle with Rational Numbers?

Several reasons have been suggested for the difficulty students experience when learning rational number concepts and skills:

1. In terms of instructional approaches, lessons are too often focused on procedures and memorizing rules rather than on developing conceptual foundations, such as the quantity represented by the numerator and denominator, prior to skill building.
2. Specific content difficulties occur when students confuse whole number computational procedures with those for fractions. For example, when adding fractions, many students combine both numerators and denominators rather than making certain there must be a common denominator and that denominators are not added. Also, students assume that multiplying fractions will always yield a product larger than the factors, as is the case with whole numbers. When multiplying 6×2, 12 is larger than 6 or 2. However, $6 \times 1/2 = 3$, a product less than one of the factors, 6. Likewise, division of fractions can result in a quotient larger than the dividend, for example $12/1/3 = 36$.
3. Estimating rational number answers can be more challenging than estimation with whole numbers. Students must be able to approximate fractions as more or less than, for example, in order to compute efficiently. Fractions have many names, thus presenting more possibilities for errors.
4. Fractions are unconnected to everyday objects and are seen as too abstract (Alverado & Herr, 2003).
5. Flexible use of notation can be confusing for students. Fractions can be renamed with larger or smaller numerals in the numerator and denominator, as mixed numbers, as improper fractions, and using decimals. It is difficult to rename fractions with limited understanding of their size and the concept of equivalence (Saxe, Tayler, McIntosh, & Gearhart, 2005).

About the Student: Tawana

Tawana is 12 years old, likes school, and is in the fifth grade. She is somewhat shy and often requests that she have the opportunity to work alone. She will make contact with her teacher easily, and often does so to the irritation of the teacher and other students. She likes the teacher to give directions orally and in small blocks of information. Her shyness surfaces when she is expected to work with her peers, any adult with whom she is not comfortable, and in large-group settings. She becomes irritated when she is expected to work in groups and will voice her objection openly during those activities. She does like to work with a single peer—usually a girl she considers her friend. It is clear that she is more comfortable with females than she is with males. Tawana is a good listener and has strong auditory skills (she picks up quickly on verbal cues). Usually, she has to be told just once, and she can grasp the ideas. If the teacher does repeat the material several times, Tawana will become irritated and will admonish the teacher for her repetitive behavior. She can express herself verbally and has good understanding of word meaning. She loves to have the teacher point out her strengths to the class. She accepts verbal rewards graciously and does not need to be redirected to her assignment after the administration of the reward.

Tawana's pencil-and-paper activities are strong. She writes well and uses the space of the paper judiciously. She will argue, verbally challenge, and name-call when she is expected to work in academic areas in which she performs poorly. She will also perform poorly when she is seated in the back or far sides of the room—especially if someone whom she doesn't like sits next to her. If instructions are given to her in written form, she will read the material too fast or will not read the material at all. Written material does not present challenges to her if the teacher stands near her and reinforces her reading behavior.

Tawana does not like to be involved in numerical activities and games. She objects greatly when the teacher gives her any form of tangible reinforcer, such as tokens, smiley faces, or atta-girl signs, but she does like getting good grades. She says those forms (smiley faces, tokens, etc.) of reinforcers are for babies. She does work diligently when she is assigned to the computer and frequently asks to be allowed to use the computer for her written assignments. She seems to rebel when she is assigned to a group, especially when the group is required to read and follow the work assignment without teacher assistance.

Tawana will work hard and accurately when she knows that the reward is social time with her female classmates. She becomes very agitated when she is put in a social setting with her male peers. This agitation is usually pronounced by her becoming verbally aggressive. The classroom has a quiet area, which is her favorite place, and she often asks to go to that area.

Error Patterns: Diagnosis, Prescription, Remediation

Rational Number Error Pattern I for Tawana

The first five test questions for Tawana focus on fundamental numeration. She is asked to connect symbols for the three interpretations of fraction concepts.

STUDENT WORK SAMPLE I FOR TAWANA

1. What fractional parts of the figures are shaded?

$\frac{4}{4}$ $\frac{9}{6}$

2. What fractional parts of the blocks are shaded?

$\frac{3}{2}$ $\frac{4}{6}$

3. Circle $^3/_4$ of the group of boxes:

4. Put a ring around $^3/_8$ of the group of triangles:

5. Draw an arrow where the $^1/_2$ mark should be:

0 1 2

6. Put a circle on the number line where $^2/_3$ should be:

0 1 2 3 4

Diagnosing the Error: The first step is to consider Tawana's conceptual and skill strengths and error patterns, which are revealed in the kinds of answers she expressed. List your ideas in the following chart:

Tawana's Error Pattern(s):
Tawana's Strengths:

Tawana knows that she is working with fractions because she records the answers in fraction form. She is aware that, in some way, fractions represent parts of a whole and she can find a point along a line segment. However, she lacks fraction number sense because she does not represent quantity connected to models.

The first and second questions are related to the interpretation of a part of a whole unit. The set model is represented by the third and fourth items. The fifth and sixth questions assess Tawana's understanding and skill with the linear model. Her answers indicate that she does not understand the various rational number interpretations. She also does not connect the drawings to the correct fraction notation. Specifically, for questions 1, 2, 3, and 4, Tawana is counting the shaded part in relation to the unshaded rather than the whole unit. With reference to the linear model, Tawana mistakes the meaning of the unit for the entire length.

Prescription: With the strengths and error patterns in mind, the teacher completes a DAS for Tawana, shown in Table 7.1.

Using the diagnosis of Tawana's fundamental understanding of fractions and symbols, an MIP should be developed. It should include broad objectives for the rational number concepts and skills for connecting the symbols to those meanings. Tawana works best with real-world, narrative examples and stories. Therefore, she should begin with verbal situations that describe the meaning of fractions and connect them with hands-on activities at the concrete level to address her need for concept development.

Remediation: An MIP for Sample Error Pattern I is shown in Table 7.2. The objective of the first activity on the MIP is to assist Tawana in understanding the region and set models, as well as the related symbolic notation. Developmentally, it is critical that Tawana begin with regions and then move to sets because that interpretation is more challenging to understand. She should cut same-sized paper rectangles, about 5 cm by 20 cm in dimension. The first strip is folded in two sections, horizontally, and then shaded in one section, as follows:

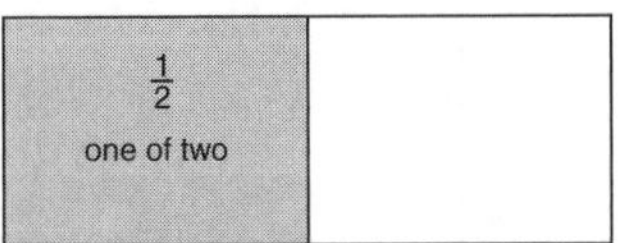

Ask Tawana about the sections to make sure she grasps the concept that they are not just pieces, but all the same size and shape—they are congruent. The words "one of two" are written in one of the sections. Above the phrase "one of two," the symbol "1/2" is written. In this way, Tawana connects the numeral representation to the meaning of the symbols. The 2 refers to the total number of sections in the region and the 1 represents the number of sections we are thinking about (the shaded section). On a separate piece of paper, or on the back of this strip of paper, Tawana should write "two of two" to represent the entire region, and "2/2" is written next to it to demonstrate that the denominator refers to the number of

TABLE 7.1 Data Analysis Sheet

Student: Tawana

Team Members:

Context	**Content Assessment**	**Process**		**Behavior**		**Reinforcement**
		Input	Output	Academic	Social	
+	+	+	+	+	+	+
• In her classroom • Close to her friends • By a peer of choice • Quiet area in the classroom • School in general • Front of room • Working alone	***Learned Concepts I*** • Numeration and notation • Understands fractions as "parts of whole" ***Learned Concepts II*** • Addition notation understood • Distinguishes numerator from denominator • Accurately computes addition facts ***Learned Concepts III*** • Subtraction facts • Whole number subtraction algorithm ***Learned Concepts IV*** • Multiplication facts for whole numbers • Meaning of multiplication sign ***Learned Concepts V*** • Multiplication facts • Fraction notation • Knows to invert and multiply to find quotient	• Good listener • Strong auditory skills • Easily talks with teacher • Written material with teacher supporting her	• Good word usage • Computer usage • Presenting in front of classmates • Good understanding of word meaning • Good pencil-and-paper skills	• Good verbal skills • Likes word activities and games • Redirects easily	• With a favorite peer • Strong sense of social justice • Working with girls • By teacher	• Verbal reinforcers, social praise • Opportunity to work with her female peers • Graciously accepts verbal praise
–	–	–	–	–	–	–
• Large-group setting • Seated in back of room or in far sides of class • Physical education class and lunchroom • Seated by a peer she doesn't like	***Error Pattern I*** • Does not understand parts of wholes embedded in a unit, parts of wholes in groups, or linear interpretations ***Error Pattern II*** • Unable to find common denominator when necessary for addition ***Error Pattern III*** • Mixed-number subtraction algorithm • Number sense ***Error Pattern IV*** • Procedures for multiplication of fractions • Does not know when to find common denominator ***Error Pattern V*** • Does not understand meaning of fraction division in "real-life problems" • Unable to apply rules correcly • Lacks fraction number sense	• Written projects • Large-group directed settings	• Presenting in front of peers who criticize • Large-group, high-activity areas	• Reads too fast or refuses to read • Doesn't like numerical games or activities	• Shy • Criticizes peers and teachers • Argues • Name-calling • Challenges teacher and peers • Boys agitate her, which causes her to be aggressive	• Smiley faces • Tokens • Atta-girl symbols • Any artificial tangible rewards

Note: The + symbols indicate strengths and the – symbols indicate areas of concern.

TABLE 7.2 Mathematics Improvement I Plan for Tawana: Developing Fraction Concepts

Time		About 30 minutes	About 20 minutes	About 20 minutes
Context		In classroom and close to friend (+)	Seated in learning group, most of whom are girls (+)	Working by herself in the classroom (+)
Content		Works in groups with fraction kit (+)	Records symbols connected to kit pieces (+)	Compares sizes of fractions with kits and records equality or inequality in math journal, makes flag in "Flag It" (+);
Process	Input	Uses fraction strips to fold (+)	Teacher verbally explains instructions to class (+)	Teacher is available to talk to her (+)
	Output	Writes answer on paper or in computer program (+)	Group has to present to class (–)	Must present her outcomes to the class with peer support (+)
Behavior	Academic	Shading and notating (+)	She likes to use words to explain herself (+)	Tawana is allowed to discuss the assignment and flag with the teacher (+)
	Social	With girlfriend who shares her social justice attitude (+)	Boys could agitate her (–) Encourage girls to respond (+)	Teacher stays in Tawana's area within the classroom (+)
Reinforcement		Teacher verbally reinforces with praise (+)	Teacher rewards the group with verbal praise (+)	Teacher gives Tawana social time with her girlfriends (+)

Note: The + symbols indicate strengths and the – symbols indicate areas of concern.

sections in the entire unit and the numerator refers to the number of sections we care about (in this case, all of them). The slip of paper would look like this:

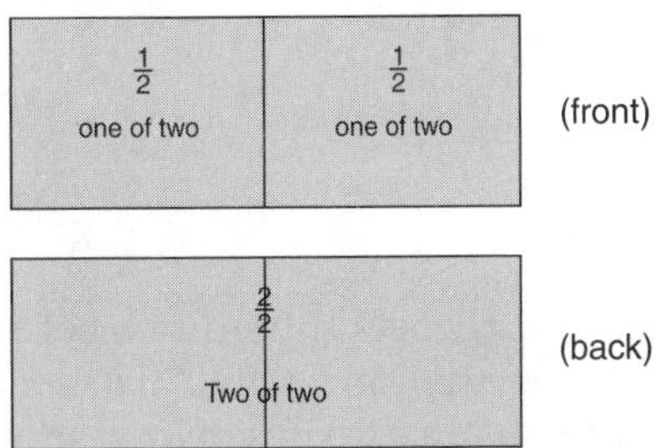

To further illustrate the concept, Tawana should fold another rectangle into four sections by folding the rectangle in half twice. She can think of sectioning off a rectangular cookie in four sections, in preparation for sharing it. She then should shade each section and name it "one of four." She no longer needs to write the words. Tawana likes to interact verbally and should explain to her teacher what the number 1 refers to (one section) and what the number 4 refers to (all the parts of the whole). She is now connecting the symbols to their meaning and can write "1/4" in each section. That paper and the first one should then be placed next to each other (as shown at top of next page).

Tawana is asked to determine the number of sections in the "four" paper that match one of the sections in the "two" paper. Because two sections in the

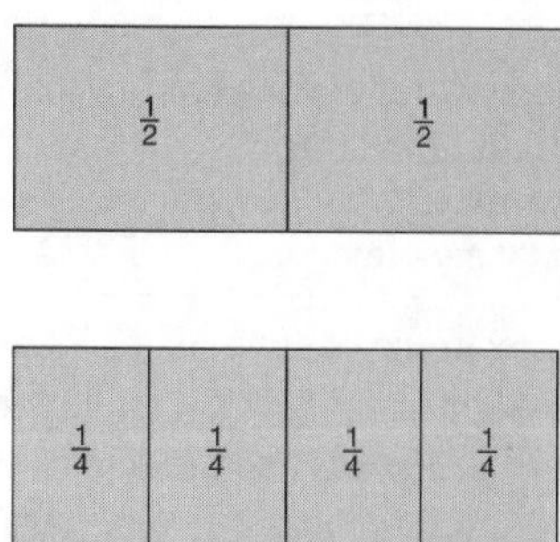

"four" paper occupy the same amount of space as one section in the "two" paper, Tawana can actually see and explain that two fourths and one half are equivalent because the regions cover an equal amount of space. These explanations should involve her in her work and reinforce her confidence through exchanges with her teacher, which Tawana enjoys. The activity continues as another strip is folded into thirds. A section of two thirds size equals the amount of space as four sixths on a strip marked off into sixths, as shown:

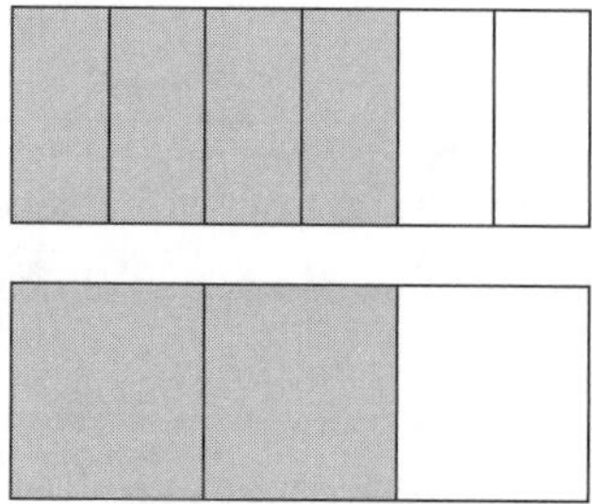

To interpret fractional parts within the same rectangle, as required in the first and second questions posed, Tawana folds a paper into two sections. She shades one half of it and folds the paper horizontally again so that four sections appear to be shaded:

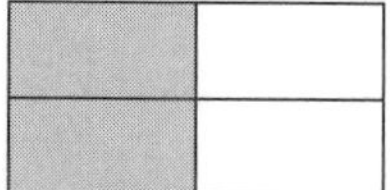

Tawana reports the number of sections that are shaded in the whole region. She can see that one out of two sections are marked off. Then, when the paper was folded again, two out of four sections are shaded. So, one half and two fourths cover the same space and are once again seen as equal in size and shape. She can continue with another example of folding a piece of paper into thirds, shading one third and then folding the paper again into fourths, horizontally. Again, it is seen that one third covers the same space and therefore is equivalent to 4 out of 12 (or 4/12). Also, 4/12 is seen as different from four eighths. Examples would look like the following:

$\frac{1}{3}$ $\frac{1}{3}$ $\frac{1}{3}$

$\frac{4}{12}$

Tawana writes the symbols, 2/4 = 1/2 and 1/3 = 4/12, as a representation of the drawings. The numerator is seen as the number that "counts" the shaded sections and the denominator is seen as the name for all the sections in the entire region—rather than as a separate quantity in relation to the numerator.

Another activity focuses on linear interpretation. The model is represented with a number line. Tawana cuts a strip of paper and marks a zero at the left edge and the numeral 1 about three inches away. She folds it into six equal-sized sections between the 0 and 1 as a number line, and labels the dividing lines with "1/6," "2/6", "3/6", "4/6", "5/6", and "6/6." The paper looks as follows:

0	$\frac{1}{6}$	$\frac{2}{6}$	$\frac{3}{6}$	$\frac{4}{6}$	$\frac{5}{6}$	$\frac{6}{6}$
0						1

It is important that Tawana marks a zero at the left edge of the number line so that she does not confuse the 0 and the 1. Students often begin counting with the number one, not realizing that a unit must first be measured to be counted. Tawana could pretend she is walking one block from her house with her friend. To find the point in the block where one half would be, Tawana should fold the strip of paper into two equal-sized sections. She finds that the one half fold lies at the three sixths mark, and can then tell you that one half is equal to three sixths in length and that they are equivalent. She can mark "1/2" on the strip of paper. The same technique can be used to find where two thirds would lie on a number line marked with sixths. In this way, Tawana learns to measure distance, not just to look at the numerals on a number line.

Each time Tawana moves within any interval, she marks the numeral "1/2" to represent that distance. From 1 to 2, one moves one half the distance and marks that amount. The same action is repeated between each consecutive whole number. Each interval is considered a whole unit:

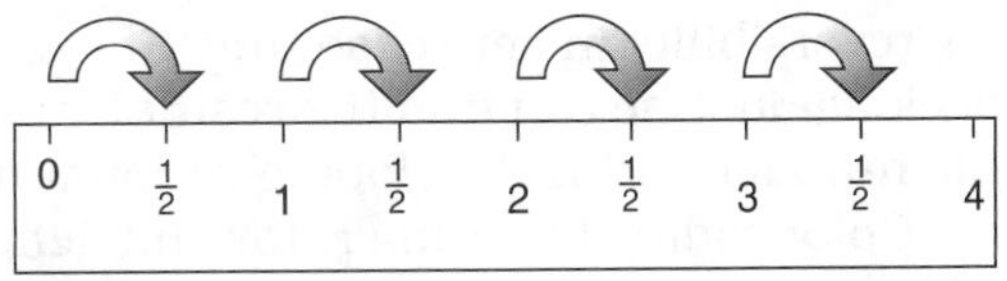

Discrete numbers, each representing separate items, can be understood by working with shapes of familiar items, such as cookies, cars, dogs, or toys. Tawana can form a set of counters to represent real-life items such as buttons.

She should write the numeral to once again represent all the members of the set, six, as the denominator. Then she should enclose any number of the circles, in this case, two, and write that numeral as the numerator. In this case she has circled two of six, or two sixths.

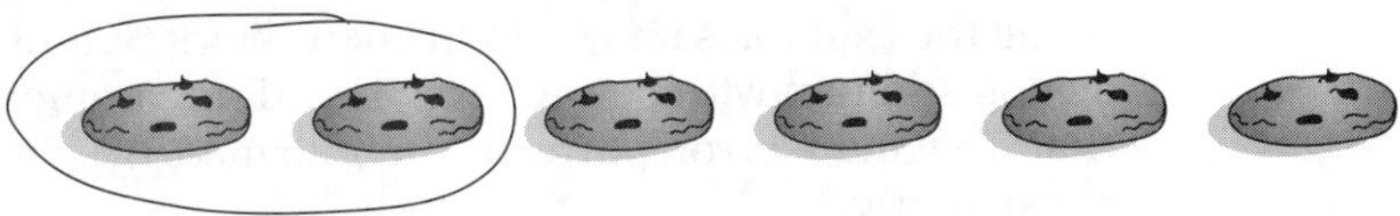

In this way, the numerator represents the number of items she is concerned about. Perhaps that amount names the number of cookies she'd like to eat, or number of pets she'd like to adopt, of the total number of cookies or pets.

Equivalence, as in 2/6 = 1/3, can be modeled when Tawana marks off the set in three equal groups:

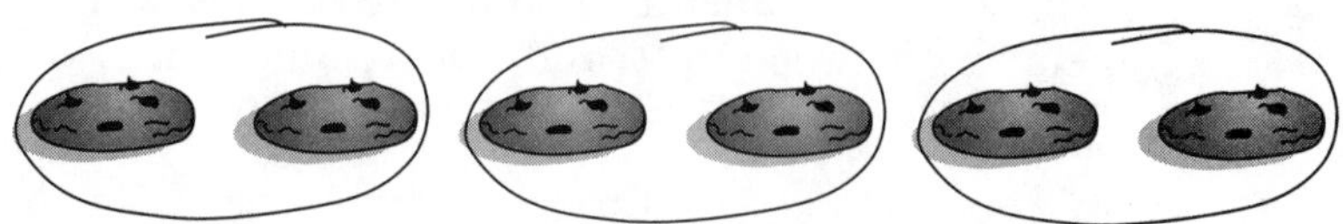

She sees that one of the three groups contains two of the six cookies. One third and two sixths name the same amount of quantity.

In another example, she can double the original group and extend the lines. For example:

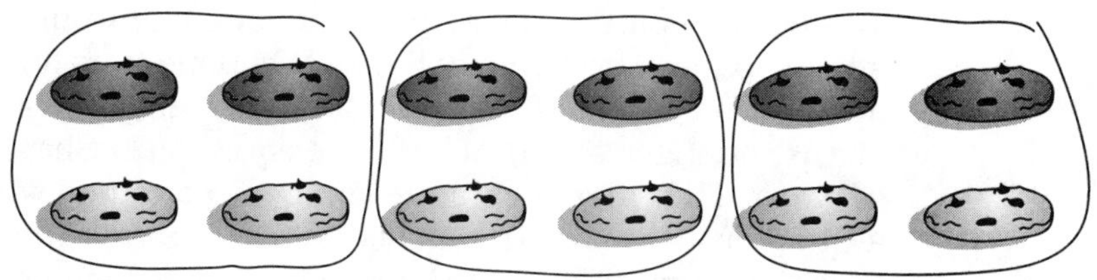

Here, 4 out of 12 is also seen as one third, and Tawana should continue to count the entire amount as the denominator and the amount marked as the numerator rather than mistakenly comparing the numerator to the denominator (as she does in the error pattern). By doing these activities, Tawana is developing reversibility in her reasoning. She can move from one half to two fourths and back again. She can find the result by understanding the relationships between the number and is developing rational number sense.

Color coding the numerator and denominator and using boxes to mark them off is another technique that can help Tawana because she also likes paper-and-pencil activities. She writes the numerator in one color and the denominator in another to separate their functions. She could also write them in a template such as:

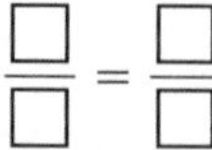

Rational Number Error Pattern II for Tawana

Diagnose the second type of error that Tawana is making with fractions by analyzing the examples shown in Student Work Sample II for Tawana. The questions assess addition with both common and uncommon denominators. Make certain that Tawana's error pattern is confirmed by checking to see that it is made consistently.

STUDENT WORK SAMPLE II FOR TAWANA

1. $\frac{2}{5} + \frac{1}{5} = \frac{3}{10}$

2. $\frac{3}{8} + \frac{1}{4} = \frac{4}{12}$

3. $4\frac{2}{4} + \frac{5}{1} = 4\frac{7}{5}$

4. $\frac{4}{9} + \frac{1}{3} = \frac{5}{12}$

5. $\frac{1}{2} + \frac{1}{3} = \frac{2}{5}$

6. $4\frac{3}{7} + 5\frac{2}{9} = 9\frac{5}{16}$

Diagnosing the Error: First, consider the type of knowledge and skill Tawana shows in the addition paper. Then, think of her addition knowledge that is faulty. Write your findings in the space provided.

Tawana's Error Pattern(s):
Tawana's Strengths:

Tawana knows that she should add numerators separately from adding denominators. She recorded the sum as a fraction. However, Tawana is adding the denominators together just as she did with numerators. There is no evidence of fractional number sense because the sums have no relationship to the addends; $2/5 + 1/5$ could not possibly add to $3/10$ (problem 1), because that sum is less than one of the addends. She is using addition procedures that do not lead to logical conclusions. Tawana needs to work with physical representations of these numbers to develop fraction number sense. A DAS can now be completed, and may look like that shown in Table 7.1.

Prescription: Tawana should begin with manipulatives such as Dr. Loyd's fraction kit, which contains plastic fraction pieces that fit within a unit-sized region. Shading graph paper will be effective for the drawing level of understanding. After representing her physical knowledge first with the materials, then with the drawings, she can move to using numerals. The progression from one level of understanding to another, along with explanations of her work, should help Tawana advance to a more complete conceptualization of addition with fractions, underpinning her algorithmic skill.

Remediation: The MIP should be written by indicating a plan of action for addition of fractions, keeping the diagnosis in mind as well as the fact that other, non-academic factors in Tawana's learning style remain unchanged (see Table 7.3). Dr. Loyd's fraction kit is a model of the unit or region interpretation of fractions. The kit contains one large plastic square that represents the unit "1." Additionally, there are squares cut into halves, thirds, fourths, fifths, sixths, eighths, tenths, twelfths, and fifteenths that fit on the unit square.

TABLE 7.3 Mathematics Improvement Plan II for Tawana: Adding Fractions

Time		25–30 minutes	30 minutes	20 minutes
Context		In classroom and close to friend (+)	Seated in learning group (+)	Working by herself in the classroom (+)
Content		Groups pieces from kit to work on concept for adding fractions with like denominators (+)	Works with group of students to create real-world problems to model and ask other students to solve (+)	Plays "Fraction Grab" and "Rolling Fractions" with other students in small group (+)
Process	Input	Oral problems posed (+)	Teachers and students suggest problems (+)	Teacher is available to talk to her (+)
	Output	Writes answer on paper or in computer program (+)	Kit is demonstrated (+)	Must present her outcomes to peer (+)
Behavior	Academic	Manipulates fraction kit (–)	Verbally explains addition for all cases (+)	Tawana is allowed to discuss the assignment with the teacher (+)
	Social	Works with peer (+)	Girls reinforce her (+)	Teacher stays in Tawana's area within the classroom (+)
Reinforcement		Teacher verbally reinforces with praise (+)	Teacher rewards the group with verbal praise (+)	Teacher gives Tawana social time with her girlfriends (+)

Note: The + symbols indicate strengths and the – symbols indicate areas of concern.

To begin, Tawana selects the unit piece of the fraction kit to place before her. All sections of the kit are seen in reference to the whole and are placed upon it to be identified. For example, Tawana covers the unit with all green strips to find that five cover the whole. Therefore, each green strip can be named "one of five," or "1/5," as established in the earlier lesson. When Tawana places a one fifth size piece on the unit to represent the size, for example, she can say she is eating one fifth of a piece of cake. When asked how much two fifths added to one fifth are together, she places another two fifths and finds that she has grouped three fifths together. To connect symbols to concepts, she writes 1/5 + 2/5 = 3/5, using a template—as she did before—for writing numerals. She concludes that adding the numerals in the numerator results in the correct sum, but would not if the denominators were added. Fifths and fifths, when combined, are still fifths—not tenths as she had marked on her paper. In this way, Tawana's own work serves to contradict her original answer. She can determine, for herself, the correct solution and explain the process.

Adding fractions with related denominators, such as halves and fourths, is the next type of algorithm with which to work. Tawana must trade one denominator for that of the other, which is its multiple (4 is a multiple of 2). Given a situation where she paints three eighths of a bedroom wall and her friend paints another one fourth of it, Tawana would want to know how much of her wall is painted (see problem 2). She begins to model the situation by covering the unit region with three of the eight sections:

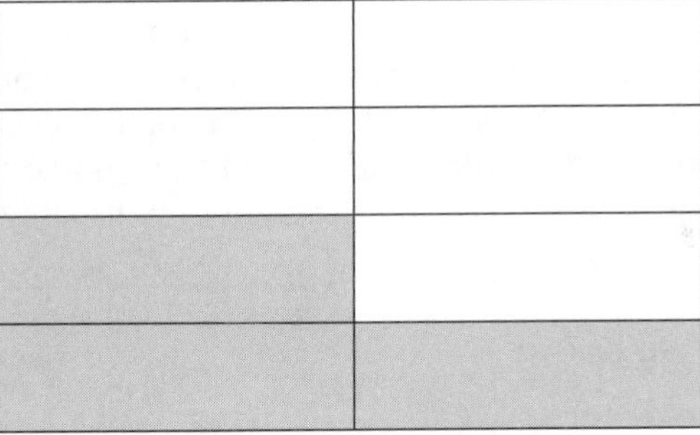

She finds that the one fourth size unit, when placed next to the three eighths, covers two of the eighths. Tawana now has placed 3/8 + 1/4 or 2/8 on the unit region. Five eighths of it is covered. Once again, she is expressing the denominator in the size of the units being joined and added. The shaded paper would look like the following:

$\frac{1}{4} = \frac{2}{8}$

$\frac{3}{8}$

When asked why she might think that four ninths and one third, the fourth question on her work paper, could or could not be five twelfths, Tawana could explain that result by demonstrating with the kit or shaded graph paper. She places ninths on the square and marks or counts off four of them. She places the one third size piece next to the four ninths so that she can find out how much of the cake she wants to eat. She then has seven ninths covered, and can compare that to the incorrect five twelfths answer. The example is illustrated below:

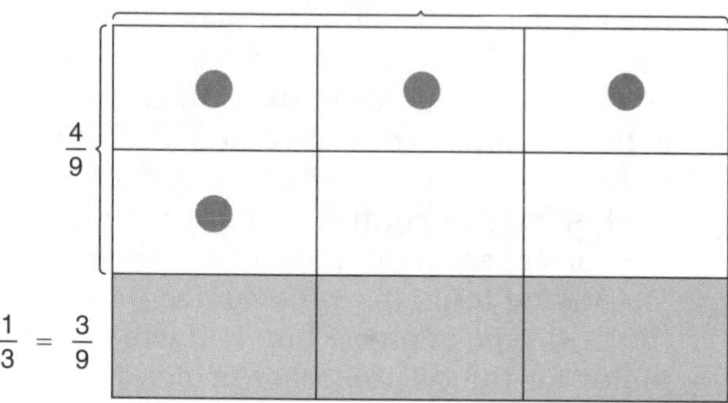

To generalize her understanding and skill, she continues with examples such as 1/3 + 1/12, in which Tawana trades enough one twelfth size pieces to match the one third piece. She will find that there are four, and then can name the amount of the unit covered, or the sum.

In some addition cases, one fraction is not a multiple of the other and so cannot be renamed by it. Examples of problems with uncommon denominators are 1/3 + 1/2 or 5/7 + 2/9. To solve a problem such as 1/3 + 1/2, pieces that represent the third and the half are placed on the unit. If they are placed vertically, next to each other, the sum is not easily seen nor understood, as in this drawing:

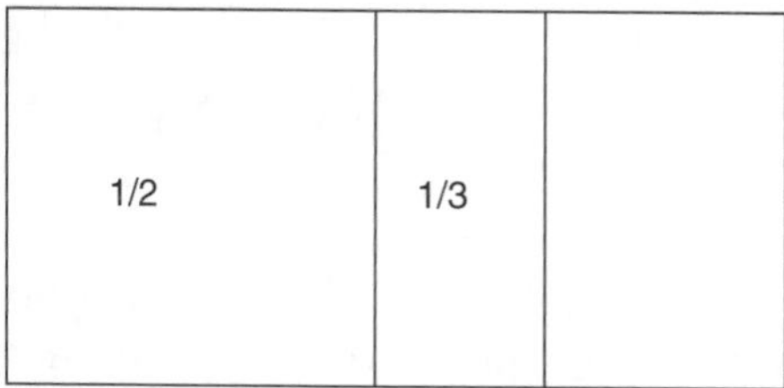

However, Tawana could place the third size piece and the half size piece at right angles to find a common area, which represents the common denominator. The pieces would be placed as follows:

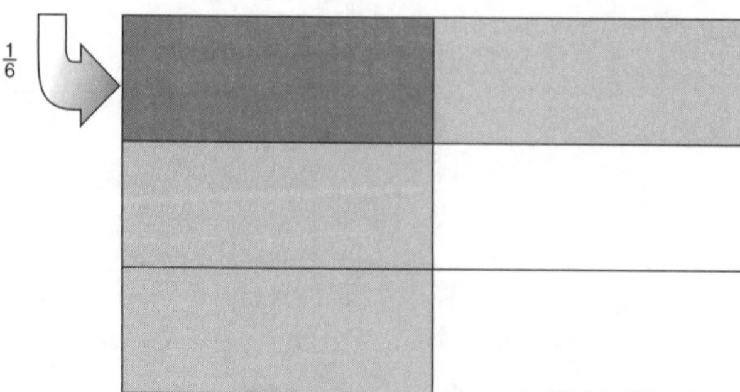

Tawana should then find the correct-sized piece that fits in the areas where the one half and one third overlap, which is the one sixth size piece. Have her replace the one third with the correct number of common-area pieces, two sixths. Then have her cover the one half with three sixths, so that both the half and the third are named by their common names. Then Tawana can see that one third and one half name the same amounts as two sixths and three sixths, for a sum of five sixths.

The algorithm can be connected to the physical representation. Have Tawana write 1/2 = 3/6 because she knows that is true. Working backward, she can write 1/2 = □/6 and fill in the missing square, which has to be 3. Helping her generalize, the teacher guides her to find equivalent fractions, by first finding the number to multiply the denominator in the original fraction by, to get the converted denominator. She would find that number, in this case, 3. She should then use that number to multiply the numerator. The "rule" to multiply both denominator and numerator by the same number can be generalized in the following example:

$$\frac{1}{2} \times \frac{\boxed{3}}{\boxed{3}} = \frac{1 \times 3}{2 \times 3} = \frac{3}{6}$$

$$\frac{1}{3} \times \frac{\boxed{2}}{\boxed{2}} = \frac{1 \times 2}{3 \times 2} = \frac{2}{6}$$

$$\frac{5}{6}$$

When Tawana has to rename both fractions to sixths, she is provided with further evidence that fractions must have the same denominator before addition takes place. Multiplying the denominators (2 × 3) will result in finding the common name (6). Tawana can use that "rule" for any addition problem. The rule can be reinforced with practice activities found at the end of this chapter. The games are especially effective with students, such as Tawana, who enjoy working with peers.

A learning activity for adding fractions could include the following steps:

1. Represent addends with appropriate sections placed on the unit region.
2. If all sections represent the same part of the whole (denominator), count the total number of sections and record the total.
3. If sections represent different parts of the whole (the denominators are related or are uncommon), exchange one or both sections so that all are the same part of the whole.
4. Count the sections and record the total.

Rational Number Error Pattern III for Tawana

The questions in Student Work Sample III for Tawana assess Tawana's ability to deal with mixed-number subtraction. She must subtract mixed numbers from whole numbers, mixed numbers from mixed numbers, and fractions from whole numbers. She was not asked to work with uncommon denominators, such as 4/5 − 2/3, so that the exercise could focus specifically on her understanding of mixed numbers and subtraction rather than renaming denominators.

STUDENT WORK SAMPLE III FOR TAWANA

1. $3 - 1\frac{1}{2} = 2\frac{1}{2}$

2. $6 - 3\frac{3}{5} = 3\frac{3}{5}$

3. $\overset{3\ 1}{\cancel{4}}\frac{1}{3} - 2\frac{2}{3} = 1\frac{9}{3}$

4. $\overset{5\ 1}{\cancel{6}}\frac{2}{9} - 3\frac{5}{9} = 2\frac{7}{9}$

5. $\overset{5\ 1}{\cancel{6}}\frac{1}{7} - 3\frac{2}{7} = 2\frac{9}{7}$

6. $7 = 6\frac{10}{6}$; $-\frac{4}{6}\quad\frac{4}{6}$; $6\frac{6}{6}$

Diagnosing the Error: First, list what you think Tawana has as strengths and error patterns by virtue of her responses. Consider how she is responding to the exercises, in terms of other operations and what she knows about whole number work. Write your response in the space below.

Tawana's Error Pattern(s):
Tawana's Strengths:

To her credit, Tawana can determine the correct answer to a subtraction problem. She knows she is working with fractions because she expresses the difference as a fraction. The difficulty is that Tawana does not rename the top number (minuend) from which to subtract the bottom number (subtrahend). In the first and second problem, she "brings down" the fraction as if it were being added for mixed-number addition. In the remaining examples, Tawana is borrowing a "10" as she would when doing whole number subtraction. The errors reveal difficulty with place value because she is following old "rules" of renaming in terms of tens. She does not connect the symbols to the process but only to remembered procedures that are not appropriate in these cases.

Prescription: Because Tawana has little concept of what rational number subtraction means, she needs to work with regions to shade or pieces of paper to cut for models of each subtraction situation involving mixed numbers. Tawana should work with manipulatives or drawings as a step before attaching the rules of the algorithm to each example. The steps she should follow are to:

1. Create models for the different fraction interpretations.
2. Record the models and results.
3. Attach symbols to the drawings.

Remediation: Considering Tawana's operational and conceptual strengths and error patterns, as well as her diagnosis, an MIP plan would be similar to that shown in Table 7.4. The first two examples in Tawana's paper involve a whole number and a mixed number. Tawana should be presented with a real-world

TABLE 7.4 Mathematics Improvement Plan III for Tawana: Subtracting Fractions

Time		**25–30 minutes**	**30 minutes**	**30 minutes**
Context		In classroom and close to friend (+)	Seated with a girl peer (+)	Working by herself in the classroom (+)
Content		Groups pieces from kit to work on concept for subtracting fractions with like and unlike denominators (+)	Works with group of students to create real-world problems to model and ask other students to solve (+)	Plays "Fraction Concentration," number line moves, and/or "More or Less" (+)
Process	Input	Class suggests real-world problems (+)	Teacher verbally explains instructions to class (+)	Teacher is available to talk to her (+)
	Output	Writes answer on paper or in computer program (+)	Group has to present to class (–)	Records winners and reports to teacher (+)
Behavior	Academic	Draws and/or uses manipulates to show answers (–)	Explains process of take away with kit and drawings (+)	Tawana is allowed to discuss the assignment with the teacher (+)
	Social	Works with girls (+)	Practices with peer (+)	Teacher stays in Tawana's area within the classroom (+)
Reinforcement		Teacher verbally reinforces with praise (+)	Teacher rewards pairs of students (+)	Teacher gives Tawana social time (+)

Note: The + symbols indicate strengths and the – symbols indicate areas of concern.

situation such as ordering three pizzas for a slumber party, serving one and one half of the pizzas, and then wanting to know how much pizza is left.

Tawana can draw three pizzas, round or rectangular, and then shade one and one half of the pizzas (amount eaten) to determine the amount remaining.

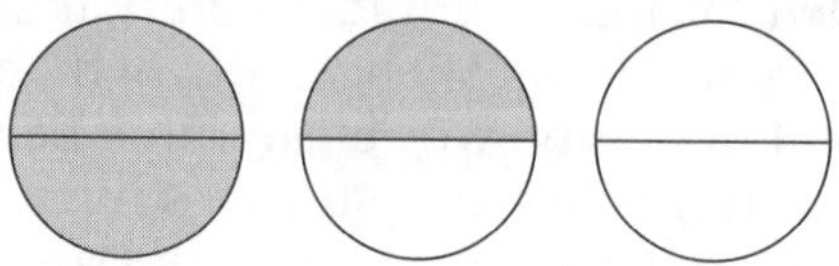

She could also use the following comparison method:

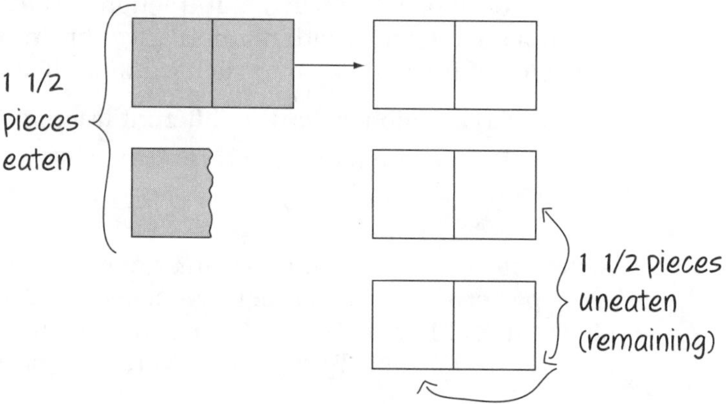

Tawana can see that there are one and one half pizzas left. She should then write "3 − 1 1/2 = 1 1/2" next to her drawings. Tawana can repeat the process for another example when she removes three and three fifths pieces from six pieces to find there are two and two fifths pieces left. Clearly, the answer is not three and three fifths, as Tawana might want to respond. Her error pattern revealed that she was subtracting the whole numbers and "brought down" the fraction. She should be asked what could be done with the numerals to be sure she could find the correct answers if she didn't have pizzas or graph paper with which to work. Tawana might respond, for 3 − 1 1/2, she could first take one from three to get two. She could then take one half more away to get one and one half remaining. That invented algorithm makes numerical sense and guided her thinking. She can then be encouraged to use a "shortcut" in which the "3" is renamed to "2 2/2" (because one half is in the subtrahend and halves must be removed from halves, as seen in the fraction kit work on addition):

Invented algorithm	*Shortcut*
3	3 = 2 2/2
− 1 1/2	− 1 1/2 = 1 1/2
2	1 1/2
− 1/2	
1 1/2	

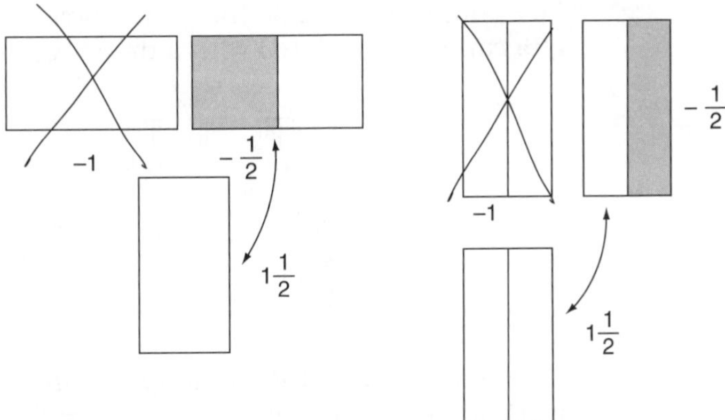

Questions 3, 4, and 5 each show a mixed number subtracted from a mixed number. Her work reveals what was done with whole numbers in that she is regrouping one group of ten from the whole number to the numerator. Many errors are meaningful as students try to follow rules they have already learned.

Tawana can find out whether her responses are correct by checking the differences with a drawing. Because she does not respond well to being corrected directly without a reason or context, she should not be told which answers are correct or not but should learn to check them herself. She can then adjust her algorithm by working backward from the iconic (illustration) result to the symbolic (numeric) stage. For 4 1/3 − 2 2/3 (problem 3), the drawing would look as follows:

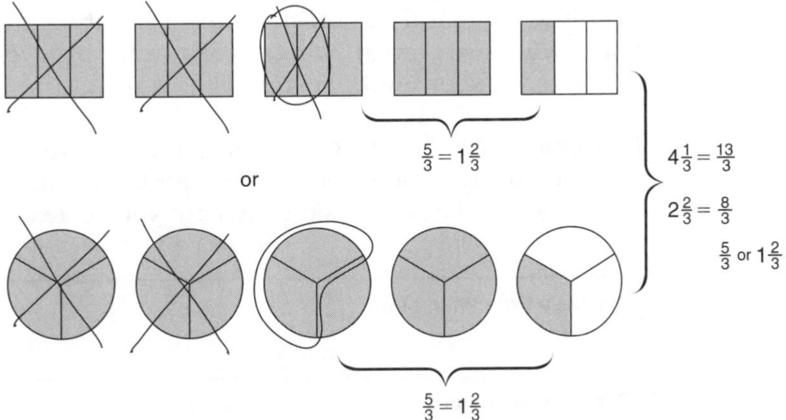

The correct answer, 1 2/3, is different from Tawana's first answer, 1 1/3. She should be asked to consider renaming both fractions to thirds. Again, the four is renamed to thirds with an improper fraction, 13/3, and 2 2/3 is renamed to 8/3. When they are subtracted, 5/3 is the difference, which can be simplified to a mixed number: 1 2/3. Tawana can conclude that changing mixed numbers to improper fractions efficiently yields a correct result, as seen in the picture she drew.

The example of a simple fraction subtracted from a whole number, such as 7 − 4/6, can be remediated with a drawing such as:

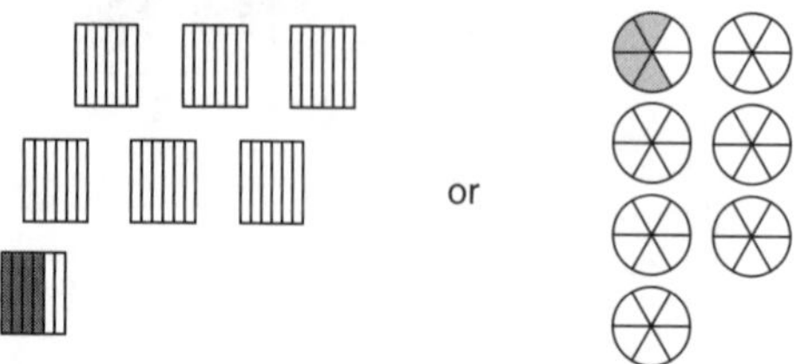

Tawana will find that the differences are 38/6, or 6 2/6. She can then use the algorithm to change the whole number to a mixed number and remove the subtrahend to find the difference. That fraction could be renamed to a mixed number to match the drawing result.

Asking Tawana to create her own problems, along with a story to explain why she chose those particular numbers, is an excellent way to check for understanding and skill. Because Tawana works best with verbal situations in a small group or one on one, she should be encouraged to choose a picture from a magazine, tell a story about it, and apply it to a fraction subtraction problem. The picture should show the answer or she could draw a picture to show the result. These are excellent ways to involve her on a personal level and continue the progress toward developing number sense about fractions in general and, specifically, work with subtracting mixed numbers.

Rational Number Error Pattern IV for Tawana

Student Work Sample IV for Tawana focuses on multiplication. Tawana must work with multiplying common fractions, multiplying mixed numbers by common fractions, and multiplying mixed numbers by mixed numbers. The questions will also reveal whether Tawana believes she must find common denominators for multiplication (which is not the case).

Diagnosing the Error: Tawana's strengths and error patterns should be considered in terms of her understanding of multiplication, multiplication of fractions, and basic fact skills. Record your observations in the following space.

Tawana's Error Pattern(s):
Tawana's Strengths:

From examining her work, we see that Tawana can find the correct product when multiplying and knows to write it as a fraction. She accurately obtains multiplication products. Tawana multiplies fractions as if they were being added, and so finds a common denominator. She is also multiplying whole numbers and fractions separately, with little idea that the mixed number represents one quantity. The DAS for multiplication would be similar to that shown in Table 7.1.

STUDENT WORK SAMPLE IV FOR TAWANA

1. $\frac{1}{2} \times \frac{3}{5} = \frac{5}{10} \times \frac{6}{10} = \frac{30}{10}$

2. $\frac{4}{5} \times \frac{2}{3} = \frac{12}{15} \times \frac{10}{15} = \frac{120}{15}$

3. $4\frac{2}{4} \times 5 = 4\frac{2}{4} \times \frac{20}{4} = 4\frac{40}{4}$

4. $6 \times \frac{2}{3} = \frac{18}{3} \times \frac{2}{3} = \frac{36}{3}$

5. $2\frac{2}{3} \times 3\frac{3}{4} = 2\frac{8}{12} \times 3\frac{9}{12} = 6\frac{72}{12}$

6. $4\frac{3}{7} \times 5\frac{2}{9} = 4\frac{27}{63} \times 5\frac{14}{63} = 20\frac{378}{63}$

Prescription: Tawana needs to work with the fraction kit and drawings to find the correct product. She enjoys working with real-life application questions, which can be incorporated into the questions she is asked about fraction multiplication. When she has solved these problems correctly, she should compare the results with those that she obtained when she found common denominators or treated mixed-number multiplication as if it were made up of four different numbers. As Tawana compares the correct product to the incorrect product, she can develop her own reasoning for finding correct and reasonable products.

TABLE 7.5 Mathematics Improvement Plan IV for Tawana: Multiplying Fractions

Time		20 minutes	25–30 minutes	30 minutes
Context		In classroom and close to friend (+)	Seated alone (+)	Playing games with classmates (+)
Content		Groups pieces from kit to work on concept for multiplying fractions (+)	Ask other students to solve problems of each type (+)	Plays "Shaping Computation" and "Bingo" to practice (+)
Process	Input	Uses own examples (+)	Teacher verbally explains instructions to class (+)	Teacher is available to talk to her (+)
	Output	Manipulates kit (+)	Presents to teacher (+)	Winners get prizes (+)
Behavior	Academic	Uses written problems from class (+)	She likes to use words to explain herself (+)	Tawana is allowed to discuss games with the teacher (+)
	Social	Works alone (+)	Keeps busy alone (+)	Teacher stays in Tawana's area within the classroom (+)
Reinforcement		Teacher verbally reinforces with praise (+)	Teacher rewards Tawana by letting her lead games next period (+)	Teacher gives Tawana time to play more games (+)

Note: The + symbols indicate strengths and the – symbols indicate areas of concern.

Question: What is the most common question students ask about fraction computation?
Answer: Do I need to find a common denominator?

Remediation: A sample MIP for multiplication of fractions can be seen in Table 7.5. Tawana should be given a real-world multiplication of a fractions situation, such as the following:

> My friends left 3/5 of a pizza after the party I gave. Later that evening I was still hungry. I decided to eat 1/2 of the leftover pizza. How much pizza will I eat?

Using the fraction kit for the first two problems, Tawana should place three of the fifths on the unit to model how much pizza was left after her party. On another unit piece, she should place halves to indicate she is thinking of eating a piece that size. The kit would look like this:

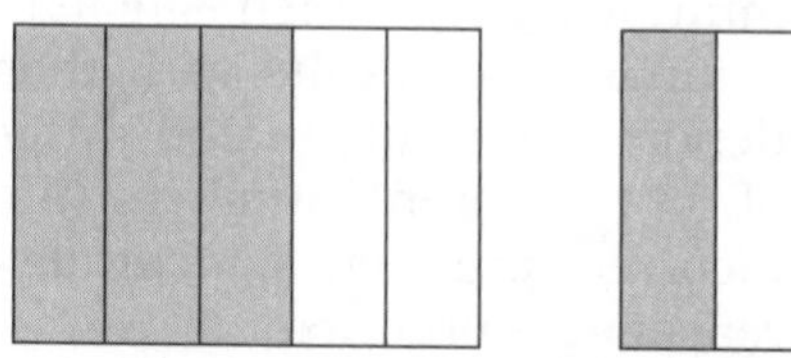

To find how much pizza she would eat if she takes one half of the three fifths of her pizza, she places the one half size unit over the three fifths as follows:

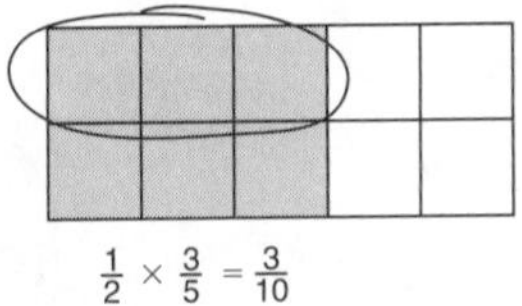

By counting the number of sections or fraction pieces in each of the groups (one half of the group of three fifths), she can find that one half of the three fifths is really the same as three tenths of the pizza. Three of the total number of sections (10) are double shaded. She should generalize the action to state that a group of a group or a piece of a piece is found by multiplying the numerators and then the denominators.

The second example is completed in a similar fashion. Tawana finds the amount represented by four fifths of a group of two thirds by covering two thirds of the square with four fifths of the pieces. The kit or a drawing would look as follows:

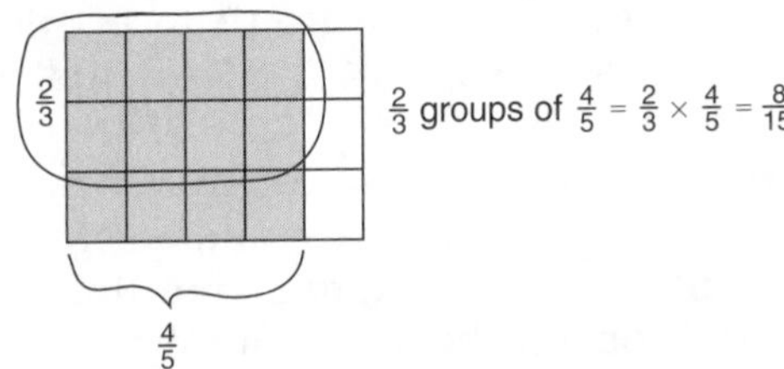

$\frac{2}{3}$
$\frac{2}{3}$ groups of $\frac{4}{5} = \frac{2}{3} \times \frac{4}{5} = \frac{8}{15}$
$\frac{4}{5}$

Tawana can then count and find that four fifths of two thirds represents 8 of the 15 sections in the square: 8/15.

If Tawana had renamed both fractions and multiplied, she would have gotten an incorrect product, as indicated in her kit work and with a drawing. Allowing her to multiply according to her error pattern and comparing it with the drawing is an effective conflict strategy. It allows her to reason that her algorithm, through which she found a common denominator for multiplication, is incorrect.

The third and fourth examples of multiplication error involve mixed numbers. It is common, as Tawana did, to multiply the whole numbers together and the fractions together, each as separate numbers. This is a similar error pattern to that of multiplying the digits of two-digit multiplication separately. Students see the tens and ones as unrelated and multiply each by only the factor in the same place. For example:

$$2\ 2/3 \times 3\ 3/4 = (2 \times 3) + (2/3 \times 3/4)$$

$$4\ 3/5 \times 6\ 1/2 = 4 \times 6 + (3/5 \times 1/2)$$

It is best if Tawana constructs her own meaning of multiplying all factors by each other. She can begin with whole numbers because she is familiar with them and connects to what is known. She shades an array for 12 × 14 and counts the total number of units marked. Comparing that product, 168, with what is found by multiplying digits in each place separately allows Tawana to recognize that she is multiplying two digits by two digits (10 × 2 and 10 × 4) and that the product is not the same as she would have gotten by multiplying only 10×10 and 2×4. The array would look like the following illustration:

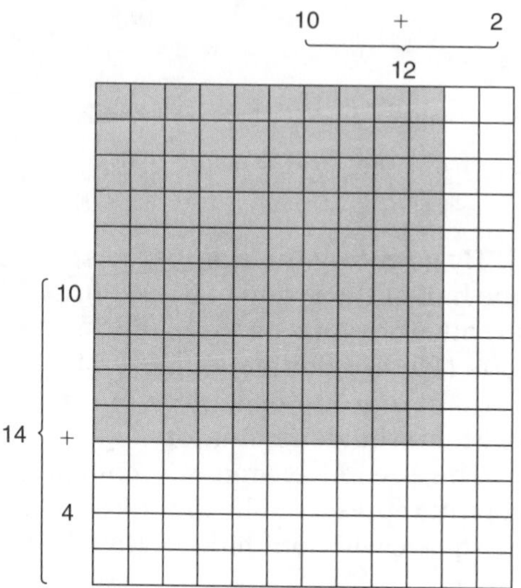

Connecting that concept to fractions, Tawana rewrites the multiplication problem as $(2 + 2/3) \times (3 + 3/4)$, just as 12×14 is $(10 + 2) \times (10 + 4)$. Tawana could multiply $(2 \times 3) + (2 \times 3/4) + (2/3 \times 3) + (2/3 \times 4)$ as multiplication is carried out in all its steps. However, that many partial products could lead to more computational error and recording difficulties. Once Tawana understands that all the factors must be multiplied by writing such examples as these, she should convert the mixed numbers to improper fractions. In that way, multiplication can be completed more efficiently and would be completed as follows:

$$2\ 2/3 = 8/3 \qquad \frac{8}{3} \times \frac{15}{4} = \frac{120}{12}$$
$$3\ 3/4 = 15/4$$

A learning activity for multiplying fractions would include:

1. Represent the second factor, the quantity being multiplied, on the unit region.
2. Represent the first factor, the amount that is a part of the second factor, on top of it.
3. Count the quantity that represents the overlapped section, which is the part of the part.

Rational Number Error Pattern V for Tawana

Tawana is being asked to divide common fractions by each other and by mixed numbers. Some examples require the division of a mixed number by a mixed number. It is important to check that the error made in one problem is consistent with the error in a similar problem so that the type of mistake is clearly identified.

Diagnosing the Error: What strengths and error patterns do you see in Tawana's work in terms of her understanding of division and division of fractions? Record your findings in the following space.

Tawana's Error Pattern(s):
Tawana's Strengths:

Tawana has learned the rule to "invert and multiply" for division of fractions but has no conceptual knowledge of why or how that works. She is following a procedure with little understanding, as evidenced by the fact that she either inverts the wrong fraction or both fractions. If she inverts the divisor, it may be only because she happened to invert both fractions. She has little understanding of what the rule means and therefore cannot proceed correctly with the algorithm because she cannot remember which fraction is which; she only knows the rule. However, Tawana does record the facts accurately and shows some knowledge of the rule. A DAS for this error would be similar to that shown in Table 7.1.

Prescription: Tawana should work again with the fraction kit to visualize the division situation and understand it. She can also work with drawings and templates to assist with connecting the symbols to the concrete and iconic representations. By doing this she can remember which fraction to invert because she has some underlying understanding of the division situation and how it operates.

Remediation: An MIP for Tawana, in terms of improving her understanding and skill with fraction division, is shown in Table 7.6. Tawana should begin with a division situation that can be modeled and has everyday application. She is told that she has one half of a birthday cake and friends who each want one quarter

TABLE 7.6 Mathematics Improvement Plan for Dividing Fractions: Student Work Sample V for Tawana

Time		**30–35 minutes**	**20–25 minutes**	**30 minutes**
Context		In classroom and close to friend (+)	Seated in learning group (+)	Play games with class and partner (+)
Content		Manipulates pieces from kit, graph paper to connect symbols (+)	Finds results to class problems and their own group's problems (+)	Plays "Equivalent Bingo" and "Shaping Fractions for Division" (+)
Process	Input	Solves class problems (+)	Teacher verbally explains instructions to class (+)	Teacher is available to talk to her (+)
	Output	Draws and records answers (+)	Explains to the teacher (+)	Records results (+)
Behavior	Academic	Uses student-created stories (+)	She likes to use words to explain herself (+)	Tawana is allowed to discuss the assignment with the teacher (+)
	Social	Works with girl partner (+)	Gets reinforcement from partner (+)	Teacher stays in Tawana's area within the classroom (+)
Reinforcement		Teacher verbally reinforces with praise (+)	Teacher rewards the group with grade (+)	Teacher gives Tawana more game time (+)

Note: The + symbols indicate strengths and the – symbols indicate areas of concern.

STUDENT WORK SAMPLE V FOR TAWANA

1. $\frac{1}{2} \div \frac{3}{5} = \frac{2}{1} \times \frac{3}{5} = \frac{6}{5}$

2. $\frac{4}{5} \div \frac{2}{3} = \frac{5}{4} \times \frac{2}{3} = \frac{10}{12}$

3. $4\frac{2}{4} \div 5 = 4\frac{4}{2} \times \frac{5}{1} = 4\frac{20}{2}$

4. $3 \div \frac{2}{6} = \frac{1}{3} \times \frac{2}{6} = \frac{2}{18}$

5. $2\frac{2}{3} \div 3\frac{3}{4} = 2\frac{3}{2} \times 3\frac{4}{3} = 6\frac{12}{6}$

6. $4\frac{3}{7} \div 5\frac{2}{9} = 4\frac{7}{3} \times 5\frac{9}{2} = 20\frac{63}{6}$

of the one half to eat. How many friends could each eat one quarter of the one half of a cake? Tawana should select the one half unit to place on the whole, to find the number of one quarter sized pieces that can be removed. She will find that there are two pieces. Then she can summarize that division of fractions can mean that she has to find out how many certain-size pieces can be removed. The following is an illustration:

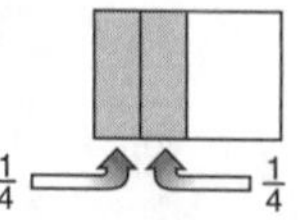

She can compare this result to that of $1/2 \times 1/4$, when the answer would be $1/8$ (not true for this situation). To connect this situation to the symbolic stage, Tawana is asked to find the result of one half divided by one fourth by writing the fractions as complex fractions or as division, which is one interpretation of fractions. The fraction would be written as follows:

$$\frac{\frac{1}{2}}{\frac{1}{4}}$$

Tawana is asked to multiply the denominator by its reciprocal in order to get 1 in the denominator:

$$\frac{\frac{1}{2} \times \frac{4}{1} = \frac{4}{2} = \frac{4}{2} = 2}{\frac{1}{4} \times \frac{4}{1} = \frac{4}{4} = 1 = 1}$$

The numerator, 1/2, is multiplied by 4/1. The product is 4/2, or 2, the quotient of 1/2 divided by 1/4.

Another example would include the following:

$$\frac{\frac{2}{3} \div \frac{3}{5} = \frac{2}{3}\cdot\frac{5}{3} = \frac{10}{9}}{\frac{3}{5}\cdot\frac{5}{3} = 1} = \frac{10}{9}$$

To assist Tawana with correcting errors that deal with whole numbers divided by fractions, she is asked to recall the example of one half divided by one fourth, in which she learned that one can multiply by the inverted divisor to find the correct quotient. She can draw the example in this way to illustrate three bags of candy. Tawana wants to determine how many little bags, each with two sixths of a bag of candy, can be given away for gifts:

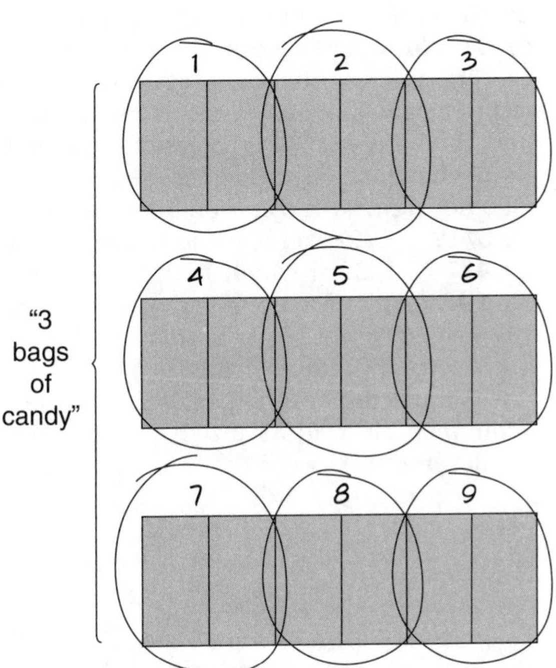

She finds that she can make two sixths sized portions nine times. Using the algorithm, she writes:

$$\frac{3}{1} \div \frac{2}{6} = \frac{\frac{3}{1}}{\frac{2}{6}} = \frac{\frac{3}{1} \cdot \frac{6}{2}}{\frac{2}{6} \cdot \frac{6}{2}} = \frac{18}{\frac{2}{1}} = \frac{9}{1}$$

When Tawana finds out that for another example of six divided by one half she can remove one half sized portions 12 times, the result reinforces the fact that inverting the denominator will result in the correct solution.

A more difficult situation occurs in the problem 2 2/3 ÷ 3 3/4 (example 6), because it is difficult to determine how to remove 3 3/4 pieces from 2 2/3. For mixed-number problems, it is more efficient for Tawana to change the fractions to improper fractions, as she did for multiplication, then follow the pattern for inverting and multiplying. This pattern has been seen to yield the correct solution in fraction pieces and in shaded boxes, so its credibility can be generalized to a more complicated fraction problem. Here, Tawana would rename 2 2/3 to 8/3 and 3 3/4 to 15/4 and proceed with the algorithm.

Conclusions: Instructional Strategies Summary

Throughout the rational number lessons and activities, it is essential that conceptual understanding be established as a foundation for mastering algorithms and procedures. Concrete, hands-on materials and drawings, to which symbols can be connected in the same lesson, are critical components for lessons in which students achieve both fractional number sense and then computational fluency. Direct connections between materials and numerals and between mathematical examples and real-life situations are keys to recognizing patterns and performing successful computations.

Fractions should be taught in a developmental, planned approach. The concept of part of a unit is more easily understood and should be introduced before the part/whole examples of sets and lines. As students understand fraction symbolism, the operations are reinforced. For addition and subtraction, students should begin with common denominator examples, move to related (1/2 + 1/4 or 5/12 − 1/2) exercises, and then to uncommon fractions such as 1/5 + 1/3 or 4/7 + 1/3, in which both denominators must be renamed. Multiplication and division of fractions is more easily understood first with common fractions (1/2 × 1/3 or 4/6 ÷ 1/3) than with mixed fractions.

As with building fraction numeration, the operations should be taught in conjunction with patterns of materials, illustrations, and authentic examples, as well as much student discussion, to establish reasoning and achievement.

Instructional Activities

ACTIVITY: Rolling Fractions

This activity is for groups of three or four students.

Objective: Order fractions from least to greatest

Materials:

Paper

Pencil

One set of dice in two different colors for each group

Directions:

1. Each group folds a piece of paper in half and then folds it in half again (this should make four columns).

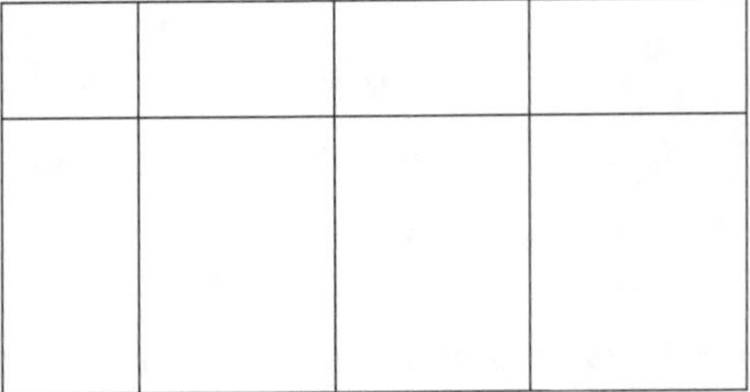

2. Players write their name at top of each column.
3. One color die is designated as numerator and the other as denominator for each group of players.
4. The first student in the group rolls a die and records the numeral seen as the numerator. The next die is thrown and the numeral seen is written as the denominator. For example, if a "3" is rolled and then a "4," the student records 3/4 under her name.
5. Play continues until all players have rolled the die 10 times and have recorded fractions.
6. Players then make a list of the fractions from greatest to least or least to greatest for their column.
7. The lists are compared and everyone who got the correct order gets one point.
8. Players with the most points at the end of the game win.

ACTIVITY: Fraction Grab

This activity is for groups of two students.

Objective: Reinforce understanding of part of a set and equivalent fractions

Materials:

A number cube with the sides labeled 1/2, 1/3, 2/3, 1/4, 3/4, and "remove 1"

24 small counters for each team of 2

Directions:

1. Players each put 24 counters on a piece of paper in front of them.
2. The first player rolls the number cube. The fraction that shows up determines the number of counters to be taken from another student's set on that turn. For example, if player A tosses 1/4, then player A takes 6 counters from B's set because 1/4 = 6/24. Player B then gets to play with a pile of 18 counters. If player B tosses "1/2", Player B can remove 12 counters from A's pile because 1/2 = 12/24. Note that any time "remove 1" is tossed, the player for that turn gets to remove one counter from the other player's pile.
3. Play continues until a player with a set of one loses.

Variations:

1. Change fractions that are written on the cubes.
2. Change the number of counters with which play is begun.
3. Players may use paper and pencil or a calculator to assist them in finding equivalent fractions.

ACTIVITY: Number Line Moves

This activity is suitable for a whole class of students.

Objective: Reinforce understanding of number line and linear interpretation of fractions

Materials: Register tape or unlined paper

Directions:

1. The number line should be divided into segments of 1/6 units (or whatever units are decided on).
2. Each student moves a marker along the line to find the missing value in each number line. For example, for number 1 below, the student follows a path starting at 1/6.
3. Students complete each number sentence, using the number line for direction, and submit the finished work to the teacher.

   1. 5/6 − 2/6 + 1/6 + 5/6 = _____.
   2. 3/6 + 5/6 − 2/6 + _____ = 8/6.
   3. _____ + 1/6 − 3/6 + 4/6 = 1 1/2.
   4. 1 5/6 − _____ + 4/6 − 1/6 = 1 5/6.

Illustration:

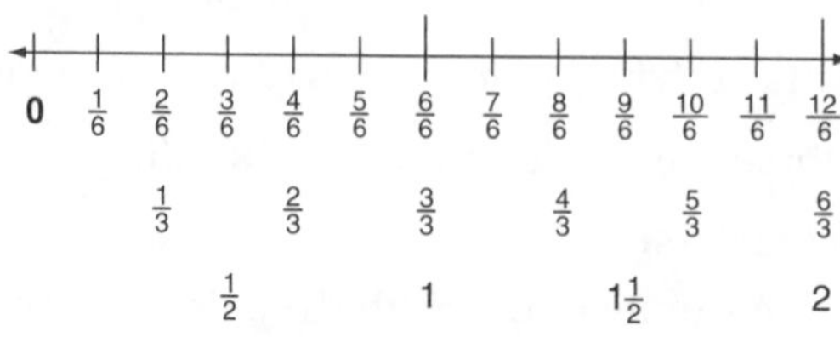

ACTIVITY: More or Less

This activity is suitable for large or small groups or pairs of students.

Objective: Reinforce understanding of rational numbers

Materials: Index cards, each marked with different fractions

Directions:

1. The class is divided into teams or pairs of two children.
2. Cards are shuffled and placed face down.
3. For round one, a card is drawn by each player on the team.
4. The student who draws the card with the greater fraction wins the other player's card.
5. The winners are the students/teams who end up with the most cards.

ACTIVITY: Making Fraction Wholes

This activity is designed for the whole class.

Objective: Identify and build units of one with equivalent fractions.

Materials:

Number cubes marked with 1/2, 1/4, 1/8, 1/16, 2/4, and 3/4

Dr. Loyd's fraction kits or two sets of cut-up strips of paper that are the size of halves, fourths, eighths, and sixteenths

Sheet of plain paper, same size as the unit square in the fraction kit

Directions: Place the fraction pieces in the center of the table. Each player needs a sheet of paper of the same size as those used to make the fractional parts for each player. Students should roll the number cube to determine the order of play; the player with the highest roll goes first. The number cube is rolled to determine the fractional part to take. The fractional part should be placed on the player's whole sheet of paper. The piece may only be placed if it will not overlap other parts and will fit on the paper. A part may not be moved once it is placed. *Note:* Before any turn, a player may return a part to the center of the table. The first player to cover the paper wins.

Example:

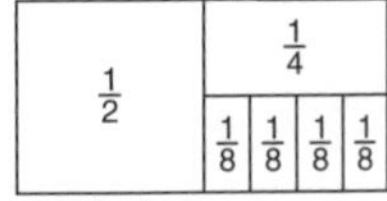

ACTIVITY: Equivalent Fractions Bingo

This activity is suitable for groups of four to five students.

Objective: Practice naming equivalent fractions and/or mixed numbers

Materials:

A 3 × 3 playing card with nine sections (sections contain fractions and/or mixed numbers)

Call cards contain different names (or notation) for the fractional numbers on the playing mat

Playing mats and the corresponding call cards may be made of posterboard

Call cards may contain a visual clue to the meaning of the fraction as a part of a whole, but that is not necessary

Directions:

1. The game is played like bingo. A caller is chosen and holds up a card from the pile.
2. Any player who has an equivalent fraction or mixed number, if that topic is being practiced, covers the corresponding call with a disc. The first player to obtain three discs in a row (vertically, horizontally, or diagonally) is the winner. Example:

Call Card

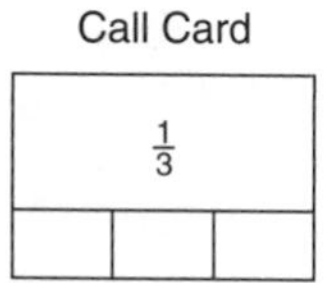

Playing Mat

$\frac{2}{3}$	$\frac{1}{2}$	$\frac{25}{100}$
$\frac{10}{12}$	FREE	$\frac{9}{15}$
$\frac{2}{10}$	$\frac{2}{6}$	$\frac{5}{10}$

Variation: Call cards can be marked with computation exercises that students solve and find on the playing mat.

ACTIVITY: Flag It

This activity is suitable for the entire class.

Objective: Reinforce understanding of concept of fractional parts of a unit

Materials:

Construction paper

Pencil

Ruler

Glue

Straws or dowel

Clay

Directions:

1. Using a pencil and a ruler, students choose a fraction for their flag. They divide each sheet of construction paper into fraction sections, according to that fraction. For example, this is the flag for "Half Land" because each section is divided in halves.

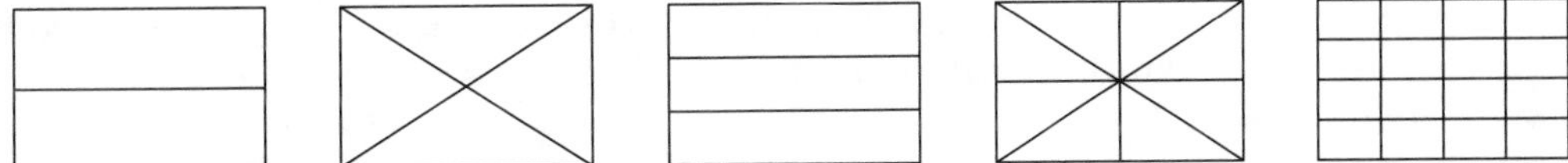

2. After the paper is divided, students should color each fraction section a different color.
3. On another sheet of paper, students should write their fraction name of the country and a story. For example, "I am writing about Fourth Land. People there live in houses that are one fourth of the size of other lands. . . . "
4. Students should then tape the flag to a straw or dowel and display it on a desk by sticking a flagpole into a small clump of clay.
5. Students can be challenged to try making a group of flags that show the same fraction in different ways.

ACTIVITY: Map Fractions

This activity can be used with the whole class, small groups, and pairs of students.

Objective: Integrate the subject of mathematics and geography

Materials:

Large United States map

Chart paper

Individual United States maps for students

Directions:

1. The teacher begins class discussion with questions such as: What fraction of the states in the U.S. are west of the Mississippi River? What fraction are islands? What fraction border Mexico? Record fractions on a chart next to the large map.
2. Students work in pairs and using a U.S. map, create additional fractions about the United States.
3. Students share results. Students identify which fraction is the largest, the fraction closest to half, and so on. Groups of students must explain their reasoning. Additional questions are written and presented.

Variations: Students take their maps home and find additional fractions from parents, siblings, and so on. Responses are share with class.

ACTIVITY: Fraction Concentration

This activity is suitable for groups of two students.

Objective: Practice finding fraction equivalences and writing notation

Materials: 30 Index cards, marked with 1/2, 1/3, 2/3, 1/4, 2/4, 3/4, 1/5, 2/5, 3/5, 4/5, 1/6, 2/6, 3/6, 4/6, 5/6 on 15 cards. The corresponding word names for the fractions are written on the other 15 cards.

Directions: Students play "concentration" using fractions and their correspond ing word names. All 30 cards are placed on the blank side on a table in rows. Students should take turns turning over two at a time. If they match, the student keeps them. If cards do not match, they are turned back over. Students continue taking turns until all cards are matched.

ACTIVITY: Shaping Computation

This activity is suitable for the whole class or small groups of students.

Objective: Reinforce fraction computation

Materials:

Game sheet of shapes for each operation or game sheet with one operation

Number cubes marked with the digits 1, 2, 3, 4, 5, 6, or 4, 5, 6, 7, 8, 9

Directions:

1. The group should decide or choose an operation and whether the "highest" or "lowest" answer will win the round. Players are told the numerals that are on the cube to be tossed.

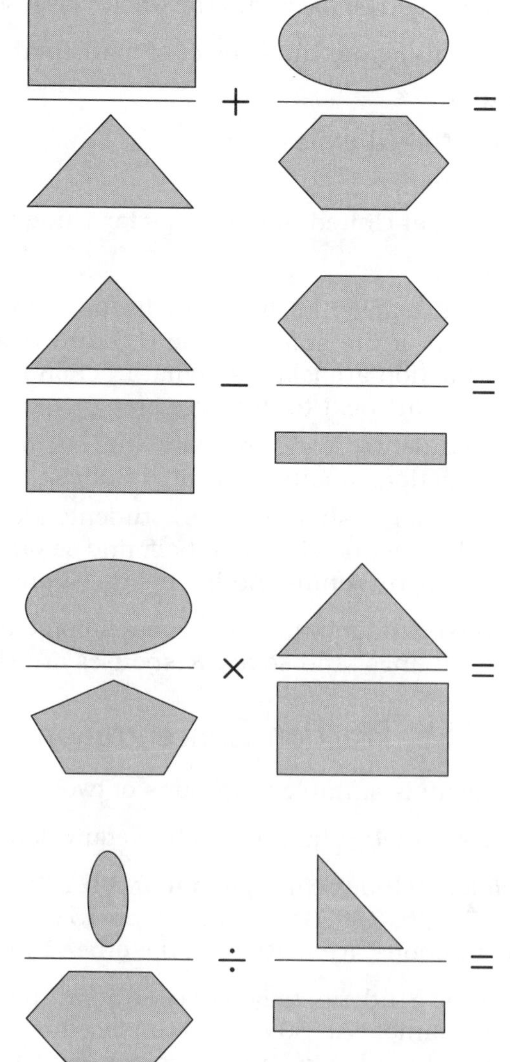

2. Leader tosses the cube.
3. Each player writes the called numeral in one shape of the problem and computes the operation.
4. Players win points by correctly computing highest or lowest answer in the class, depending on the agreed-upon goal for that round.

Discussion Questions

1. Identify the part–whole interpretation of the fractional situation for each of the following examples:
   a. pumpkins on a farm: ____________________
   b. amount of lawn to be mowed: ____________________
   c. number of crayons in a box: ____________________
   d. amount of pie eaten from one pie: ____________________
   e. amount of milk remaining in a glass: ____________________

   Explain your reasoning.
2. Provide a real-world example of a misconception students hold with regard to estimating the fractional size of something, such as food they have on a plate, homework completed, time watching television, or amount of candy eaten.
3. Describe a whole number algorithm that does not hold for rational numbers. Explain why the same procedures do not work for fraction as they do for whole numbers.
4. Was the study of fractions difficult for you? Why or why not?
5. What curricular or everyday materials, other than rectangles, are effective for teaching students concepts and operations for fractions?
6. What is an advantage of teaching related fractions (e.g., $1/2 + 1/4$) prior to teaching unrelated fractions (e.g., $1/3 + 1/2$.)? Explain your reasoning.
7. Explain why modeling related fractions ($1/2 + 1/4$) is presented prior to students' modeling ($1/3 + 1/2$).
8. Explain why modeling $3\ 1/4 = 12/4$ with drawing and materials is effective for learning about fractions. What is an example of materials students could use to derive meaning when renaming mixed numbers and improper fractions? List three questions would you ask of students.
9. Draw a diagram to represent the physical representation of $2/3 \times 5$ and $2/3 \div 5$. Describe a real-world example that would illustrate the need to find $2/3 \times 5$ and $2/3 \div 5$.

References

Alverado, A. E., & Herr, P. R. (2003). *Inquiry-based learning using everyday objects: Hands-on instructional strategies that promote active learning in grades 3–8.* California: Corwin Press.

Behr, M. J., Lesh, R., Post, T. R., & Silver, E. A. (1983). Rational number concepts. In R. Lesh & M. Landau (Eds.), *Acquisition of mathematics concepts and processes,* (pp. 91–126). New York: Academic Press.

Behr, M. J., Wachsmuth, I., Post, T. R., & Lesh, R. (1984). Order and equivalence of rational numbers: A clinical teaching experiment. *Journal for Research in Mathematics Education, 15,* 323–341.

Bezuk, N. D., & Bieck, M. (1993). Current research on rational numbers and common fractions: Summary and implications for teachers. In D. T. Owens (Ed.), *Research ideas for the classroom: Middle grades mathematics* (pp. 118–136). *New York: Macmillan.*

Crouch, R., & Baldwin, G. (1964). *Mathematics for elementary teachers.* New York: John Wiley and Sons, Inc.

Empson, S. B. (2003). Low performing students and teaching fractions for understanding: An interactive analysis. *Journal for Research in Mathematics Education,* 34(4), 305–343.

Flores, A., & Klein, E. (2005). From students' problem solving strategies to connections in fractions. *Teaching Children Mathematics, 11*(9), 452–457.

Huinker, D. (1998). Letting fractional algorithms emerge through problem solving. In L. J. Morrow & M. J. Kenney (Eds.), *The teaching and learning of algorithms in school mathematics* (1998 Yearbook of the National Council of Teachers of Mathematics, pp. 170–182). Reston, VA: NCTM.

Kieren, T. E. (1992). Rational and fractional numbers as mathematical and personal knowledge: Implications for curriculum and instruction. In G. Leinhardt & R. T. Putnam (Eds.), *Analysis of arithmetic for mathematics teaching* (pp. 323–371). Hillsdale, NJ: Erlbaum.

Kieren, T. E. (1995). Creating spaces for learning fractions. In J. T. Sowder & B. Schappelle (Eds.), *Providing a foundation for teaching mathematics in the middle grades* (pp. 31–65). Albany, NY: SUNY Press.

Kilpatrick, J., Swafford, J., & Findell, B. (Eds.). (2001). *Adding it up, helping children learn mathematics.* Washington, DC: National Academy Press.

Lappan, G., & Bouck, M. K. (1998). Developing alogorithms for adding and subtracting fractions. In L. J. Morrow & M. J. Kenney (Eds.), *The teaching and learning of algorithms in school mathematics* (1998 Yearbook for the *National Council of Teachers of Mathematics, pp. 183–197*). Reston, VA: NCTM.

Lesh, R., Post, T. R., & Behr, M. (1988). Proportional reasoning. In J. Hiebert & M. Behr (Eds.), *Number concepts and operations in the middle grades* (pp. 93–118). Reston, VA: National Council of Teachers of Mathematics.

Mack, N. K. (1995). Confounding whole number and fraction concepts when building on informal knowledge. *Journal for Research in Mathematics Education, 26,* 422–441.

Markovits, Z., & Sowder, J. T. (1991). *Students' understanding of the relationship between fractions and decimals.* Focus on Learning Problems in Mathematics, *13*(1), 3–11.

National Council of Teachers of Mathematics. (2000). *Principles and standards for school mathematics.* Reston, VA: Author.

Neumer, C. (2007). Mixed numbers made easy: Building and converting mixed numbers and improper fractions. *Teaching Children Mathematics, 14*(4), 488–492.

Ortiz, E. (2002). A game involving fraction squares. *Teaching Children Mathematics, 7*(4), 218–222.

Ploger, D., & Rooney, M. (2005). Teaching fractions: Rules and reason. *Teaching Children Mathematics, 12*(1), 12.

Post, T. R., Cramer, K. A., Behr, M., Lesh, R., & Harel, G. (1993). Curriculum implications of research on learning, teaching, and assessing rational number concepts. In T. P. Carpenter, E. Fennema, & T. A. Romberg (Eds.), *Rational numbers: An integration of research* (pp. 327–362). Hillsdale, NJ: Lawrence Erlbaum Associates.

Post, T. P., Wachsmuth, I., Lesh, R., & Behr, M. J. (1985). Order and equivalence of rational numbers: A cognitive analysis. *Journal for Research in Mathematics Education, 16*, 18–36.

Richardson, L. I. (1996). *Dr. Loyd's fraction kit.* St. Louis, MO: Pegasus Publishing.

Saxe, G. B., Tayler, E., McIntosh, C., & Gearhart, M. (2005). Representing fractions with standard notation: A developmental analysis. *Journal for Research in Mathematics Education, 36*(2), 135–157.

Sowder, J. T. (1995). Instructing for rational number sense. In J. T. Sowder & B. P. Schappelle (Eds.), *Providing a foundation for teaching mathematics in the middle grades* (pp. 15–30). Albany: State University of New York Press.

Streefland, L. (1993). Fractions: A realistic approach. In T. P. Carpenter, E. Fenneman, & T. A. Romberg (Eds.), *Rational numbers: An integration of research* (pp. 289–325). Hillsdale, NJ: Erlbaum.

Chapter 8

Decimal Fractions

Decimals are easy . . . you just stick a dot into a regular number and you're done.

You can tell which is the biggest decimal by picking the number with the highest number at the end.

We had to learn about decimals because we have to learn money . . . that's all they're used for.

Decimals are the numbers with the "th" in them.

Decimals hurt my head.

What Are Decimals?

Students often think decimal fractions are whole numbers with arbitrarily placed decimal points. That misconception can lead to difficulties in both understanding and computational skill. Clearly, the concepts and procedures associated with decimal fractions require careful study and frequent reinforcement.

There are two essential aspects of the decimal system: "a) the quantities that are being represented and b) the written symbols of the rational number system that represent the quantities" (Leinhardt, Putnam, & Hattrup, 1992, p. 285). The terms *decimal fraction* and *decimal* refer to notation that represents fractions with denominators written as powers of 10, as in .1, .01, .001, and so on. Decimal fractions serve to extend the whole number place value system to the right of the ones place.

The following diagram illustrates the number line that is extended to the right of the ones place to indicate the value of decimal fractions.

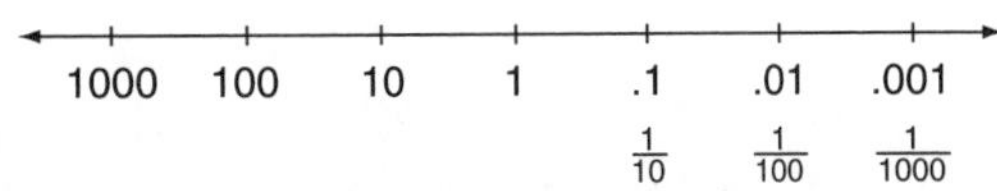

Not all fractions have denominators that are powers of 10. To find the decimal representation for a fraction such as 1/4, the interval between 0 and 1 can be divided first into tenths and then into fourths. One fourth is located between the two tenths and three tenths points, as in the illustration:

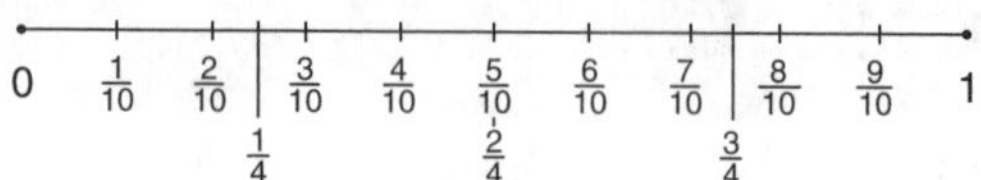

The number line can be further divided to find the exact representation of 1/4. When the interval between 2/10 and 3/10 is divided into 10 sections, the location of 1/4 corresponds to 25/100. The following number line illustrates the location of the rational numbers.

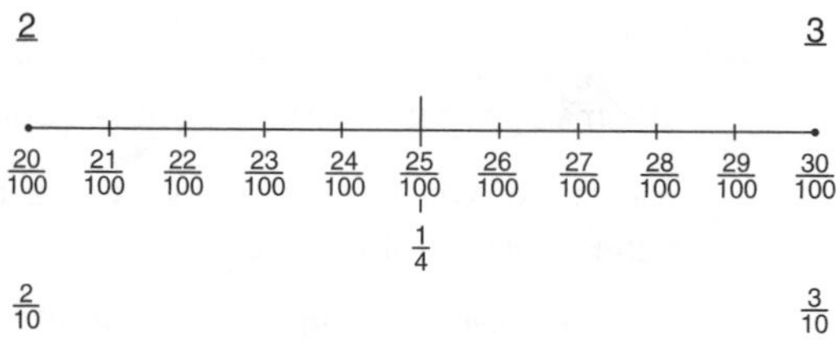

Another representation of 25/100 is the decimal fraction 0.25. The purpose of the decimal point is to designate the unit's position by being placed to its right. In the case of 0.25, the unit number is "0" and the decimal point is placed to its right.

To summarize, decimal fractions with one place to the right of the decimal point represent tenths, two places to the right represent hundredths, three places to the right notate thousandths, and so on. Examples are:

$$2/10 = 0.2$$

$$25/100 = 0.25$$

$$125/1000 = 0.125$$

Using money notation as an example, $27.59 would equal 2(10) [20 dollars] + 7(1) [7 dollars] + 5(.1) [50 cents] + 9(.01) [9 cents]. Seven is in the units place, and the decimal point is written to its right. The metric system is another expression of decimal numbers. The distance 43.85 meters can be expressed as:

4(10) + 3(1) + 8(.1) + 5(.01).

[40 meters] + [3 meters] + [.8 meters] + [.05 meters]

Decimals are read as mixed fractions. That is, 43.85 would be read as 43 "and" 85 hundredths. The word "and" is spoken only in reference to the decimal point. It is incorrect to say "two hundred and fifty nine" for the numeral 259.

Why Do Students Struggle with Decimals?

Evidence from mathematics education studies (Heibert, 1992; Heibert & Wearne, 1986; Heibert, Wearne, & Taber, 1991; Kieren, 1992, 1995; Markovits & Sowder,

1991; Sowder, 1997) indicates that both children and adults experience difficulties with understanding and computing decimals in terms of:

1. fully understanding the meaning of decimal number size and/or symbols
2. correctly ordering decimals with reference to size
3. being able to choose the correct operation to apply in a given situation
4. making sense of answers
5. rounding numbers

The instructional priority should be to help students create meaning for written symbols. Teachers must design instruction to promote meaningful experience with quantity to hook with symbols and actions as a referent to operation symbols. (Leinhardt et al. 1992, p. 317)

Connecting the symbols and procedures with actions on quantities and helping students judge the reasonableness of answers are of paramount teaching and learning importance.

About the Student: José

José is a 12-year-old middle school student. He is liked by his peers and enjoys sports. José has experienced difficulty with school for several years and socially presents challenges to his teachers. He is shy, he talks quietly, and he does not like to be the center of attention in the classroom. He has friends and does try to be close to them whenever possible.

José's oral expression is poor; he prefers to write rather than talk. His written work is usually acceptable when he understands the work at hand and has ample time to complete his task. His "attention to task" is about 10 minutes and he prefers to be busy. José is very successful if tasks are presented in small blocks of work.

José shows difficulty with directions and often misunderstands oral directions the teacher gives. He is a visual learner and will ask to have the task explained by an example on the board. He does become angry when his peers try to coach him too much and feels they are babying him. José does not mind the teacher staying close to him as long as attention is not brought to him.

José will ask the teacher for directions. He likes tangible rewards and will accept them for his good work. However, he becomes upset when the teacher praises him publicly and will misbehave soon after such rewards are given to him.

José will work in small cooperative groups but is also comfortable working independently. He particularly likes the computer and is becoming quite good at using it in the classroom. He will ask for computer-assisted learning exercises.

Error Patterns: Diagnosis, Prescription, Remediation

Decimal Error Pattern I for José

The first Student Work Sample for José deals with decimal numeration. That is, José is dealing with ordering decimal fractions in terms of size. He must also write the symbol that correctly represents the illustrations. Examine his responses to determine what pattern you see for his understanding of these concepts.

STUDENT WORK SAMPLE I FOR JOSÉ

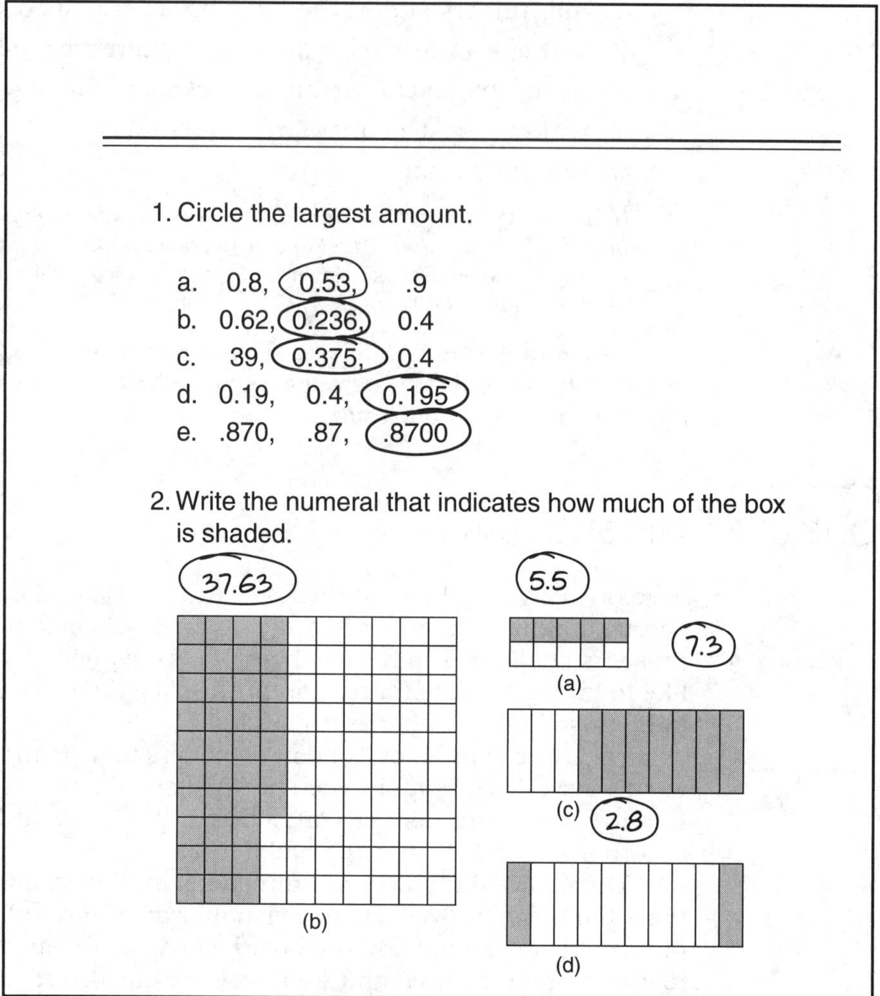

1. Circle the largest amount.

   a. 0.8, (0.53,) .9
   b. 0.62, (0.236,) 0.4
   c. 39, (0.375,) 0.4
   d. 0.19, 0.4, (0.195)
   e. .870, .87, (.8700)

2. Write the numeral that indicates how much of the box is shaded.

Diagnosing the Error: Classify José's strengths and error patterns in terms of his understanding of decimal numeration and sequence in the variety of expressions. Use the space provided.

José's Error Pattern(s):
José's Strengths:

José can write numerals with decimal notation. However, he is confused about the order and size represented by the numerals. He compares the decimals as if they were whole numbers. For question 1, his answers indicate that he believes that the largest amount is always that which is expressed with more digits. The answers marked in question 2 would support the assumption that José cannot relate the meaning of the decimal fraction symbol to its physical representation; he writes the places as if they were a combination of a whole number and a decimal fraction. He does not understand the base-10 place value system as applied to decimal fractions. Because José has difficulty understanding fundamental numeration ideas, he is experiencing conceptual difficulties.

Prescription: Suggestions related to this error pattern for José's DAS are found in Table 8.1.

José should begin working with learning aids such as graph paper, divided in tenths and hundredths, and coins. Though coins do not represent a value one can actually observe from their appearance, their practical connection to the drawings and notations will help José make sense of decimal fractions. He should not use base-10 blocks if they were used in whole number computation lessons. It can be confusing for students to grasp that the flat that represented 100 ones for whole numbers now represents the quantity of "one" in decimal notation. That connection can be made at a later time when José is more advanced in his understanding and procedures.

Remediation: An MIP for Error Pattern I can be found in Table 8.2. José should begin by comparing tenths and hundredths with real-world application problems. Because José enjoys sports, he should consider the following:

> José and his friend are each running in a 3.5-kilometer race in a school track meet. José ran 2.6 km in 10 minutes and his friend, Roy, ran 2.45 km in the same amount of time. José said that 2.45 km, which has three digits, should be longer than 2.6, which has two digits. But, he ran further than Roy! Help José find out why 2.6 km represents a longer distance than 2.45 km.

Comparing Tenths: José is a visual learner and would benefit by illustrating the problem. He should draw a line segment(s) for each of the kilometers the boys ran. The following illustrates:

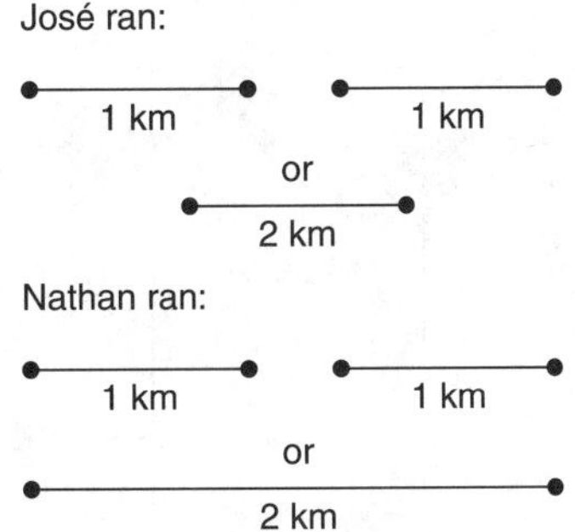

José now needs to know how much .6 and .45 represent so he can compare the entire quantities to solve his problem. To connect what he already knows about fractions to these new lessons on decimals, he should:

1. draw a box to represent 0.6 and one to represent 0.45
2. divide each box vertically, in red, into tenths and shade the appropriate amount; he writes the fractions 6/10 and 4/10 to represent those shaded quantities

TABLE 8.1 Data Analysis Sheet

Student: José

Team Members:

Context	**Content Assessment**	**Process**		**Behavior**		**Reinforcement**
		Input	Output	Academic	Social	
+	+	+	+	+	+	+
• Works well in small groups or near his teacher	***Learned Concepts I*** • Sequencing • Reads whole numbers • Writes whole numbers ***Learned Concepts II*** • Addition • Basic fact skill proficiency • Whole number regrouping • Algorithm proficiency ***Learned Concepts III*** • Subtraction • Basic fact skill proficiency • Whole number regrouping • Algorithm proficiency ***Learned Concepts IV*** • Multiplication • Basic fact skill proficiency • Algorithm proficiency ***Learned Concepts V*** • Division • Proficiency with whole number algorithm • Division facts and estimation	• Visual directions • Small task activities • Demonstrations	• Writing his answers out on paper and on a computer	• Responds well to demonstrated task with examples on board • Likes to be busy • Short time activities	• Small groups • Close to teacher • With boys and girls alike • Strong sense of right and wrong	• Tangible rewards such as "atta-boys" and smiley faces • Telephone call to his mother • Working with a peer of his choice
–	–	–	–	–	–	–
• Does not work well in large-group setting	***Error Pattern I*** • Sequencing • Lacks concept of place value of decimal fractions • Determines size by length of numerals: the more the numerals, the larger the decimal • Compares decimals as if they are whole numbers ***Error Pattern II*** • Addition • Lacks place value concept for decimal fractions • Does not line up decimals in like places to add ***Error Pattern III*** • Subtraction • Procedural error of not regrouping "over" the decimal point from ones place to tenths ***Error Pattern IV*** • Procedural error of incorrect placement of decimal point in product, counts the number of places from opposite direction ***Error Pattern V*** • Concept of dividing by decimal divisor and renaming it to whole number to divide • Division • Concept error of place value • Incorrect placement of decimal point in product • Does not rename divisor and dividend correctly from incorrect place	• Written directions • Large task activities	• Called upon to talk in front of his peers • Expected to grade his peers' work	• Activities during transition times	• Talking to the class • Will tear up his work when he is frustrated	• Notes home to his mother • Public praise from the teacher

Note: The + symbols indicate strengths and the – symbols indicate areas of concern.

TABLE 8.2 Mathematics Improvement Plan I for José: Understanding Decimal Numeration and Sequencing

Time:		35 minutes	25–30 minutes	20–25 minutes
Context		He is with a small group of his peers (+)	Assignment given to entire class by the teacher with a director on board (+)	He plays a game with a partner (+)
Content		Solve real-world problems on decimal order with diagrams and symbols; play "Mix and Match Decimals" (+)	Shade rectangles and place value charts to identify and compare decimals (+)	Solve word problems, play "Build Decimals," "Reasoning About Decimals," or "Fill 'er Up" (+)
Process	Input	Directions from teacher are given in oral form (+)	Directions demonstrated to the class by use of the chalkboard (+)	Directions are given by students for the game (+)
	Output	Students write their answers on their study sheets (+)	He recites his answer to the teacher (+)	He can put his answers on the classroom computer (+)
Behavior	Academic	Completes diagrams and game (+)	Produces drawings, symbols, and game answers (+)	He can complete small blocks of his assignment and present that work to his teacher for correction (+)
	Social	With peer group of his choice (+)	He talks to the teacher about the assignment (+)	Begins to talk to a peer who is seated next to him about the assignment (+)
Reinforcement		Teacher praises with verbal comments (+)	Teacher tells José she will call his mother in the evening and tell her how hard José has worked (+)	The teacher awards him a smiley face for his hard work (+)

Note: The + symbols indicate strengths and the – symbols indicate areas of concern.

3. record the decimals—it may be necessary to tell José that the first numeral to the right of the decimal point indicates the number of tenths so that he can write the decimal correctly if that lesson has not already been taught
4. divide each box horizontally in tenths, in blue, and shade the number of hundredths (5)
5. mark the rectangle with the appropriate decimal notation

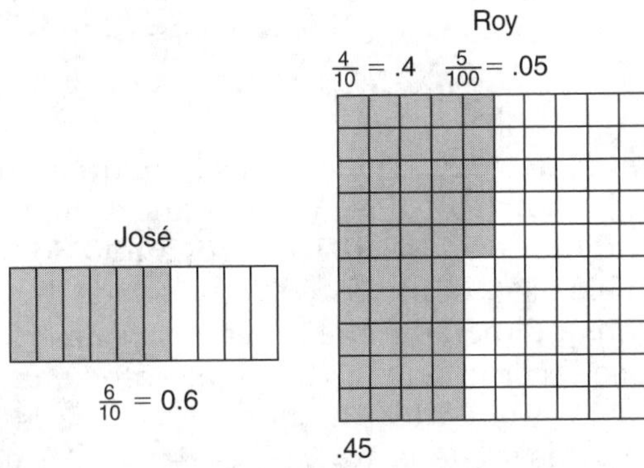

José compares the two diagrams to find which quantity covers more space.

José should also mark the decimal notation in a place value chart, as seen below:

	0.1	0.01
Roy	XXXX	XXXXX
José	XXXXXX	

José can generalize that to compare decimals, he should consider first the largest decimal place value position, which is closest to the unit number. If the same number is in both those places (two decimals with the numeral 5 in the tenths column, for example), he checks the next largest place to the right. When he compared 0.60 to 0.45, José found that 6/10 and 4/10 are each located next to the unit "1." Tenths represents a larger quantity than all the other decimal places. Even though there are 2 digits in .45 and only one in .6, the extra digit cannot compensate to make 0.45 larger than 0.6. Six tenths is larger than four tenths. Also, he sees that zeros to the right of any decimal do not change the value, because no more boxes have been shaded.

José should continue comparing decimal fractions such as 0.25 to 0.3 or 0.6 to 0.57. This activity provides a foundation for an understanding that one has to consider each decimal fraction by beginning with the tenths place. The number of digits in the numeral does not determine decimal fraction size, as José had erroneously believed.

Money is a useful tool for teaching tenths and hundredths places in decimal fractions with applications. José could also find out which is more, $0.25 or $0.20, by marking the number line and a place value chart. He could create his own real-world problems, finding the cost of items in newspaper advertisements and then drawing the products to determine which items cost more, less, or the same, as in:

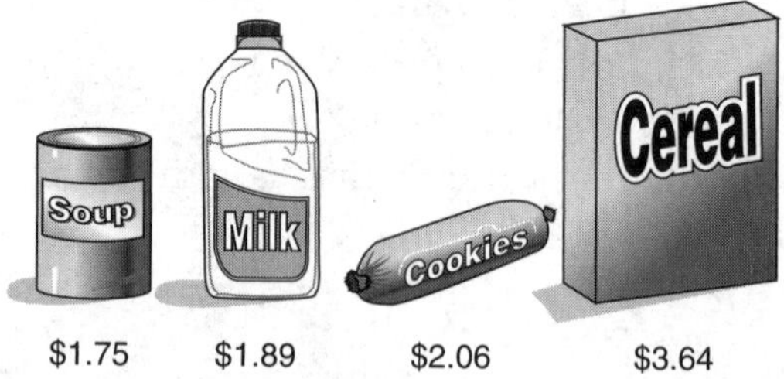

Decimal Order: Placing decimal fractions in correct numerical order is the next step in helping José understand decimal numeration. He shades the hundreds grid to show 0.13, 0.10, 0.46, and 0.30 to represent amounts of money he found in his piggy bank. José should shade the quantities in different colors in the same grid and then put them in order from smallest to largest in a second grid. He can also record them in the place value chart.

To work with thousandths, José is given chart paper on which the thousandths sections are already drawn. He observes their small size and can tell that one thousandth is one tenth of one hundredth. José can try to divide a hundredth into 10 sections to appreciate the small size of this decimal amount. These ideas can be extended to have José express the tenth, then the hundredth, then the thousandth in any decimal fraction amount, such as 3.4, 3.45, and 3.456.

Decimal Error Pattern II for José

The second Student Work Sample for José deals with decimal fraction addition. Determine what consistent error is being made in terms of addition and the placement of the decimal point.

STUDENT WORK SAMPLE II FOR JOSÉ

1. (carry 1) 24.3 + .59 = 30.2
2. (carry 1) 6.7 + .88 = 15.5
3. (carry 1 1) 4.52 + .078 = 5.30
4. (carry 1) 379.432 + 23.556 = 61.4992
5. (carry 1) 72.34 + .6672 = 1.3906
6. 8.216 + .797 = 16.186
7. (carry 2 2) .543 + 33.64 + 57 + .9821 = 1.03461
8. (carry 2 1, 1) 2.67 + .3793 + 854.2 = 1.2602

Diagnosing the Error: First, classify José's strengths and error patterns related to his ability to add decimal fractions using the algorithm. Use the following space to record your findings.

José's Error Pattern(s):
José's Strengths:

José can compute addition facts correctly. He is also able to regroup whole numbers in the base-10 place value system. However, he does not align the decimal places correctly. He lacks an understanding of the reason for and procedure of adding like units to each other. Information regarding addition is found in José's DAS in Table 8.1.

Prescription: José should begin working with decimal squares and place value charts to model addition examples. He needs to understand that the place value system extends to decimal fractions as it does with whole numbers.

Remediation: A sample MIP for Error Pattern II is shown in Table 8.3. José should begin with decimal models of squares divided in tenths, as he did in

TABLE 8.3 Mathematics Improvement Plan II for José: Addition of Decimal Fractions

Time:		**30 minutes**	**20 minutes**	**30–35 minutes**
Context		He works with another student (+)	Assignment given to entire class by the teacher on board (+)	He is expected to study and complete his assignment by himself (+)
Content		Add decimals from travel problem with place value chart, check with calculator; play "Add On," and "Fill 'er Up" (+)	Solve word problems for "Using Food for Thought in Math" (+)	Play "Add on" and "Fill 'er Up" with a partner (+)
Process	Input	Directions from teacher are given in oral form (+)	Directions were then demonstrated to the class by use of the chalkboard (+)	Directions are given to small groups for games (+)
	Output	Students write their answers on their study sheets (+)	He is expected to recite to his partner (+)	He can put his answers on the classroom computer (+)
Behavior	Academic	Completes assignment as given (+)	Creates more problems (+)	He can complete small blocks of his assignment and present game answers to teacher (+)
	Social	With peer of his choice (+)	Assignment given part by part (+)	Begins to talk to a peer (+)
Reinforcement		Teacher praises with grade (+)	Teacher tells José how hard he has worked (+)	The teacher awards him a smiley face for his hard work (+)

Note: The + symbols indicate strengths and the – symbols indicate areas of concern.

remediating the first error pattern. He should be provided with a real-world problem such as the following:

> Paul is working on a geography unit with his class. He is recording how far it is to travel from town to town in his state, to determine the distance traveled for a possible family trip. He is supposed to find the total distance from his home town to others that the family chose. If he travels to Healthy Town, which is 135.78 away from his home, then to Happy Town, going 458 km more, and then ends at Sleepy Town, which is 367.8 km from Happy Town, how many total miles would they travel?

Using the Internet, José could first research information about his state and produce a printed map, indicating distances between various cities, to show the class. Connecting mathematics to other subject areas is vital to helping students value the importance of mathematics in their daily lives. José is motivated by using technology.

It is very important that José creates his own dissonance between his original sum and the correct result. He needs to understand for himself where and how he is making his errors, rather than depending on the instructor's feedback. This process is facilitated as José uses graph paper and follows a pattern of remediation to add decimals that includes:

1. Shading the amounts he is comparing on hundreds squares. For 135.78 José shades 78 hundredths on his hundredths grid to find that he covered 7 tenths and 8 hundredths. He shades 5 tenths, for the 367.5, on a second grid. Vertical lines are drawn in red and horizontal in blue. José counts the red columns for tenths and the smaller blue squares for hundredths. The following is an example:

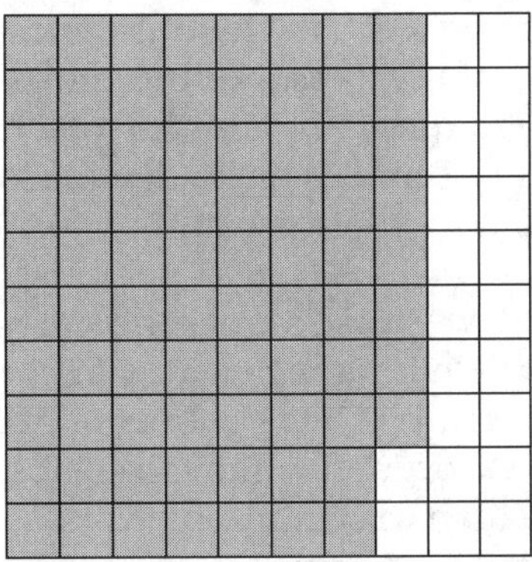

2. Completing a place value chart to record quantities and find the sum. The following is an example of the chart, which could be made by simply turning his notebook paper at right angles to form vertical columns:

100	10	1	0.1	0.01	0.001
1	3	5	.7	8	
4	5	8			
3	6		.5	0	

3. Adding decimals on paper and/or with a calculator to reinforce the necessity to line up decimal points to find the correct sum. This type of activity also provides opportunities for increasing estimation and provides practice.

Decimal Error Pattern III for José

Score José's decimal fraction subtraction Work Sample III. Note his pattern of errors related to subtracting decimals rather than only in terms of the whole number subtraction algorithm. Determine whether his errors are consistent.

Diagnosing the Error: Consider the strengths and error patterns of José's understanding and procedures used to subtract decimal fractions. Record your observations in the following space.

José's Error Pattern(s):
José's Strengths:

José can use the subtraction algorithm when regrouping for whole numbers and correctly finds the difference in subtraction facts. However, he fails to regroup from the ones to the tenths place. He either inserts another digit to finish regrouping the tenths place before dealing with the ones column (see problems 1 and 4) or he disregards borrowing from the ones place entirely. His subtraction information, in a DAS form, is found in Table 8.1.

Prescription: José's work indicates more of a procedural than a conceptual error pattern. He knows how to work with the subtraction algorithm when grouping is involved, but he is confused about recording a value that moves from tenths to ones—"over" the decimal place. As such, it is not necessary for him to start remediation with manipulatives because he understands the regrouping concept. He should use models such as graph paper, place value charts, and money examples to work on procedural rules.

Remediation: The MIP for subtracting decimals can be found in Table 8.4. José can construct a place value chart using his notebook paper. For a real-life example, he should think about a situation in which he had $22.34 in savings and wanted to purchase an item costing $7.58. His parents ask him to find out how much of his savings he would have left, to help him learn to save money for the future.

José records the amount of savings using his error pattern solution. He then subtracts, using the chart, to find that the difference is $14.76. The discussion would center around the fact that the minuend, the top number, had to be

STUDENT WORK SAMPLE III FOR JOSÉ

1. 24.30 − .59 = 24.171 (regrouping marks: 2 1)	2. 6.70 − .88 = 6.182 (regrouping marks: 6 1)	3. 4.520 − .878 = 4.1642 (regrouping marks: 4 1 1)
4. 379.432 − 23.556 = 356.1976 (regrouping marks: 8 13 12 1)	5. 72.3400 − .6672 = 72.6828 (regrouping marks: 12 1 9 1)	
6. 8.216 − .797 = 8.419 (regrouping marks: 7 1 10 1)	7. 2.6700 − .3796 = 2.3004 (regrouping marks: 9 1)	8. 33.64 − 5.7 = 28.94 (regrouping mark: 1)

renamed from ones to tenths and tenths to hundredths. Regrouping took place across the decimal point to get a correct answer.

Specifically, 58 hundredths must be removed from 0.34. José groups 10 of the tenths together and moves them to the hundredths column. Now seeing that there are 14 hundredths, he removes 8 and records a 6. He renames 10 tenths from the ones to get 13 tenths, from which he can remove 5 tenths. A chart and drawing would look like this:

TABLE 8.4 Mathematics Improvement Plan III for José: Subtraction of Decimal Fractions

Time		20 minutes	25–30 minutes	20–25 minutes
Context		He is with a small group of his peers (+)	Story problems and game sheets are distributed (+)	He is expected to study and complete his assignment by himself (+)
Content		Solves real-world subtraction problems using coins and place value charts (+)	Compute missing price lists using addition and subtraction; play "Add on" as a subtraction game (+)	Work on budget for his own version of "Using Food for Thought in Math" (+)
Process	Input	Stories created by class (+)	Directions were then demonstrated to the class by use of the chalkboard (+)	Directions are given to him separately (+)
	Output	Students write their answers on their study sheets (+)	He is expected to submit answers (+)	He can put his answers on the classroom computer (+)
Behavior	Academic	Completes assignment as given (+)	He moves to game when ready (+)	He can complete small blocks of his assignment and present that work to his teacher for correction (+)
	Social	With peer group of his choice (+)	He will work alone on price list and choose partner for game (+)	Works alone or with peer for game (+)
Reinforcement		Teacher praises him after lesson (+)	Teacher tells José how hard he has worked (+)	The teacher awards him time to play "Bingo" (+)

Note: The + symbols indicate strengths and the – symbols indicate areas of concern.

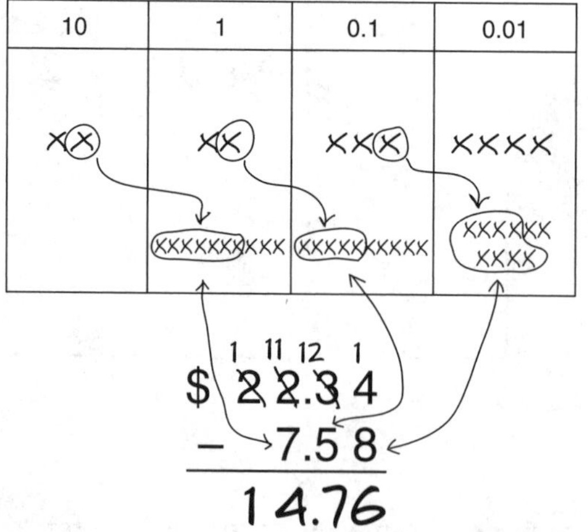

Additional examples to foster estimation and mental math strategies, as well as correct paper/pencil calculations, could include a problem in which José and his friends have to "fill in" a missing price, requiring both addition and subtraction computation. José is told that his sales receipt was torn and he needs to find a missing price to make certain the total was correct. The items bought were:

Corner Store Sales Slip

Items	Price
Soda:	$ .55
Pretzels:	$ 2.89
Apples:	
Hot dogs:	$ 5.68
Total:	$ 9.12

Decimal Error Pattern IV for José

Score José's Student Work Sample IV for decimal fraction multiplication. Determine any error patterns regarding the use of the algorithm, placement of decimals, and accuracy of basic facts. Confirm the pattern by checking similar examples on the paper.

Diagnosing the Error: Examine the types of errors in multiplication that José made. List the strengths and error patterns of his work in the space provided.

José's Error Pattern(s):
José's Strengths:

José is able to complete the algorithm in terms of the order of steps. His knowledge of basic facts is accurate. However, he counts the number of places for finding the decimal point from the wrong direction. He is unsure of the site of the quantity represented by the product, so he does not know how to make sense of where the decimal point should go. Information for multiplication is found in the DAS in Table 8.1.

Prescription: José multiplies using the correct procedures, except for recording the decimal point. His error is more of a procedural matter, rather than a conceptual matter. The product is not so far off from the correct one; even if José used number sense, his answers would not be entirely unreasonable.

José can benefit from using clues and cues to help him remember where to place the decimal point. It is not necessary for him to begin with manipulatives or drawings because he already understands the multiplication process.

STUDENT WORK SAMPLE IV FOR JOSÉ

```
1.  24.30        2.  6.70        3.  4.52
   ×  .59           ×  .88          × .078
   21870            5360            3616
   12150           5360            3164
 1433.70         5896.0         03525.6

4.  .3793        5.  33.64       6.    .76
   ×  2.67          ×   5.7        ×    .18
    26551          23548              608
   22758          16820               76
  7586            191.748           1368.
 101273.1
```

Remediation: José's MIP for multiplication is found in Table 8.5. He should begin with a real-world situation such as the following:

> José earns $25.46 for each of seven weeks as a helper in a bakery. He wants to know how much money he earned in all during the time period so he can help his family afford to take a vacation across the state.

Before José begins, he should be asked to estimate the dollar amount. If he has difficulty, he should be guided to think of the product of 7 × $25. To help him do so he should think about the product of 4 × 25, 100, and then mentally add it to the product of 3 × 25, to find $175. Continuing, 7 × 46 cents is

TABLE 8.5 Mathematics Improvement Plan IV for José: Multiplication of Decimal Fractions

Time:		30 minutes	20 minutes	25 minutes
Context		He is with a small group of his peers (+)	Assignment given to entire class by the teacher orally (–)	He works alone and with peer (+)
Content		Solve real-world problems involving rounding and estimates, develop strategy for both to tell class, illustrates with charts (+)	Using currency and word problems, class solves computation using cues and arrows (+)	Practice multiplying by powers of 10, do worksheet of "How much is your word worth?", plays "Move On" using multiplication (+)
Process	Input	Directions from teacher are given aloud (+)	Directions were then demonstrated to the class by use of the chalkboard (+)	Directions are given to the entire class (–)
	Output	Students write their answers on their study sheets (+)	He is expected to recite to teacher (+)	He can put his answers on the classroom computer (+)
Behavior	Academic	Completes assignment as given (+)	He creates his own new problems (+)	He can complete small blocks of his assignment and present that work to his teacher for correction (+)
	Social	With peer group of his choice (+)	He works alone (+)	Begins to talk to a peer who is seated next to him (+)
Reinforcement		Teacher praises with check marks (+)	Teacher tells José how hard he has worked (+)	The teacher awards him a smiley face for his hard work (+)

Note: The + symbols indicate strengths and the – symbols indicate areas of concern.

approximately the same as about 7 × 50 cents, or \$3.50. Adding \$175 to \$3.50, he estimates a total of \$178.50. He writes the problem as:

$$\begin{array}{r} \$25.46 \\ \times \quad 7 \\ \hline \end{array}$$

He now knows that the product is about \$178.50. If José continued his error pattern, he would have counted over two places from the left to mark the decimal point. He can see that \$17.822 could not have been correct, according to the actual results. Therefore, he will learn that counting from the left of a number is an incorrect procedure.

He should circle the 6 or put an arrow above the ones place such as:

$$\begin{array}{r} \downarrow \\ \$25.46 \\ \times \quad 7 \\ \hline \end{array}$$

In this way, he is using his visual learning style strength to provide a cue and remind him to begin counting places from the right, or the ones, place. When he finds the place, between the eight and the two, he finds that \$178.22 is, in fact, close to his estimated answer.

To extend the lesson, José examines the pattern in the following table. He could actually multiply those numbers and write all the zeros to check the pattern he found.

Decimal multiplication: Powers of ten

$0.1 \times 1 = 0.1$	$0.01 \times 1 = 0.01$	$0.001 \times 1 = 0.001$
$0.1 \times 0.1 = 0.01$	$0.01 \times 0.1 = 0.001$	$0.001 \times 0.1 = 0.0001$
$0.1 \times 0.01 = 0.001$	$0.01 \times 0.01 = 0.0001$	$0.001 \times 0.01 = 0.00001$
$0.1 \times 0.001 = 0.0001$	$0.01 \times 0.001 = 0.00001$	$0.001 \times 0.001 = 0.000001$

Decimal Error Pattern V for José

Score José's Student Work Sample V for division of decimal fractions. Look for error patterns in his dealing with the placement of the decimal point as well as the ability to do long division.

Diagnosing the Error: Analyze José's error pattern with respect to division and identify what he knows and what mistakes he is making. Include your findings in the space provided. Consider his understanding of the algorithm, specifically, his ability to divide by decimal fraction divisors.

José's Error Pattern(s):
José's Strengths:

It can be observed that José knows how to work with the division algorithm and can estimate accurate whole number dividends. He does not, however, move the decimal point in the divisor when necessary. He marks the decimal point in the quotient above the place it is found in the dividend. José does not seem to understand or use the correct procedure for renaming the divisor to a whole number for division by a decimal. Table 8.1 contains DAS information related to division.

Prescription: José should use the aid of manipulatives, drawings, and symbol cues in correcting this error pattern to model the concept of "moving" the decimal point in the divisor and dividend. Once José understands the reason and ease of that step, his work with the remaining steps in the division algorithm should be more successful.

Remediation: José's MIP for division can be found in Table 8.6. José begins by relating division with a decimal divisor to division with a whole number divisor. For example, José is asked the following:

> If you and your friend, Carl, were paid $2.30 to divide equally between yourselves for work you did after school to straighten up the classroom, how much money would each of you receive?

To solve the problem, José could use real currency to measure out groups with the same amount of money in each group. That process would look like the following:

STUDENT WORK SAMPLE V FOR JOSÉ

1. $3.2\overline{)673.4}$ — answer 21.0; work: 64, 33, 32, 14

2. $5.21\overline{)9.543}$ — answer .18; work: 521, 4333, 4168

3. $.43\overline{)5.06}$ — answer .11; work: 43, 76, 43, 33

4. $3.75\overline{)987}$ — answer 2; work: 750, 237

5. $.5\overline{)43.1}$ — answer 8.6; work: 40, 31

6. $.765\overline{)945.6}$ — answer 1.2; work: 765, 1806, 1530, 276

José's money	Sarah's money
$1.00, Dime .10, Nickel .05	Nickel .05, $1.00, Dime .10

TABLE 8.6 Mathematics Improvement Plan V for José: Division of Decimal Fractions

Time		30 minutes	20 minutes	20 minutes
Context		He completes written work alone (+)	Class presents stories (–)	He is expected to study and complete his assignment by himself (+)
Content		Solve real-world problems with money coins and diagrams to show rest of class (+)	Review placement of divisor and dividend regarding decimal point, related fractions to decimal fractions, and equivalencies; complete algorithms and show arrows to explain work to teacher (+)	Solve division exercises; play "Fill 'er up" independently by recording decimals and shading appropriate grids to show answers (+)
Process	Input	Directions come from partner, if needed (+)	Directions provided to the class by use of the chalkboard and discussion (+)	Directions are given to José (+)
	Output	Students write their answers on their study sheets (+)	He is expected to recite his answer to the teacher (+)	He can put his answers on the classroom computer (+)
Behavior	Academic	Completes assignment as given (+)	When he finishes, he can play "Move On" or "Mix and Match" (+)	He can complete small blocks of his assignment and present that work to his teacher for correction (+)
	Social	With peer group of his choice (+)	He works alone and with friend for games (+)	Begins to talk to a peer who can help when needed (+)
Reinforcement		Teacher praises with marks on papers (+)	Teacher tells José she will call his mother in the evening and tell her how hard José has worked (+)	Teacher awards him a smiley face for his hard work (+)

Note: The + symbols indicate strengths and the – symbols indicate areas of concern.

José can see that he and his friend would each receive \$1.15. He divided the money in two equal groups by distributing the currency.

Dividing \$2.30 by 0.02, rather than 2.0, is much more difficult to handle. He would have the tedious task of measuring out the strips by groups of 0.2 size each or by somehow distributing the money in 0.2 groups rather than in 2 groups.

José concludes that it would be more efficient to calculate division with a whole number divisor than a decimal divisor. He should complete these steps:

1. Review the concept that it is necessary to multiply both the numerator and the denominator by the same number to find an equivalent fraction.
   For example:
   $$\frac{3 \times 2}{5 \times 2} = \frac{6}{10}$$

2. Convert fractions to decimals, 2/10 = .2.
3. Model the concept that 0.2 can be renamed as a whole number, 2.0, when multiplying by 10, just as 2/10 × 10/1 = 20/10 = 2.0. As a result, he is moving the decimal place one place from the left of the two to the right of the two in the product.

$$\begin{array}{r} 0.2 \\ \times \quad 10 \\ \hline 00 \\ 02 \\ \hline 02.0 \end{array}$$

4. Write the division problem as a fraction to connect this new idea to finding an equivalent fraction when multiplying the numerator and denominator by the same number, as done in step 1. Multiply the numerator and denominator by the same number, 10, to find that the denominator is now a whole number, 2.0.

$$\frac{2.30}{.2} \times \frac{10}{10} = \frac{2.30}{2}$$

5. Write the problem as the division algorithm and divide using the standard division procedures:

$$.2\overline{)2.30} \qquad\qquad 2.\overline{)23.0}$$

The decimal point is recorded in the quotient above the dividend to keep the place values correct, and the division algorithm is completed.

When José understands and can perform the division algorithm, he can generalize "moving the decimal" for any decimal divisor. Reminding him of the table he produced for multiplication is helpful. José would see what power of 10 to choose for getting a whole number divisor.

Practice should include exercises such as:

1.	4	×	?	=	4
2.	0.45	×	?	=	45
3.	3.265	×	0.01	=	?
4.	0.32	×	0.001	=	?

Conclusions: Instructional Strategies Summary

The study of decimal fractions is based upon expressions of the quantity with models of number lines, hundreds squares, place value charts, and currency in everyday experiences. Many students mistake decimal problems for whole number computation and apply procedures that do not exist or are mistakenly created to solve problems. These learners can develop conceptual fluency by illustrating decimal fractions for themselves and connecting them to what is previously understood, common fractions. Relating $3/10 = 0.3$ in drawings and on square paper are very effective strategies. Decimal number sense should be a focus throughout the lessons and activities so that students can correct themselves when they realize their results are not reasonable. Students should strive to make their own decisions as to the accuracy and usefulness of their results.

Decimal number computation has often been learned as a series of rules, as in "line up the decimal places" or "count over to put the decimal in the product." When misunderstood, these procedures become forgotten or are applied incorrectly. Students and their teachers must take the time, in developmental steps, to carefully use materials and illustrations to make sense of the algorithms. Place value lessons are essential so that computation is completed accurately and with understanding.

Computation examples should be created that connect the lessons to authentic applications of decimal amounts, such as using money, reading food labels, buying gasoline at the service station, or a myriad of other daily occurences. Numeracy can be achieved for decimals when students understand and compute with fluency.

Instructional Activities

The following games and activities are suitable for supporting students' understanding of and skill level with decimal fractions. Students will work with numeration or place value, sequencing, and computation by engaging in this work. The activities can be utilized for the whole class, small groups, pairs, or individual work.

ACTIVITY: Mix and Match Decimals

Objective: Connect symbols to drawn representations

Materials:

Game boards with a variety of decimal numeral shaded grids. They can be made with 100s square grid stamps on posterboard. Grids are shaded with a variety of decimal representations and are laminated.

Cards with decimal fractions on them that match the game boards

Directions:

1. The object of the game is to match the drawings on the game boards to numerals on the cards.
2. Cards are placed in a stack.
3. Players take turns drawing cards, or the leader shows a card to the group of players.
4. When the drawing on a grid matches the numeral on the player's card, she covers it with a counter.
5. Play continues until all the numeral cards are drawn.
6. The player who has all pictures covered, or a row of them covered, wins. The game board could look as follows:

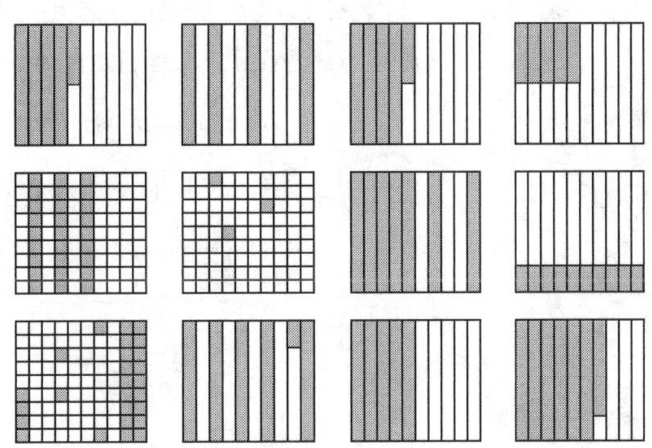

ACTIVITY: Building Decimals

Objectives: Estimate decimal size and reinforce number sense

Materials:

Paper

Pencil

Puzzle

Directions:

1. Write decimal notation from the information given in each exercise.
2. More than one answer is possible for each item.

a. Greater than 600 ___ ___ ___ . ___

b. Less than 4 ___ . ___ ___ ___

c. Between 4 and 6 ___ . ___ ___ ___

d. Between 200 and 300 ___ ___ ___ . ___

e. As near 205 as possible ___ ___ ___ . ___

f. Less than 1 ___ . ___ ___ ___

g. Greater than 890 ___ ___ ___ . ___ ___

h. Between 50 and 51 ___ ___ . ___ ___ ___

ACTIVITY: Reasoning About Decimals

Objective: Reinforce decimal place value, concepts, and number sense

Materials:

Paper

Pencil

Directions:

1. Students use clues in the box to match each decimal with its letter.
2. Decimals A, B, C, D, and E are shown in the box below.
3. Students can make up their own puzzles for others to solve.

A is greater than C but is less than D.

B and E have the same digit in the thousandths place.

B is the least of the five decimals.

4.318	4.752
0.4752	0.47062
0.4301	

ACTIVITY: Using Food for Thought in Math

Objective: Problem solving, practicing addition, and subtracting of decimals.

Materials: Grocery store ads from a variety of stores or newspapers

Directions:

1. Prior to this activity, talk with the class about food groups.
2. Tell students that they need to design a nutritious meal for a family of four for $20 or less.
3. Discuss the different plans the students create and reasons for food choices.
4. Plan meals for a day or a week. Change total dollar limits.

ACTIVITY: Guess My Number

Objective: Practice decimal algorithms

Materials:

Deck of cards, each with a different decimal numeral

Directions:

1. Players decide which operation (+, −, ×, ÷) will be used for the game round.
2. Each player chooses a card from the deck. He/she does not show it to anyone.
3. One person is designated as the leader.
4. The leader shows his/her card to the other players.
5. Each player adds, subtracts, multiplies, or divides his/her number to the leader's number, depending on the operation for that round.
6. Students then turn in their answer sheets to the teacher to be checked, or check them themselves with a calculator.
7. Students with correct answers win a point for that round.

ACTIVITY: Fill 'er Up!

Objective: Connect decimal fraction concepts to symbols

Materials:

100 squares grid

3 sets of cards numbered 1–9 (each set is a different color) or different colored wooden cubes. Cubes have numerals written on them. Red cubes represent tenths, green cubes represent hundredths, and white cubes represent thousandths.

Directions:

1. Each player has a grid. The object of the game is to fill the grid.
2. Each person rolls the cubes or selects three cards.

3. The first player fills in the grid according to the amount indicated on the cube rolled or card selected. Example: red "3," green "4," means to fill in three tenths and four hundredths. A shaded grid is shown on the next page.
4. The first player who has a covered grid wins.
5. Computation version: Pick three different cube colors, roll, and multiply or divide the result. Shade in the answer. More than one grid may be needed for each player when the result is more than 1.

   Example: red 3, green 7, white 4

$$\begin{array}{r} .37 \\ \times \quad 4 \\ \hline 1.48 \end{array}$$

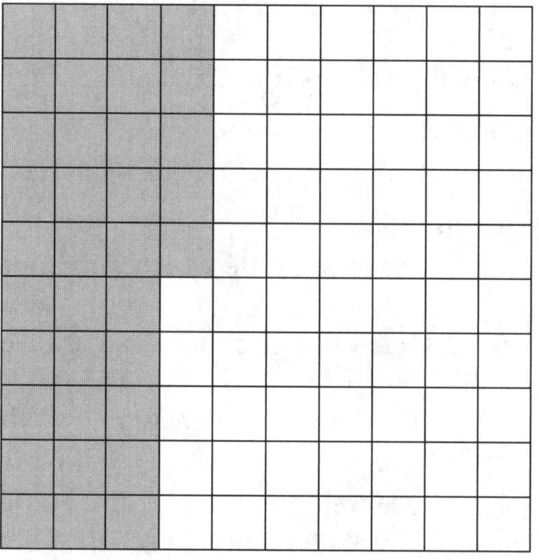

ACTIVITY: How Much Is Your Word Worth?

Objective: Practice addition of decimal numerals

Materials: Worksheet like the following (numbers are cents each letter is worth):

a	b	c	d.	e	f	g	h	i	j	k
0.10	0.20	0.30	0.40	0.50	0.60	0.70	0.80	0.90	0.01	0.02

l	m	n	o	p	q	r	s	t
0.03	0.04	0.05	0.06	0.07	0.08	0.09	1.10	1.11

u	v	w	x	y	z
1.12	1.13	1.14	1.15	1.16	1.17

Directions:

1. Write a word on the board and have students calculate its worth.

   Example: smile

s =	$1.10
m =	.04
i =	.90
l =	.03
e =	.50
	$2.57

2. Students should choose their own words for practice.
3. Challenge the students to see how many $1.00 or more words they can find.
4. Change the letter values for other games.

ACTIVITY: Move-on

Objective: Practice addition, subtraction, and multiplication of decimal fractions

Materials:

Playing board

Movable objects to mark the spaces

Wooden cube marked with the following letters: R for right, L for left, U for up, D for down, C for diagonal, and N for any direction

Directions:

1. Players choose the operation to use for the game and a target number to reach.
2. Players put their objects on the square marked "Start."
3. First player rolls the cube and moves the marker in the direction indicated by the letter appearing on the cube.
4. That number is recorded as that player's score.
5. The next player rolls the cube and advances according to the cube letter.
6. The first player rolls again and, depending on the operation chosen, adds, subtracts, or multiplies the second number by the first.
7. The second player rolls the cube and uses the same operation with the first two numbers.
8. The first player who achieves the target number wins.

Example:

The operation chosen is addition and the target number is 10

First player rolls R and moves the marker from Start to 0.8

Second player rolls D and moves the marker from Start to 0.5

First player next rolls U and moves the marker to 1.98, which is added to "0.8" to get a partial sum of 2.78

Second player rolls L and moves to 0.056, which is added to 0.5 for a partial score of .556

Play continues until one player reaches the target of 10

0.76	9.54	0.49	3.62	0.52
1.1	1.57	0.32	1.98	2.5
1.45	0.702	**Start**	0.8	0
2.13	0.056	0.5	2.68	0.3
7.5	4.06	0.12	0.15	6.3

Discussion Questions

1. How would you help a student who thinks that decimals are whole numbers with different names?
2. What real-world examples could you utilize for decimals, other than money examples?
3. Describe an activity in which students could use a number line or place value chart to develop the meaning of each decimal place in terms of the number each represents. How would you assess the students' undrstanding?
4. How would you help a student who believes that multiplication always produces a larger result than the factors involved and division always yields a smaller quotient than the number being divided?
5. Why isn't the size of a decimal number not necessarily determined by the number of decimal places notated?
6. Why is mental estimation difficult for students when working with decimals? Explain how you would help a student estimate the product of 0.58×756.
7. Suggest a remediation plan for the following types of errors.
   a. Write the following common fractions as decimal fractions:

      4/10 = 4.10
      56/100 = 56.100
      372/1000 = 372.1000

   b. Fill in the missing blanks in this sequence:
      1.13, 1.12, 1.11, ____, ____
      Answer: 1.10, 1.09
8. How does analyzing the pattern of multiplying by zeroes assist students in their understanding of the placement of the decimal point in the product? Describe an activity you would use to help students understand the effect of multiplying numbers by powers of 10.
9. Develop a DAS and MIP for the following error patterns.
   a. Estimate the sum of:

148.72 + 51.351	Answer: 150.470
25.46 + 56.84	Answer: 50.80
789.32 + 42.63	Answer: 800.60

   b.

$$\begin{array}{r} 3.24 \\ \times\ .53 \\ \hline 70.17 \end{array} \qquad \begin{array}{r} .123 \\ \times\ .24 \\ \hline 0.029 \end{array} \qquad \begin{array}{r} 45.67 \\ \times\ 6.26 \\ \hline 2858.94 \end{array}$$

c. Interpreting the following as 1.5 and 2.4 respectively:

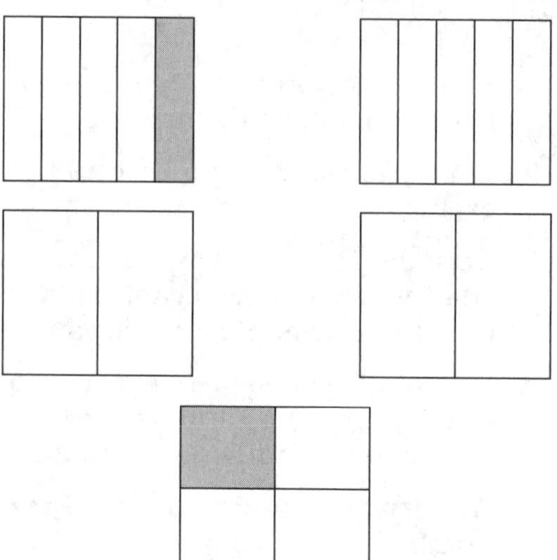

References

Crouch, R., & Baldwin, G. (1964). *Mathematics for elementary teachers.* New York: John Wiley and Sons, Inc.

Fennema, E., & Romberg, T. A. (Eds.). (1999). *Mathematics classrooms that promote understanding.* Mahwah, NJ: Lawrence Erlbaum Associates.

Hiebert, J. (1992). Mathematical, cognitive, and instructional analyses of decimal fractions. In G. Leinhardt, R. Putnam, & R. A. Hattrup (Eds.), *Analysis of arithmetic for mathematics teaching* (pp. 283–322). Hillsdale, NJ: Lawrence Erlbaum Associates.

Hiebert, J., & Wearne, D. (1986). Procedures over concepts: The acquisition of decimal number knowledge. In J. Hiebert (Ed.), *Conceptual and procedural knowledge: The case of mathematics* (pp. 199–223). Hillsdale, NJ: Lawrence Erlbaum Associates.

Hiebert, J., Wearne, D., & Taber, S. (1991). Fourth graders' gradual construction of decimal fractions during instruction using different physical representations. *Elementary School Journal, 91*, 321–341.

Irwin, K. C. (2001). Using everyday knowledge of decimals to enhance understanding. *Journal for Research in Mathematics Education, 32*(4), 399–420.

Kieren, T. E. (1992). Rational and fractional numbers as mathematical and personal knowledge. In G. Leinhardt, R. Putnam, & R. A. Hattrup (Eds.), *Analaysis of arithmetic for mathematics teaching* (pp. 323–371). Hillsdale, NJ: Lawrence Erlbaum Associates.

Kieren, T. E. (1995). Creating spaces for learning fractions. In J. T. Sowder and B. P. Schappelle (Eds.), *Providing a foundation for teaching mathematics in the middle grades* (pp. 31–65). Albany: State University of New York Press.

Kilpatrick, J., Swafford, J., & Findell, B. (Eds.). (2001). *Adding it up, helping children learn mathematics.* Washington, DC: National Research Council.

Leinhardt, G., Putnam, R., & Hattrup, R. A. (Eds.). (1992). *Analysis of arithmetic for mathematics teaching.* Hillsdale, NJ: Lawrence Erlbaum Associates.

Markovits, Z., & Sowder, J. T. (1991). Student's understanding of the relationship between fractions and decimals. *Focus on Learning Problems in Mathematics, 13*(1), 3–11.

Oppenheimer, L., & Hunting, R. P. (1999). Relating fractions and decimals: Listening to students talk. *Mathematics Teaching in the Middle School, 4*(5), 318–321.

Resnick, L. B., Nesher, P., Leonard, F., Magone, M., Omanson, S., & Peled, I. (1989). Conceptual bases of arithmetic errors: The case of decimal fractions. *Journal for Research in Mathematics Education, 20*, 8–27.

Sowder, J. (1997). Place value as the key to teaching decimal operations. *Teaching Children Mathematics, 8*, 450–453.

Sweeney, E. S., & Quinn, R. J. (2000). Concentration: Connecting fractions, decimals, and percents. *Mathematics Teaching in the Middle School, 5(5)*, 324–328.

Tracy, D. M., & Gibbons, M. K. (1999). *Deci-mania! Teaching teachers and students conceptual understanding of our decimal system* (ERIC Document Reproduction Service No. ED 433 237).

Chapter 9

Problem Solving

I hate word problems.

I can do word problems if you tell me how to start but otherwise I can't do them.

I can do word problems with the teacher but not by myself.

I can't do word problems because the words make no sense . . . how do I know what to do?

Word problems are boring . . . who cares?

What Is Problem Solving?

Students often make these comments when discussing their experiences with mathematical problem solving or word problems. Many people feel confused about the meaning, paths to follow, and reasonableness of solutions. Although students are more comfortable "solving" computational exercises, often misnamed as "problems," learners find them more difficult when words are included in the question; procedures are not as clearly identified. Frequently students believe they are incapable of understanding and/or solving for the answer.

This apprehension and avoidance are unfortunate and debilitating. It is most important for students to realize that the reason they study and learn algorithmic rules and computation facts is actually for the purpose of solving problems.

What Does Problem Solving Involve?

The document *Principles and Standards of School Mathematics* (NCTM, 2000) defines problem solving as "engaging in a task for which the solution method is not known in advance. In order to find a solution, students must draw on their knowledge, and through this process, they will often develop new mathematical understanding" (p. 52). Further, "solving problems is not only a goal of learning mathematics but also a major means of doing so. Students should have frequent opportunities to formulate, grapple with, and solve complex problems that require a significant amount of effort and should then be encouraged to reflect on their thinking" (p. 52).

Clearly, problem solving is a process of thinking mathematically. The term has also been defined as "strategic competence," which describes the "ability to formulate, represent, and solve mathematical problems" (Kilpatrick, Swafford, & Findell, 2001, p. 5).

Problem solving, as a goal, process, and skill, is contrasted with completing computational exercises with which students are already familiar. To solve problems, one must combine and recombine known algorithmic procedures in a new way. Students often think they "can't do" problem solving because they are unsure of ways to apply their own reasoning to questions. Yet, "good problems give students the chance to solidify and extend what they know and, when well chosen, can stimulate mathematics learning." (NCTM, 2000, p. 52). Because the purpose of mathematics is to solve problems, students and their teachers should not view computation as an end in itself, but as a means to problem solving.

Consider the following question:

> How many cookies would Craig have if he had three cookies and got five more?

This situation is really an addition computation exercise, if addition has already been introduced. The words do little to stimulate creative thinking or encourage reasoning. Students most likely add three and five because they see the numbers, know the previous questions were all addition types, and think little about the action really involved. If many number stories follow that example, each requiring the combination of two addends to rename the sum, there is little novel, adaptive thinking going on in the classroom.

However, students could be asked:

> Craig is supposed to buy cookies for his class party. He has $5.00 to spend for himself and 25 classmates. The students want three kinds of cookies: 9 chocolate chip, 8 oatmeal, and 9 sugar. Cookies are sold in this way:
>
> Chocolate chip: $.25 each
>
> Oatmeal: $.20 each
>
> Sugar: $.15 each
>
> Craig can also buy the cookies in packages this way:
>
> Chocolate chip: 1-pound bag for $1.75
>
> Oatmeal: 1-pound bag for $1.50
>
> Sugar: 1-pound bag for $1.00
>
> Each bag contains 12 cookies. What is the most economical way for Craig to buy the cookies? How much did he spend? Explain your reasoning.

Solving this problem requires reasoning, number sense, computation, and combining that information with knowledge of currency to find the result. If that process is unique in the problem set, then students are not merely doing algorithms that have words in them, but are, in fact, solving problems.

Problem solving, rather than the memorization of facts, should be considered the "basics" of mathematics. Understanding how to find results in a wide variety of settings, as well as the purpose of their work, helps to prevent mathematics from becoming a ritualized chore for students. Problems must be valued, not only as a purpose of learning mathematics, but also as the primary means of doing so.

Types of Problems

In general, problems can be classified as either real-world application or process problems. The former refers to the type of problems that require adaptive reasoning in authentic, everyday situations (Silver, Kilpatrick, & Schlesinger, 1990). An example is the following:

> Nate and Matt are friends at school. Nate likes to play at Matt's house in the afternoon. Matt lives nine miles from the school. How far does Nate travel back to his house when he goes from school to Matt's house and then back to his house, if he lives five miles on the other side of the school?

In contrast, a process problem is considered nontraditional. It describes a situation in which the solution path is not as readily discernable from the story as the application problem presents. Examples include:

1. If an 8-inch pizza serves two people, how many should two 12-inch pizzas serve?
2. Find two consecutive numbers whose product is an even number.
3. Arrange the digits 1–6 in six slots on the perimeter of a triangle so that all three sides add up to the same sum.

Using Heuristics

Both types of problems require the solver to apply some type of heuristic. The word *heuristic* derives from the Greek word for *discover* and means a general strategy used to guide the problem solver in finding a solution (Charles & Lester, 1982). Typical heuristics include:

- drawing a picture
- using manipulatives
- working backward
- acting it out
- making a table or list
- using smaller numbers
- looking for a pattern
- guessing and checking

Unlike algorithms, which prescribe specific procedures that yield a result, the application of heuristics does not guarantee career solutions. One could draw a diagram or construct a table, for example, and not necessarily arrive at a logical or correct result. However in the absence of knowledge of exactly what to do, a heuristic helps students begin to solve the problem—the more heuristics with which students are familiar, the greater the likelihood of finding a solution.

Why Do Students Struggle with Solving Problems?

The most common struggle students report when attempting to solve problems is not understanding what is being asked of them. That is, the context of the problem does not make sense and/or is not clearly translatable to a number sentence. Additional reasons for poor achievement follow.

Literacy Issues

Little Understanding of Mathematics Vocabulary: For some learners, the meaning of terms such as *added, sum quotient, divisor, dividend, factor, numerator, denominator*, and *difference* is unknown or confusing. For example, when sixth-grade students were asked to find the difference in a plant's height during a month's growth, they did not understand that they were to subtract the initial measurement from the final measurement. Students did report that the term for the answer to a subtraction problem is called the difference. But they did not connect the term to its application or authentic situations. Also, mathematical terms are easily confused or unknown; many students cannot, for example, distinguish the divisor from the dividend in terms of the quantities they represent.

Limited Ability to Read Problems: This difficulty is related to students' reading levels. If the vocabulary is beyond students' comprehension, the mathematics of the problem is compromised. Students' abilities are also limited by difficulty with complex sentence structure and vocabulary.

Limited Verbal Ability to Explain Thinking: Students who lack verbal skills have trouble expressing or explaining their thinking both aloud and on paper. This error pattern has serious implications for current testing practices in which students must explain their reasoning. Students may also be unable to discuss their thoughts and strategies in group work or with the teacher. Poor verbal skills often discourage students from attempting to take first steps to solve a problem.

Number Sense Issues

Difficulty Focusing on Important Information: Some students are unable to understand what is being asked in the problem because shapes, numbers, and/or symbols distract them. These students can neither choose the most important information nor compose a plan of action because they do not understand what information is relevant or unnecessary for the solution.

Limited Ability to "Picture" the Situation: For learners with this difficulty, the problem has no contextual meaning. For example, if students were asked to find the length of a shadow thrown by a ladder leaning on a wall, there might be little understanding of where that shadow could be located if they have limited experiences with ladders. If students have limited experiences with purchasing, they would have no idea what a discount means. Likewise, if students have never ordered a meal from a menu, they will struggle with determining totals and budgets.

Limited Self-Checking Ability: Some students have little experience in determining whether answers are reasonable. They often ask the teacher whether or not work is correct, or they might accept any answer just to finish a problem. For example, when students were asked how many buses, each with a capacity of 24 passengers, were needed to take 56 children on a field trip, some replied that two and a half buses would be logical. This response revealed a lack of number sense and an inability to picture reasonable situations.

Instructional Issues

Limited Personal Appeal: Most students must want to solve problems. Motivation is limited when learners feel there is little connection and relevance to their experiences. Students then often question the usefulness of mathematics in daily life situations or in their future. Time and energy for problem solving are diminished when students feel unconnected to mathematics.

Limited Time to Solve Problems: When students feel rushed or do not take sufficient time to think through a problem, errors result. Students must be provided enough time to check their work to thoroughly evaluate each step of the problem-solving process.

Improving Students' Problem-Solving Ability

There are many ways in which teachers can help students become better problem solvers. This section will focus on general methods to encourage improvement that can be applied to process or application problems. Improving dissimilar learners' problem-solving abilities occurs in lessons and activities that focus on the following suggestions, and proceed carefully through step-by-step instruction and feedback to and from teachers and students.

Instructional Strategies

Establishing a Context for Interest: An important instructional technique is to embed problem solving in mathematics lessons by relating the problem to students' interests. For example, the teacher could pose this problem:

> A young boy, Daniel, wants to go to a theme park. He must earn his ticket, which costs $10.00. He can wash dishes and clean his room for $.50 per hour and rake leaves for $.75 per hour. How many hours should he work in each location to earn the ticket money?

In this problem, students are engaged in a situation in which they may have personal interest. They are encouraged to understand that the reason they are learning mathematics is to solve specific problems with number operations.

Teaching a Variety of Heuristics: Equally important is that specific problem-solving heuristics be taught. The teacher focuses on how to use a particular strategy, such as drawing a picture, using manipulatives, or finding patterns, by carrying them out with students during lessons. The teacher and students brainstorm and verbalize all the thinking done before, during, and after work. Class discussions include plans of what to do, when certain steps are taken, why steps are used (or not used), and how and why to proceed with each thought. Even second guessing is important to verbalize aloud because it helps students learn to think logically.

Not all students will learn to use all the strategies in an efficient manner. However, pupils must be familiar enough with the techniques to choose the strategies. To solve a question about buying gum, for example, students can draw a picture, act it out with currency, or use smaller numbers.

Grouping Similar Types of Problems That Call for Similar Strategies: This strategy helps students find patterns in solution attempts. Lessons on organizing data tables, drawing diagrams, or working backward toward solutions are helpful tools to increase familiarity with heuristics. Solution patterns can then be applied to new problems.

Working Cooperatively Toward a Solution: Group efforts can be less threatening to students than working individually (Johnson & Johnson 1980). "Problem solving ability is enhanced when students share opportunities to solve problems themselves and to see problems being solved" (Kilpatrick et al., 2001, p. 420).

Starting with Simple Problems: Solutions are more easily found and confidence is built when students experience success quickly. They are more willing to take risks after knowing they are, in fact, able to find solutions correctly.

Rewarding Students for Small Steps of Success: Frequent words of praise and positive comments on written work for step-by-step improvement are powerful instructional strategies for encouragement. Suggestions and hints are also helpful to students throughout the problem-solving process.

Compiling a Mathematics Dictionary Journal with Students: Important mathematics terms should be discussed in class. The words should be defined and further identified with drawings. For example, students record a definition for *dividend* and draw an arrow to the dividend in a long division problem. Geometric shapes can be drawn and their components, such as perimeter, area, edges, and vertices, can be marked and defined. These vocabulary words should include those that can confuse children. For example, *volume* refers mathematically to geometry and measurement but also to decibels of sound.

Providing Sufficient Time for Solving Problems: Solving a variety of fewer, quality problems rather than many similar problems allows time for:

- estimation
- use of alternate strategies and processes
- detection of errors
- search for additional solutions
- everyday applications to other problems
- discussion

Simplifying Numbers: An example of using smaller numbers follows:

A sporting goods store has 247 soccer balls worth $5.97 each and 375 footballs worth $2.95 each. What is the total value of soccer balls and footballs?

To complete the problem, students could substitute:

- 2 instead of 247 soccer balls
- $1.00 instead of $5.97
- 3 instead of 375 footballs
- 2 instead of $2.95

Reduce Reading Difficulties: Reduce the number of words and/or record the problem on a tape recorder in the same example:

247 baseballs worth $5.97
375 softballs worth $2.95
Worth how much all together?

Learning to Solve Problems

Instruction designed to assist students in problem solving is enhanced when students are taught specific strategies and receive frequent feedback. Moreover, when problems are integrated as a story or a real-life situation in daily lessons, problems are solved more intuitively and language becomes much more familiar. These instructional techniques are critical for implementing the classic approach to teaching problem solving in George Polya's book, *How to Solve It* (Polya, 1945). Polya identifies four specific steps to find solutions:

- understanding the problem
- devising a plan
- carrying it out
- assessing its accuracy or looking back

These steps provide a structure that teachers can use to improve students' problem-solving abilities.

Both students' and teachers' behaviors will be described in the following sections with reference to these problem-solving steps. When problem solving is taught within these defined stages, misunderstandings are less likely to arise. If difficulties do arise, they can be dealt with at the point of error.

Problem Solving: Step by Step

This section will present a sample of steps teachers and students can take to solve authentic problems. The following is an example of an application problem that could relate to students' interests or, if not, could be modified to do so.

> Karen and Henry did some work for their family and as a reward, they got a gift of green bean plants from "Plants For Us." The store clerk told the children that the plants were magic. The clerk said that Karen's plant would double its size each day and that Henry's would grow taller by 2 cm each day. The children took the plants home on Monday and put them near the kitchen window. Both were 2 cm tall. The children were surprised to see that, by Tuesday, the plants had already grown to be 4 cm tall, so they took them to school that day for everyone to see. The class wanted to know which plant would be taller on Friday or if they would be the same height. Can you tell them and explain how you know?

Understanding the Problem—What to Do: The teacher and students need to discuss the problem to understand its intent. This first phase involves the following instructional steps, with questions, and possible student responses:

1. **Teacher:** We must find out what the whole problem says by reading it through entirely from beginning to end. What do we know for sure? What is the unknown? Anything else?
   Response: We know that Karen and Henry both have plants. We don't know which plant will be taller on Friday.
2. **Teacher:** What is the data? What is the situation we know?
   Response: We know that the plants were 2 cm tall when the children got them. Karen's plant doubles in size each day and Henry's plant gets taller by 2 cm each day.
3. **Teacher:** What are we trying to find out?
   Response: We want to know which plant will be taller on Friday, or if they will be the same size.
4. **Teacher:** Is there enough, or too much, information provided? Why do you think so? Is it clear to you?
   Response: We could mark out the name of the store, the reasons the children got to buy the plants, and where the plants were placed.
5. **Teacher:** Are there any math words you do not understand?
   Response: We need to talk about what "double its size" means.
6. **Teacher:** Underline the sentences and words that you need to solve the problem. Explain your reasoning.
   Response: We should underline the information telling us how tall the plants were on Monday and that one doubles its size and one gets 2 cm taller each day. We should underline "Friday" because that's the day the plants will be compared for height.
7. **Teacher:** Retell the problem to another person, the teacher, or to yourself.

Devising a Plan to Find the Answers—What to Do? This is the step in which heuristics are applied. The teacher and students must decide which type of plan is best. The teacher should list all possible heuristics and then discuss which are most appropriate to this problem and why they were chosen. Students could then decide upon one or all of the following strategies:

1. Draw a picture of the plants each day as shown in the following:

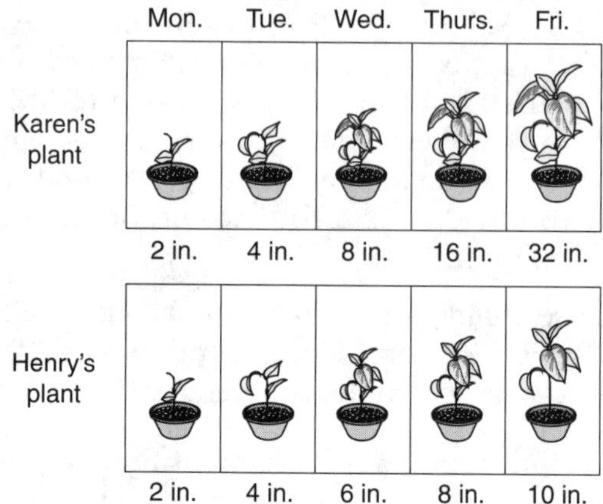

2. Make a table of the information known so that a pattern can be seen and completed:

	Day 1	Day 2	Day 3	Day 4	Day 5
Karen's plant	2	4	8	16	32
Ellen's plant	2	4	6	8	10

3. Explain a pattern and how you decided what you found:

For Karen, the number of the day is the exponent for the root number, "2."
$2^1, 2^2, 2^3, 2^4, 2^5$

For Henry, the number of the day 1's multiplied by 2.
2 x 1 2 x 2 2 x 3 2 x 4 2 x 5

4. Students could make a graph to demonstrate what happens each day as the plants grow. An example is shown in Figure 9.1.

If it helps students become more involved, they could use their own names when identifying the plants and explaining the problem to others.

Carrying Out the Plan with Heuristics: Students work in groups to utilize their plan to find a solution. Teachers ask the following:

1. Which plant was taller? How do students know?
2. Why did groups of students use the heuristics they chose and how did that strategy lead to a solution?

If a plan did not work, as seen when they could not answer the question or when others pointed out mistakes, groups should try another one of their chosen heuristics. Students show their work and explain it to the whole class.

FIGURE 9.1

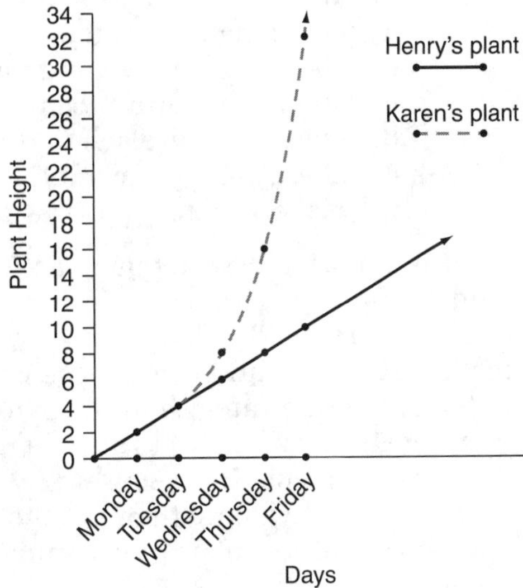

Examining Solutions: Checking for Results—Which Were Right? Looking back helps students reflect upon what was done to solve a problem, which leads to better problem solving. It helps check arithmetic mistakes. Students discuss what worked, what did not, and why. Questions that help students assess their own work and thinking are very important for students who struggle with problem solving. They can think through ideas such as:

- What else could we try?
- How did we know we were finished?
- How did we know we were right or wrong?
- How can we explain our steps and results?
- How do we know that our answer is reasonable?

Suggested Lesson Plan Structure

A general lesson plan for classroom instruction in problem solving over a one-week or two-week period can be organized in this way:

1. Several problems that relate to students' interests are presented or created for the entire class.
2. Problems are solved aloud as teachers and students think through processes and solutions.
3. Small groups of students complete problems together. These problems follow the same patterns, in terms of types of strategies to be used, as the whole-class experience.
4. Small groups share their thinking processes and results.
5. Students work independently on three or four similar problems.
6. Individual students share their thinking and results.

7. The teacher or students can produce variations to an original problem by:
   a. changing the content
   b. changing the size and type of numbers
   c. changing the number of conditions
   d. reversing the given and wanted information
   e. changing some combination of the above
   f. personalizing problems for individuals

It is important to establish an atmosphere in the classroom that encourages students to solve problems. Learners should feel that all their ideas and their attempts are valid, though incorrect answers should be discussed and corrected. Students, and teachers as well, should be encouraged to take risks and to try different strategies in order to solve problems. They should understand that the erroneous answers are discussed and used as learning devices in a positive environment. By discussing why a strategy did not work, students are encouraged to evaluate their results and move forward. They should also know that solving problems is given primary importance.

Conclusions: Instructional Strategies Summary

Problem solving is a creative process and a skill. It is the goal of mathematics. As such, problem solving must be approached, for those who have difficulties, in a carefully planned, methodical, guided manner that provides opportunities for students to learn to reason for themselves. Students improve their problem solving by participating in activities that focus on finding patterns and utilizing specific heuristics or strategies that modify their attempts, based on the problem outcomes in a variety of lessons. Students should learn to solve problems in an open, accepting, and discussion-laden environment. Students should learn to share their approaches and model logical thinking with each other.

Tools for solving problems can be learned and include drawing pictures, making tables, working backward, acting problems out, using manipulatives and models, applying logic, and finding patterns. When these methods are taught in conjunction with appropriate problems that appeal to students' interest, improvement is seen. Problems are valued not only as a purpose for learning mathematics but also as a primary means of doing so.

Discussion Questions

1. How is the definition of problem solving more inclusive than "completing computational procedures correctly"? What are the major components of problem solving? Provide an example for each.
2. Identify two problem-solving heuristics you consider to be most challenging to students. Explain your reasoning.
3. How do process problems and authentic problems differ in their instructional focus?
4. Write five process problems and five authentic problems to solve. List three questions you would ask of students in helping them to find the solutions for each of your problems.
5. Which of Polya's problem-solving steps involves the use of heuristics? Why?
6. Choose two of the reasons students experience difficulty in problem solving with which you most identify. What experiences did you have in learning mathematics that influenced your choices? Explain your reasoning.
7. Why is important to express the problem-solving process aloud with students?
8. Interview five people you know who are not teachers. Ask them if they had difficulty with problem solving in mathematics—if so, why?
9. What are good everyday examples for application types of problems?
10. What are important everyday activities families can engage in to provide experiences to which mathematics can be related?
11. Based on your reading, how early in their schooling do you think students can learn to solve novel problems? Explain your response.

References

Andres A. G., & Trafton, P., (2002). *Little kids—powerful problem solvers: Math stories from a kindergarten classroom.* Westport, CT: Heinemann Publisher.

Artzt, A., & Newman, C. (1990). *How to use cooperative learning in the mathematics class.* Reston, VA: National Council of Teachers of Mathematics.

Bransford, J., & Stein, B. (1984). *The ideal problem-solver.* New York: W. H. Freeman & Co.

Charles, R., & Lester, F. K. (1982). *Teaching problem solving: What, why and how.* Palo Alto, CA: Dale Seymour.

English, L. D., Fox, J. L., & Watters, J. J. (2005). Problem posing and solving with mathematical modeling. *Teaching Children Mathematics, 12*(3), 156.

Flores, A., & Klein, E. (2005). From students' problem solving strategies to connections in fractions. *Teaching Children Mathematics, 11*(9), 152–157.

Hartman, Hope J. (1996). Cognitive learning approaches to mathematical problem-solving. In A. S. Posmentier & W. Schulz (Eds.), *A resource for the mathematics teacher.* Newbury Park, CA: Corwin Press, Inc.

Jitendra, A. (2002). Teaching students math problem-solving through graphic representations. *Teaching Exceptional Children, 24*(4), 34–38.

Johnson, D., & Johnson, R. (1980). Using cooperative learning in math. In N. Davidson (Ed.), *Cooperative learning in mathematics*. Tucson, AZ: Zephyr Press.

Kilpatrick, J. (1987). Problem formulating: Where do good problems come from? In A. V. Schoenfeld (Ed.), *Cognitive science and mathematics education* (pp. 123–148). Hillsdale, NJ: Lawrence Erlbaum Associates.

Kilpatrick, J., Swafford, J., & Findell, B. (Eds.). (2001). *Adding it up: Helping children learn mathematics*. Washington, DC: National Research Council.

National Council of Teachers of Mathematics. (2000). *Principles and standards for school mathematics*. Reston, VA: Author.

Polya, G. (1945). *How to solve it*. Princeton, NJ: Princeton University Press.

Polya, G. (1965). *Mathematical discovery* (Vol. 2). New York: John Wiley & Sons.

Rigelman, N. R. (2007). Fostering mathematical thinking and problem solving: The teachers' role. *Teaching Children Mathematics, 13*(6), 308–314.

Schoenfeld, A. (1989). Teaching mathematical thinking and problem-solving. In *Toward a Thinking Curriculum: Current Cognitive Research*. Alexandria, VA: Association for Supervision and Curriculum Development Yearbook.

Sheffield, L. J., & McGatha, M. B. (2006). Mighty mathematicians: Using problem posing and problem solving to develop mathematical power. *Teaching Children Mathematics, (12)*5, 79–85.

Silver, E. A., Kilpatrick J., & Schlesinger, B. (1990) *Thinking through mathematics, fostering inquiry and communication in the mathematics classroom*. New York; Collage National Examination Board.

Silver, E. A., & Philip Smith, J. (1980). Think of a related problem. In S. Krulik (Ed.), *Problem Solving in School Mathematics, Yearbook of the National Council of Teachers of Mathematics* (pp. 146–156). Reston, VA.: The Council.

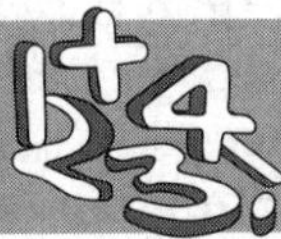

Chapter 10

Time and Money

I don't pay attention to my brother when he says he'll be off the phone in just a minute, because he never is.

—*Fourth grader*

I'm not going to figure out how much money I have to spend on something from the school store because I'm waiting for the stuff to go on sale.

—*Second grader*

Time and Money as Measurement Topics

Teaching students to use the measures of time and money is critically important for student success in managing daily life experiences. The National Council of Teachers of Mathematics recommends, in the Measurement Standard in *Principles and Standards of School Mathematics* (PSSM), that as early as preschool to second grade, students should "recognize the attributes of length, volume, weight, area, and time" (NCTM, 2000, p. 102). Standards for grades 3 through 5 include the expectations that "students select and apply appropriate standards units and tools to measure . . . time" (p. 170).

Although the PSSM document does not specifically discuss money concepts and skills, students should be able to recognize all the coin amounts and write their correct values . . . as well as the dollar amounts, in order to deal with everyday currency experiences. The study of money is most often dealt with as a measurement topic, though it is also used as an application of place value and/or problem-solving activities (Carlsson, & Cohen, 2002). Forming different values and decimals by combining the dollars and coins, adding and subtracting monetary values, converting money values, and learning to give and receive the correct change after making a purchase are essential objectives for succeeding in the elementary-level mathematics curriculum and throughout the grades.

Learning About Time

The topic of time can be separated into two areas for instructional purposes: the skill of reading the clock and the concept of time duration. The latter refers to understanding the length of a particular time period, such as a minute, or the interval between two time slots that is, the amount of time between two clock times. Teaching students to read clocks should be connected to students' activities, both in and out of school. The skill is more successfully learned in the context of informal or authentic experiences, much like number sense is meaningfully developed when students have opportunities to relate reasonable quantities to their daily lives (Brownell, 1935).

Learning About Money

Recognizing the values of coins and dollars in relation to the monetary system is an important first step in learning to understand and use currency. Students advance to combining coins and bills to find total value. For example, students would find that the value of a quarter and a dime can be exchanged for that of 35 cents, or that 14 dimes and 6 pennies can also be named as $1.46. Fundamental concepts and skills associated with money exchanges include:

- Currency recognition
- Currency value
- Currency exchange
- Currency computation

Why Do Students Struggle with Learning About Time and Money?

Time and money measurements can pose difficulties because they require the application of indirect scales. That is, when measuring the length of a room or the capacity of a glass of milk, one could place a meter stick end to end from one side of a room to the other or pour liquid into a calibrated measuring container; rocks can be placed on a scale to measure their mass as indicated on the the instrument's dial. However, clocks cannot be placed next to an hour to measure time, nor a dime next to an object to determine its monetary value. Measuring time is complex because it requires the knowledge and skill of reading an analog clock and the understanding of points in and duration of time periods. As well, determining currency value is challenging because coins have no visible measurement markings on them and coins and paper bills are not proportional to their value; a nickel is physically larger than a dime but represents less purchasing power.

An additional reason that the expression of time and money measures is challenging is the issue of new and confusing vocabulary. For example, 45 minutes after 6:00 can also be referred to as 6:45 or 15 minutes before 7:00. *A quarter until 7:00*, or *a quarter of 7:00*, and even *a quarter before 7:00* all refer to the same clock time. With reference to the clock, "before and after" are not clear to many students. Fifty cents can also be called "half dollar" and expressed as $0.50 or 50 cents.

The scales of clock and currency must be understood, in terms of both their own structure and their application. Students' errors, then, have much to do with the understanding and skill of reading the instruments, using unfamiliar notation correctly, understanding time duration as well as the value and system of combining coins and bills, and dealing with confusing vocabulary terms.

About the Student: Sarah

Sarah is an active, curious third-grade student who wants to learn how to tell time and to determine the amount of allowance she gets and saves. She has had little experience with telling time because she has used only digital, rather than analog, clocks in her home. She does go to the store with her parents and watches them use money but has not paid for items herself without someone telling her what coins to use and how much change she received. She works well with others but prefers to work in small groups rather than to present her work to the entire class or the teacher alone. Sarah enjoys drawing and illustrating. She enjoys rewards such as verbal praise but would rather others did not know when she makes errors by seeing marks or stickers on her papers; she does not offer responses to the whole class willingly. Sarah does like role-playing situations with others in contexts where she can talk to her friends and show her drawings, as long as she does not have to show her written work to everyone or speak to all of her classmates at once.

Error Patterns: Diagnosis, Prescription, and Remediation

Time Error Pattern I for Sarah

The first type of error dealing with telling time is found in Student Work Sample I. Sarah responded to six illustrations asking her to express the time with correct numerals and notation.

Diagnosing the Error: The teacher examines the child's responses and identifies the type of mistake Sarah is making as conceptual or procedural. Sarah's strengths in clock reading and recording as well as errors should be noted. Record your own analysis of the error pattern you detect in the space provided.

Sarah's Error Pattern(s):
Sarah's Strengths:

A diagnosis of Sarah's work reveals that although she can record single-digit numerals, she is confusing the hour- and minute-hand readings on the clock.

STUDENT WORK SAMPLE I

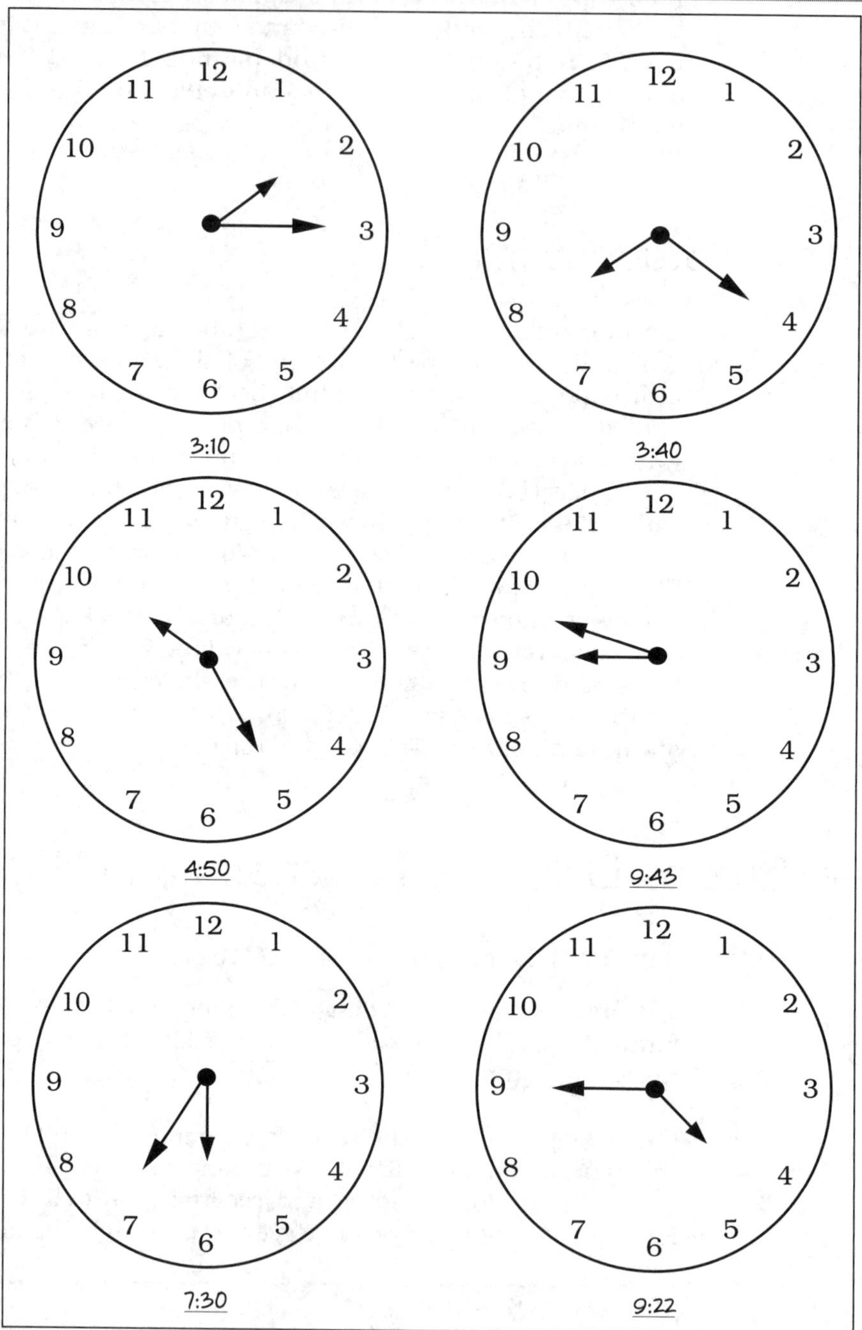

The hour hand is read as the minute hand and the minute hand is considered as the hour hand. Her answers would be inaccurate if she attempted to indicate the time when a television program began or when school actually ended. Her content strengths include the fact that she can read and write numerals and knows that the hour and minute hand differ in function. She also knows that

TABLE 10.1 Data Analysis Record

Student Name: Sarah **Data Analysis Record**	**(area of concern)**						
Context	**Content**	**Process**		**Behavior**		**Reinforcement**	
		Input	**Output**	**Academic**	**Social**	**Strong**	**Weak**
+	+	+	+	+	+	+	+
• Likes to draw • Likes to work with hands-on activities • Likes to learn in small groups • Likes to play games	***Learned Concepts I*** • Reads numerals • Knows directionality ***Learned Concepts II*** • Reads analog clock ***Learned Concepts III*** • Reads numerals • Finds dates/days on calendars ***Learned Concepts IV*** • Recognizes coins and paper bills in appearance • Knows value of coins and paper bills • Can skip count ***Learned Concepts V*** • Recognizes coins and paper bills in appearance • Knows value of coins and paper bills	• Reads and records whole numbers well • Likes to construct hands-on aids • Accepts suggestions from other students	• Willl show and express work to small groups of students • Will show work to teacher when feeling confident	• Will express answers in drawings nd symbols • Needs real-world experiences	• Enjoys working with others in small groups • Comfortable expressing herself verbally and with drawings • Positive attitude toward value of learning	• Likes verbal praise from small groups • Keeps rewards (stickers, marks) to herself	
–	–	–	–	–	–	–	–
• Lacks real-world experiences • Does not like to present work to whole class or alone to teacher	***Error Pattern I*** • Confuses hour and minute hand on clocks ***Error Pattern II*** • Cannot determine delayed time or time duration for hours and minutes ***Error Pattern III*** • Cannot determine how many days between two dates on calendar ***Error Pattern IV*** • Cannot calculate correct change in money transaction ***Error Pattern V*** • Cannot rename money accounts with decimals/franctions/ other names	• Lacks real-world experiences • Difficulty with expressing decimals and fractions • Unable to read clocks • Unable to read calendar for delayed time	• Does not observe details carefully on clocks or calendars • Is hesitant to express answers to others in large group	• Does not like to respond until certain she is correct • Will check her work before responding	• Not comfort-able with real-world experiences • Accepts correction privately only	• Sensitive about accepting knowledge of her mistakes from teacher • Uncomfortable with attention or criticism from entire class at one time	

some times are read as "before" and "after" the hour. Her weaknesses are related to the fact that she does not understand the operation of the clock in terms well enough to accurately tell time.

An example of a completed data analysis sheet (DAS) for Sarah's error is included in Table 10.1.

Prescription: Because Sarah has little experience with analog clock reading, she is confusing the minute and the hour hands. Sarah should actively engage in learning by physically moving the hands to notice how the minute hand moves as the hour hand also advances around the clock. Sarah likes to draw and work with her hands. She would profit from expressing time by making a clock, marking the numbers on it, and watching it work. Because she has little daily experience reading the analog clock, the lessons should focus directly on working with the clock hands, position of the numerals, and connecting those clock readings to actual events in her life to provide a sense of time periods. Instructional approaches are included in Sarah's MIP in Table 10.2.

Remediation: Sarah begins the lesson on clock reading by notating the positions of 12, 3, 6, and 9 with numerals and marks around the circumference of a large paper plate. She then fills in the numerals and tick marks for 1, 2, 4, 5, 7, 8, 10, and 11. Sarah can use a real clock or a commercial teaching clock as a model to make the marks on the circumference as evenly as possible. It is helpful to point out that "12" is considered as a "0" or starting point on the clock.

Sarah traces and cuts out a clock minute hand, which is attached to the middle of the clock with a brad fastener. She then draws in 60 shorter tick marks evenly around the clock face. An illustration is shown in Figure 10.1.

Working with the teacher or another student, Sarah points the minute hand at the "12" and begins to count aloud by ones as she moves the hand around the clock. Sarah reports that the direction in which the hand moves on the clock is to the right or "clockwise." Sarah and her partner or teacher

TABLE 10.2 Mathematics Improvement Plan for Sarah: Reading Clock Time with Hours and Minutes

Time		30 Minutes	20–30 Minutes	15–20 Minutes
Context		Works with a small group of students on clock reading project	Works independently on guided practice papers	Works with one other student
Content		Constructs paper plate clock by marking intervals of ones fives, and moving clock hands separately and together	Records clock times and draws clock face form times given on worksheets checks answers with students-made clock	Plays game with another student to create times for each other to show on their clocks and check with each other for accuracy
Process	Input	Creates student-made clock and responds to oral and written questions	Worksheet and hand-made clock	Hand-made clocks; student-created stories/problems
	Output	Completes answers by moving hands on clock, and discusses intervals and positions with other students	Recorded responses and drawings	Clock faces fixed to correct times
Behavior	Social	Works with peers	Works individually	Works with one other student
	Academic	Completes work paper with correct clock faces and correct times	Completes work paper alone with aids	Students discuss their answers with each other
Reinforcement		Verbal praise from peers	Receives quiet praise from teacher	Praise from partner

FIGURE 10.1

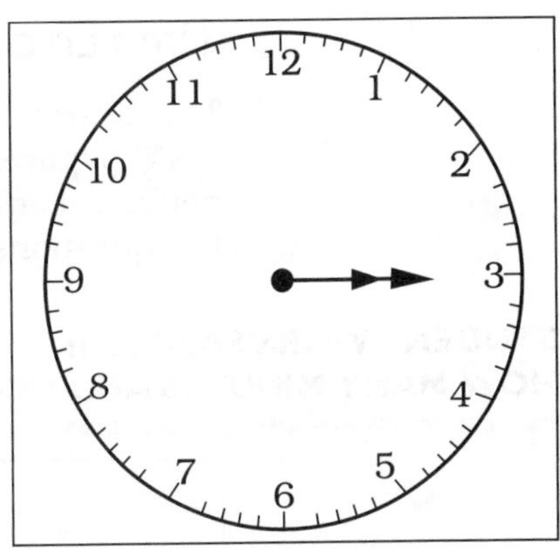

repeat this activity, starting again at the 12 and counting by fives, to stress the importance of 5-minute intervals on the clock. As an example, when Sarah puts the minute hand on 10 and moves it to 15, she calls out "15 minutes" and "5 minutes is between 10 and 15." Sarah can then point to the minute hand and report the number of minutes that have passed between that number and any number before it. To provide an authentic reference to a time period, Sarah describes activities that could be accomplished in 5-minute intervals, such as tying shoes, brushing teeth, or making a sandwich.

Next, Sarah traces an hour hand and attaches it to the center of the clock, in the same center hole as the minute hand. Sarah should describe the hour hand in relation to the minute hand in terms of length, so that she sees that the hands are, indeed, physically different. She positions both the minute and hour hand on the 12 and is guided to call that time, "12:00," though a.m. and p.m. times are not yet discussed. Her partner or teacher then leaves the minute hand on the 12 and moves the hour hand to each numeral as Sarah names that hour. For example, Sarah names the time for which the hour hand points to the "1" and minute hand to "12" as "1:00." Although the manner in which a clock operates is guided for Sarah, she is directly engaged by explaining the way in which each hand works, moving each hand separately, and naming times.

Sarah now needs to read both the minute and hour hands together to read clocks accurately. She should work with a partner so that she can identify each hour as she moves the minute hand completely around the clock. It is important to guide Sarah to realize that as the minute hand is advanced, the hour hand is being moved between two numbers. That is, she needs to identify the two numerals the hour hand is positioned between when the minute hand points to the "25." Sarah should then set her clock herself for specific times asked of her and draw the position of the hands on the clock on blank clock work papers.

To record her work for current and future reference, Sarah should draw pictures of clocks, mark them with the times modeled, and label them with standard notation. Sarah could choose various times to read aloud and write a number sentence or story to indicate what she is doing at that time. For example, she might select 4:00 or 4:30, write it under clock face, and write about her after-school activities at that time.

Time Error Pattern II for Sarah

The second type of time/clock error is found in Student Work Sample II. The task requires that Sarah determine the duration of time or delayed time between two clock times indicated on the drawings and respond to three written questions.

STUDENT WORK SAMPLE II
HOW MANY MINUTES AND HOW MANY HOURS ARE BETWEEN EACH PAIR OF CLOCKS?

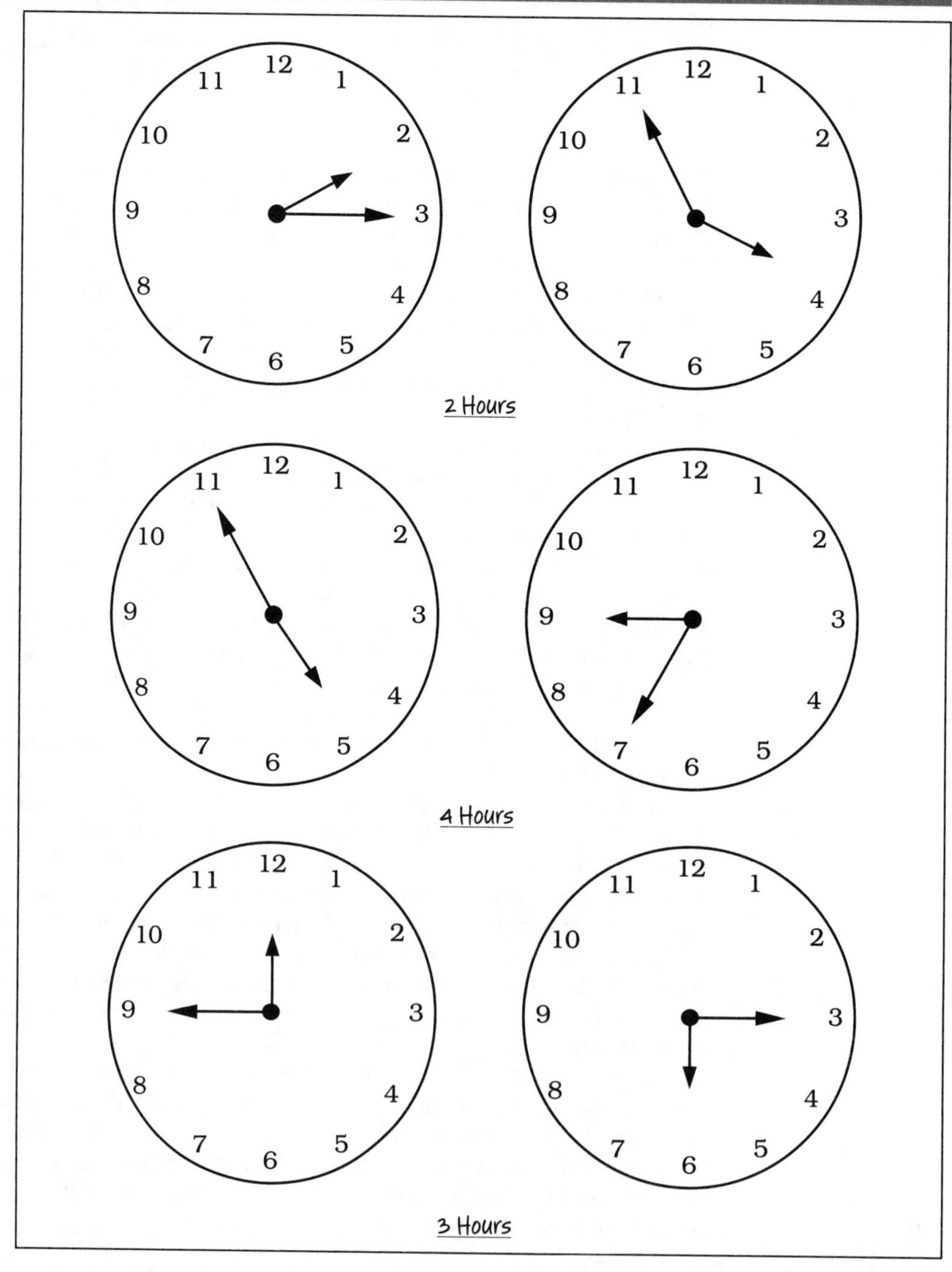

Diagnosing the Error: In these examples, Sarah's strengths include her ability to accurately read a clock and record the times shown. What additional strengths and concerns can you detect? Record your analysis of Sarah's strengths and the error pattern you detect in the following space.

Sarah's Error Pattern(s):
Sarah's Strengths:

Although it is evident from her computation that Sarah is aware that there is a difference in the two clock times, her response is limited to the duration of hours, rather than minutes. She appears to understand the concept of delayed time because she can find the number of elapsed hours but not the number of elapsed minutes. Sarah understands the concept of a period of time, although her responses are not entirely sensible, but needs to correct the procedural error of not computing the minutes between two points in time.

Prescription: Sarah needs to work with everyday examples of her activities and those of friends or her family to gain time sense with respect to minutes and the procedures for counting them. In this way, she can assess her own responses in terms of authentic examples. Sarah needs to know she can check her answers in accordance with a specific situation. This student enjoys drawing and learning with others. Games, student-made clocks and data charts, as well as discussing her results with peers would be beneficial. Refer to the completed DAS for Sarah's error in Table 10.1.

Remediation: The suggested remediation activity is described in this section and listed in Sarah's MIP in Table 10.3.

Sarah begins by recording the start and approximate finish times of some of her favorite daily or weekly activities (Figure 10.2).

Sarah draws the times for each example on the blank clocks on her work paper. Sarah can determine the amount of elapsed time for each example by first moving the minute hand on her student-made clock and then recording the number of minutes. She goes back to the start time and moves the hour hand to the finish time, recording the number of hours that have passed.

Sarah progresses from the manipulation and drawing phases of the lesson to recording symbols. To find the difference using computation, she records the two times as follows:

```
  8:30  time I finish breakfast
– 8:00  time I start breakfast
  ----
```

Sarah should discuss reasons that the finish time is written as the minuend, on top, in the subtraction problem. She is subtracting the beginning time, or the start time, from the finish or last time to find the difference—the amount of time that had elapsed between the two time periods. She can see that the difference is one-half hour. This example will serve to begin the lesson with

TABLE 10.3 Mathematics Improvement Plan for Sarah: Reading Delayed Time

Time		30 Minutes	20–30 Minutes	15–20 Minutes
Context		Works with a small group of students on clock reading project	Works independently on guided practice papers	Works with one other student
Content		Constructs two paper plate clocks with minute and hour hands that move; times are set on each clock related to student activities and duration time is determined aloud	Records clock times on each clock; draws clock faces from times given on worksheets with symbols and written problems; checks delayed time answers with student-made clock	Plays game with another student to create times for each other and report delayed time; check with each other for accuracy
Process	Input	Creates student-made clocks and responds to oral and written questions	Worksheet and hand-made clock	Hand-made clock; student-created stories/problems
	Output	Completes answers by moving hands on clock, and discusses intervals with other students	Recorded responses and drawings	Written record of correct delayed intervals of time in hours and minutes
Behavior	Social	Works with peers	Works individually	Works with one other student
	Academic	Completes work paper with correct delayed times	Completes work paper alone with aids	Students discuss their answers with each other
Reinforcement		Verbal praise from peers	Receives quiet praise from teacher	Praise from partner

FIGURE 10.2

SARAHíS TIMETABLE				
	Start Time	Finish Time	Time Between Number of Hours and Minutes	
Eating breakfast (example)	7:00	7:45	0	45
Eating lunch				
Eating dinner				
Watching my favorite TV show				
Playing outside after school				
Reading a book				
Playing a game with my friends				
Doing homework				

an answer that is easy to assess in terms of number sense. Sarah should then move on to times such as

```
  4:45  time I finish playing after school
– 3:15  time I start playing after school
  ----
```

and to examples requiring renaming, such as:

```
  6:35  time I finish dinner
– 5:50  time I start dinner
  ----
```

Sarah can create a similar table for her family or friends to complete and then report the duration of times. She should also write a story to tell about her activities during two of the times, to more fully relate her knowledge to her own experiences.

Calendar Time Error Pattern I for Sarah

The third type of time error is found in Student Work Sample III, which deals with reading calendars. Sarah is asked to determine the number of days between two dates, some of which are in the same month and some of which fall in different months.

Diagnosing the Error: Sarah's strengths in calendar reading should be noted. What strong points and weaknesses can you identify? Record your own analysis of Sarah's strengths and the error pattern you detect in the following space.

Sarah's Error Patterns:
Sarah's Strengths:

A diagnosis of student work indicates that Sarah can identify dates on the calendar and understand that she is counting the number of the days between two dates. However, she counts the number of days incorrectly. Sarah is counting the first date, rather than the day after, as one of the days between two indicated dates. She is not using the calendar dates as a number line and recognizing that a unit of time is an interval between two dates. She does not understand the concept of "numberness" in that she is counting as "one" the unit where she began rather than the interval between it and the next numeral it represents. Although she can read a calendar and write the dates, she is lacking an understanding of quantity represented by intervals, much as a student who reads a ruler incorrectly counts the "0" as a unit of measure.

Prescription: Because Sarah does not understand the concept of measuring an interval, she would profit from using a number line. This manipulative will help Sarah measure and grasp the concept of quantity and transfer that knowledge to the principle of using a calendar to measure the length of time between two dates. Starting lessons with a number line she creates and then applying it to a calendar will help Sarah actively engage in determining the correct counting of days and help her to self-monitor her readings. An example of a completed DAS for Sarah's error is included in Table 10.1.

STUDENT WORK SAMPLE III

Record the number of days between

1. April 7 and April 19: 13
2. December 4 and December 21: 18
3. October 20 and November 30: 11
4. February 17 and March 2: 14
5. In any month, first Saturday and third Saturday: 21
6. In any month, Tuesday in one week and Wednesday in the next week: 9
7. In any month, Monday in one week and Friday in the next week: 12
8. If my birthday is on September, 2 and I got a gift on September 14, how many days did I have to wait for my present? 13

Remediation: The suggested remediation activity is described in this section and listed in Sarah's MIP in Table 10.4.

Sarah should construct a number line with adding machine tape. She can fold the paper in seven equal sections and mark the intervals as "0" at the edge. She marks the tape from 1 to 7 as follows:

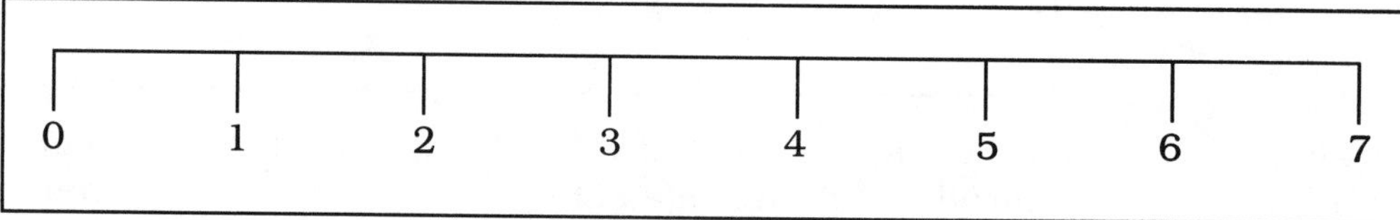

Sarah places a counter on 0 and moves it to 1. When she puts the counter over the number 1 and its interval dash, she says "1." She continues to move the counter and count aloud, making sure that she announces the number she lands on with the counter and the number of units in the interval. If needed, Sarah shades each interval as she counts along the number line so that she actively moves through the interval before counting the number of days represented. The number line can then be continued to 31 intervals or units.

To use the number line on the calendar, Sarah and her partner choose a special or favorite date in a chosen month and circle the date. Either Sarah or her partner then chooses a date, before or after the first date, on which they would like to have an event. In order to count the days between the two dates, Sarah places her number line on the calendar and uses it to count the intervening period of time. The number line and calendar would look like the illustration in Figure 10.3.

In order to count the days from May 8 to May 12, for example, Sarah places her number line on the calendar, positioning it so that "0" is over the first date. She then counts the number of marks, each representing an interval, to the next date and reports the number of days.

TABLE 10.4 Mathematics Improvement Plan for Sarah: Calendar Reading

Time		30 Minutes	20–30 Minutes	15–20 Minutes
Context		Works with a small group of students on calendar reading to count days between dates with real-world situations	Works independently on guided practice papers	Works with one other student
Content		Constructs number line and uses counters to mark dates and count correct number of days between them in same or different months	Records calendar dates and number of days between using counter checks with number line	Plays game with another student to create times for each other and reports days in intervals; check with each other for accuracy
Process	Input	Creates student-made clocks and respond to oral and written questions	Worksheet and calendars	Creates stories with activities and dates between them, recording number of days on story papers
	Output	Completes answers by moving hands on clock, and discusses intervals with other students	Recorded responses and drawings	Written record of correct intervals of time
Behavior	Social	Works with peers	Works individually	Works with one other student
	Academic	Completes work paper with correct delayed times	Completes work paper alone with aids	Students discuss their answers with each other
Reinforcement		Verbal praise from peers	Receives quiet praise from teacher	Praise from partner

FIGURE 10.3

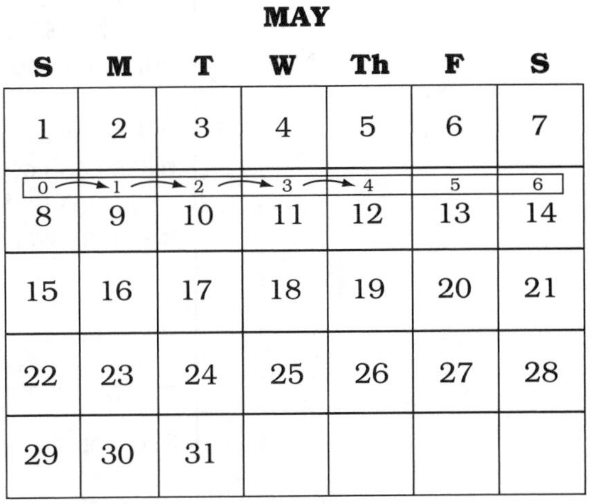

MAY

S	M	T	W	Th	F	S
1	2	3	4	5	6	7
0 →	1 →	2 →	3 →	4	5	6
8	9	10	11	12	13	14
15	16	17	18	19	20	21
22	23	24	25	26	27	28
29	30	31				

After taking several turns, Sarah is directed to choose two dates that are in different weeks and determine the number of days between the dates using the number line or counters. She should put one on the first date, May 8, and call it "0" as she did with the number line. Then she moves the counter to May 9 and counts "1." She continues moving and counting until she reaches May 12 to find that, again, there are 4 days between May 8 and 12.

The last step in this process would entail using subtraction as a number operation to find the difference between the dates. If, for example, the chosen dates were December 7 and December 16, Sarah should move the counter to find the number of days in the interval. She could then subtract the two dates to find the difference—that there were 9 days in between. To move to different months, as in the amount of days between November 20 and December 7, she would move her counter until the end of the month of November. She would then count the remaining days in December. She could also use mental mathematics to count up from November 20 to November 28 and from December 1 to December 7, to find that there are 8 days in November and then 7 in December, totaling 15 days between the dates. Counting-up and counting-on activities are very useful for this measurement and provide students useful and authentic examples for mental mathematics strategies.

Money Error Pattern I for Sarah

The first type of money error is found in Student Work Sample IV. The task requires that Sarah calculate the correct change when given a purchase price and the amount paid.

STUDENT WORK SAMPLE IV

Determine the change owed to the customer and record on the lines provided:

1. Jackie, a clerk in a bookstore, sold a book for $13.90. The customer gave her $20.10. Jackie returned $7.20. Was that the correct change? If not, what should it have been? It was correct.

2. Rachel and Ari rented bicycles for a ride along a river path. The two bikes each cost $19.95, no tax charged, per 2 hour rental. List the bills and coins that should be counted out for change if Rachel and Ari gave the bike owner $50.00 in payment.

1 dollar

10 cents

3. Compute the correct amount of change in the following chart.

Cost of Item	Amount Paid	Change
a. $4.32	$ 5.00	$ 1.00
b. $21.81	$ 25.00	$ 4.00
c. $643.89	$ 700.00	$ 100.89
d. $72.59	$ 80.01	$ 10.01

Diagnosing the Error: Sarah is able to write dollar and cents amounts correctly. Consider her additional strengths related to making change and the types of errors she is making. Record your observations of Sarah's strengths and your own analysis of the error pattern in the following space.

Sarah' s Error Patterns:
Sarah's Strengths:

A diagnosis of Sarah's work reveals that although she can record dollars and cents symbols correctly, she is unable to determine the correct amount of change in an exchange of money. Her answers are not completely unreasonable. She shows evidence of understanding money values. Sarah does not appear to be proficient in using procedures to count change correctly when using a variety of coins and dollar bills. She rounds the dollar and/or cents amount to find an answer close to the amount she thinks reasonable.

Prescription: Sarah is incorrectly expressing currency notation. Because she enjoys working with others and needs to experience authentic situations, she should handle money in practice sessions with other students. "Buying" and "selling" items in a classroom store setting and other authentic examples would provide the real-world experiences Sarah lacks in handling money and determining correct amounts. As well, she would be less hesitant to try new examples with a small group of classmates rather than in front of the whole class or with the teacher alone. Table 10.1, the DAS, lists Sarah's strengths and weaknesses for this pattern.

Remediation: The suggested remediation activity is described in this section and listed in Sarah's MIP in Table 10.5.

Sarah can learn to make change by working with skip counting and practicing that activity with real or play money exchanges. She needs to practice skip counting by intervals of 5, 10, 25, 50, and 100 to work with dollars and cents.

Sarah begins by counting out five counters and calling out "5." She then moves five more counters to the set and says "10." She continues skip counting or counting by fives by joining more counters or continuing to count aloud without them, if possible. She should combine the group of fives with ones. For example, to count from 10 to 43, Sarah could count "10, 15, 20, 25, 30, 35, 40, 41, 42, 43." Sarah can also use a calendar or hundreds chart to practice tracking the skip counting and pointing to the correct numbers. Sarah enjoys working with drawings and charts, so she can record her solutions on a hundreds chart to visually see the patterns of skip counting by fives or tens. Multiples of 5 could be shaded in blue and multiples of 10 could be shaded in red to make the patterns more obvious.

Sarah and her student friend should advance to examples with larger numbers, randomly chosen by the leader. If Sarah begins with "32," she and her partner circle it and continue from there to a predetermined final number up to 100. This activity should be used to work on the intervals of 10, 25, and 50. The teacher can ask Sarah to circle what would be 5 more than any new number,

TABLE 10.5 Mathematics Improvement Plan for Sarah: Making Change

Time		**30 Minutes**	**20–30 Minutes**	**15–20 Minutes**
Context		Works with a small group of students on making change with school store purchases	Works independently on guided practice papers	Works with one other student
Content		"Buys and sells" items with a peer to record sale, amount paid, and change using play coins, paper money, and skip counting	Records change for items on a worksheet that includes those in which student would be interested—tapes, sports equipment, clothes	Cuts out pictures from magazines of items she'd like to buy and creates problems with amount paid and change received; could be checked with calculator
Process	Input	Play currency and play sales reports	Worksheet and calendars	Creates stories with activities and dates between them, recording number of days on story papers
	Output	Responds to oral and written questions	Recorded responses and drawings	Written record of correct change
Behavior	Social	Works with peers	Works individually	Works with one other student
	Academic	Completes work paper with correct amounts of change given	Completes work paper alone with aids	Students discuss their answers with each other
Reinforcement		Verbal praise from peers	Receives quiet praise from teacher	Praise from partner

13 more than that number, and so on, randomly selecting a number and checking out the number that is 2, 5, 10, 25, or 50 more than that number.

To transfer skip-counting skills to those required for counting change, Sarah should be shown some items that could be sold in a store, such as books, with price tags. Another student is told to pay for the item with a certain amount of play bills and coins; Sarah is to count, using skip counting as a strategy, from the amount charged to the amount paid to determine correct change. It is helpful, for organizational purposes, to put the coins in zip-lock plastic bags and write the amount in the bag using a dry erase marker. Sarah should record the amount paid for each item and the change returned, as in the chart shown in Figure 10.4.

It is important for Sarah to count using different combinations of coins to make change. If she skip counts from $1.57 to $2.00 by fives, she will conclude the counting at $0.97. In order to determine correct change for $2.00, she will have to count by ones, or count up, mentally subtracting, to return the remaining 3 cents. If Sarah has difficulty with counting the remaining amount of 3 cents, she can be asked to write the subtraction problem and/or compute mentally. Examples that require combining various coins are essential in this lesson.

Money Error Pattern II for Sarah

The second type of money error is found in Student Work Sample V. The task requires that Sarah rename money values in ways other than using money symbols, including decimals and fractions.

FIGURE 10.4

These items are for sale in the classroom store:

Action Figure 26 cents

Toy Car 38 cents

Book 14 cents

Fill in the blanks that show how much change is due to the customer.

Items	**Paid**	**Change**
1. Isaac bought 1 action figure and 1 book.	75 cents	________
2. Teddie bought 2 cars and 1 book.	95 cents	________
3. Chan bought 3 books and 2 action figures.	$2.50	________
4. Chrystel bought 3 books.	60 cents	________
5. Tia bought 2 of each of the items.	$3.00	________

STUDENT WORK SAMPLE V

Circle the correct equivalent notations for these money amounts:

		a.	b.	c.
1.	$0. 25	a. (25)	b. 2.5	c. 1/4
2.	50 cents	a. 1/2	b. (50)	c. 5
3.	10 cents	a. 1.0	b. $0.10	c. (10)
4.	$1.50	a. (150)	b. 150/10	c. 1 1/2
5.	40 cents	a. 4/10	b. 40/100	c. (40)
6.	62 cents	a. 62/100	b. (62)	c. 6.2
7.	75 cents	a. 3/4	b. (75/10)	c. (75)
8.	$10.76	a. (1076)	b. 10 76/100	c. (10 76/10)
9.	$1.00	a. (1/100)	b. 1/10	c. 100/100
10.	$25.25	a. 25 25/100	b. (2525)	c. 25 25/10

Diagnosing the Error: Sarah is able to read dollar and cents amounts correctly. Consider her strengths related to reading money notation and finding equivalent amounts. Record the correct aspects of her work and the errors you detect in the space provided.

Sarah's Error Patterns:
Sarah's Strengths:

An examination of her work reveals that Sarah can read dollars and cents symbols correctly. However, she is unable to relate them to equivalent fractions, decimals, or other currency notations. Her difficulty with identifying, for example, 50 cents as a symbol representing one half of a dollar indicates her lack of understanding or familiarity with quantities represented by money notation. Her answers also indicate that she thinks that she can express an amount of money with whole numbers, ignoring the decimal notation.

Prescription: Sarah would profit from illustrating fraction and decimal quantities by shading in a chart. She should connect the symbols by writing them on the amount shaded on the chart. Sarah likes to work in small groups and draw, so she might show and explain her work in her group to further reinforce concepts for herself and fellow students. The suggested remediation activity is described in this section and listed in Sarah's MIP in Table 10.6 and her DAS for Error Pattern II with money is found in Table 10.2.

TABLE 10.6 Mathematics Improvement Plan for Sarah: Making Change

Time		**30 Minutes**	**20–30 Minutes**	**15–20 Minutes**
Context		Works with a small group of students on place value charts and hundreds chart, using play coins	Works independently on guided practice papers	Works with one other student
Content		Renames coins with decimals and fractions using place value charts and play coins and bills	Records renaming values on a place value chart, drawing play coins and bills using decimal and money notations	Cuts out pictures of item from magazines, prices them, and expresses the amounts with decimals, fractions, and money symbols
Process	Input	Play currency and place value charts	Worksheet and place value charts	Creates stories with items selected for purchase, recording amounts under pictures
	Output	Responds to oral and written questions	Recorded responses and drawings	Written record of money value
Behavior	Social	Works with peers	Works individually	Works with one other student
	Academic	Completes work paper with correct amounts of change given	Completes work paper alone with aids	Students discuss their answers with each other
Reinforcement		Verbal praise from peers	Receives quiet praise from teacher	Praise from partner

Remediation: Sarah needs to work with actual coins or play coin replicas. She could begin with a hundreds chart of decimal numbers such as that shown in Figure 10.5.

Sarah places a penny on the 0.01 symbol and square to connect the fact that there are 100 pennies in a dollar and that each penny or cent is worth one hundredth of a dollar. She should also notice that the value of penny can be expressed as 1/100 because there are one hundred squares in the whole, which is called, in this case, one dollar. She should be shown the symbol of 1¢ because students cannot "discover" symbol notations. Sarah continues this pattern by identifying the amount of squares shaded by 10 of the 100, symbolizing the quantity with 1/10 and 0. 10. She then learns to call that amount both 10 cents and a dime. Similar activities are carried out for 25 cents, 50 cents, the entire one dollar, and then any amount of money in the dollar she would like to express in multiple ways. She should complete a chart such as that shown in Figure 10.6.

Sarah could also work with a place value chart in order to express the money amount in a variety of ways. She should count out the bills and coins and then record the numbers of each in the proper place. Sarah is asked to identify the number of dollars and coins that constitute a given amount or one that she creates, using her own work or newspaper ads, for example. She would express $4.32 as 4 dollars, 3 dimes, and 2 pennies. She should also express those amounts in decimals and fractions by referring to her hundreds chart. Setting the dollars and coins on the place value chart provides additional reinforcement of the concept and skill. An example of a place value chart is shown in Figure 10.7.

FIGURE 10.5

.01	.11	.21	.31	.41	.51	.61	.71	.81	.91
.02	.12	.22	.32	.42	.52	.62	.72	.82	.92
.03	.13	.23	.33	.43	.53	.63	.73	.83	.93
.04	.14	.24	.34	.44	.54	.64	.74	.84	.94
.05	.15	.25	.35	.45	.55	.65	.75	.85	.95
.06	.16	.26	.36	.46	.56	.66	.76	.86	.96
.07	.17	.27	.37	.47	.57	.67	.77	.87	.97
.08	.18	.28	.38	.48	.58	.68	.78	.88	.98
.09	.19	.29	.39	.49	.59	.69	.79	.89	.99
.10	.20	.30	.40	.50	.60	.70	.80	.90	1.00

FIGURE 10.6

Money Amount	Dollar Sign	Decimal	Fraction
Penny	$0.01		
Nickel		.05	
Dime			1/10
Quarter			1/4
Dollar	$1.00		
Fifteen cents		.15	
Twenty cents			1/5
One dollar and fifty cents		1.50	

FIGURE 10.7

Complete the chart by writing the correct decimal for each place value in the amount of money shown. The first example is done for you.

	100.00	10.00	1.00	0.10	0.01
$4.32			4.00	.30	0.02
$18.75					
$135.42					
8.89					
674.58					
62.63					

Complete the chart by filling in the fraction that is the same as the decimal place for each place value in the amount of money shown. The first example is done for you.

	100	10	1	1/10	1/100
$4.32	0	0	4	3/10	2/100
$18.75					
$135.42					
8.89					
674.58					
62.63					

(*continued*)

Complete the chart by filling in the amount of money and number of bills or coins for the amount of money shown. The first example is done for you.

	Hundred Dollars	Ten Dollars	Dollars	Dimes	Pennies
$4.32	0	0	4	3	2
$18.75					
$135.42					
$8.89					
$674.58					
$62.63					

Conclusions: Instructional Strategies Summary

Time and money are abstract measurement topics that pose several teaching and learning challenges. The concepts and procedures for understanding points and duration of time, reading and interpreting a clock, determining coin values, and exchanging currency are unique to these measurement actions. New vocabulary must be learned and utilized to successfully measure time and money. Coins pose special issues in that they are not proportional to their value and must be exchanged to gain experience with making change. School stores and participation in buying and selling provide opportunities for making correct change and identifying coin amounts in a variety of ways. Students' work with decimals and fractions can help them understand and use renaming to bring meaning to the value of coins and their use. Numerous opportunities to physically work with a clock to understand the relationship of the hands and numerals as well as activities involving exchanging currency and attaching value to coins with multiple symbols must be provided to enable students to gain a sense of these indirect scales.

Calendar reading is also essential to successful everyday living; procedures can be understood and practiced with the use of learning aids such as number lines and/or counters. Time dimensions of days, weeks, and months should be incorporated into activities with accurately reading dates and finding the length of time between identified periods of time. In all cases, activities should be introduced and practiced in relation to real-world examples.

Instructional Activities

ACTIVITY: Money Baseball Money Baseball

Objective: Express amounts of money with multiple combinations of coins and bills

Materials: Index cards with the following written on them:

20 or fewer problems of dimes and pennies, such as "4 dimes and 2 pennies is ___________?" "Singles" is written on card.

20 or fewer problems involving pennies, dimes, quarters, and dollars, such as "5 quarters less 3 dimes and 5 pennies is ___________?" "Doubles" is written on card.

20 or fewer problems involving 10 or more dollars and forms of coins, such as "Provide a different name for $50.00 using 10-dollar, 5-dollar, and single dollar bills." "Triples" is written on card.

15 problems that are more challenging. "Home run" is written on card.

Marker to more around game board.

Baseball game board: Example

Money Baseball Game Board

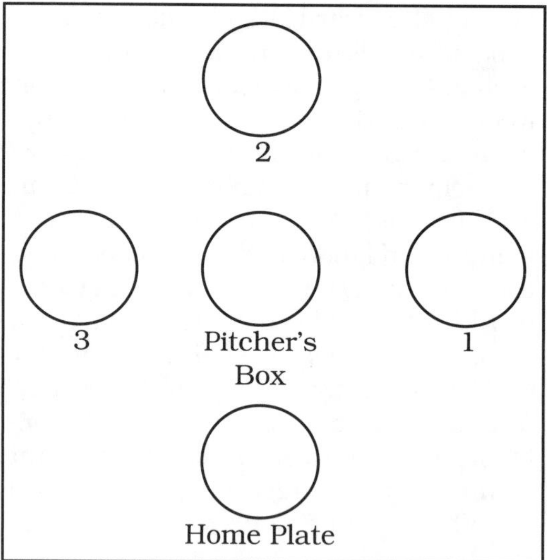

Directions:

1. Students are grouped in two teams.
2. Index cards are placed, face down in a "pitcher's box" between the teams or on game board.
3. One player on each team is the pitcher.

4. When one team is "at bat," the pitcher from the other team reads a problem chosen from the "pitcher's box."
5. If the "batter" answers the question correctly, she goes to the base designated by the problem (set up areas in the class for bases or moves the team's marks to the appropriate base).
6. If the "batter" answer incorrectly or does not answer the question, that player is "out".
7. When a player on one team score three outs, then the next team "bats".
8. When both teams make 3 outs, 1 inning is completed.
9. Each game lasts 5 innings. The team with the most runs wins.

ACTIVITY: Money Dominoes

Objective: Express money values with fractions, decimals, and currency notation

Materials: 30–40 dominoes on card stock. Each domino shows a variety of names for currency. A sample would look this way:

10 Cents	50¢

$ 0.10	Half of a dollar

Nickel	$ 1.00

ONE DOLLAR	5¢

Directions:

1. This game can be played by two or more students.
2. Each player takes seven dominoes for his own hand. The remaining dominoes are placed in a "pot" in the center of the play area.
3. The first player places a domino in the center of the area.
4. The next player must place a domino with an equivalent money name on one of its sections next to one section of the first domino, in the following fashion:

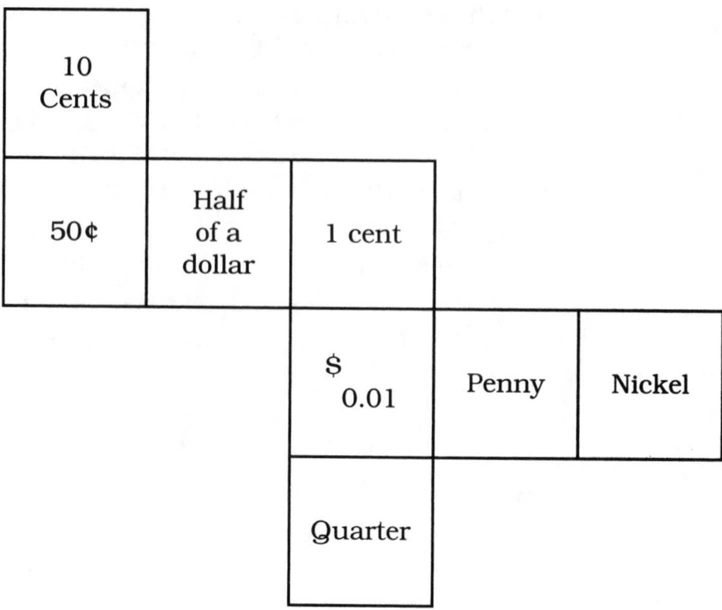

5. Play continues as each player plays a domino that can be matched for equivalent symbol form.
6. If a player does not have a domino to play, one is taken from the pot.
7. The first player to play all the dominoes in her hand is the winner.

ACTIVITY: Let's Play Store!

Objective: Make purchases and determine change

Materials: Plastic coins, laminated money cards, items to buy and sell (such as empty cereal boxes, empty cans, toys, pencils), and sales record sheets

Directions:

1. Students work in groups and decide on prices for each sale item.
2. Sale prices are marked on index cards and attached to each item.
3. Student is chosen as sales clerk and another as buyer.
4. A buyer from one group makes 2 purchases with his/her coins from the sales clerk and receives change.
5. After one group makes its purchases, a clerk from that group is chosen and items bought. Several groups can work at the same time in the store in the same manner.
6. The purchase costs, amount paid, and change returned are recorded on a worksheet to be given to the teacher at the end of the sales period.
7. After each student has had a chance to be a clerk, a group of students "marks down" the items for a classroom sale. The activity is then repeated in terms of sales and making change.
8. Students can also write advertisements for each item, stating both the original price and the new sale price.

ACTIVITY: Food for Thought

Objective: Compute using currency and determine a budget.

Materials: Grocery store ads from a variety of stores or newspaper, payment cards

Directions:

1. Prior to this activity, the teacher should talk with class about food groups.
2. Each student designs a nutritious meal for a family of four by listing foods from the advertisements to buy for the dinner that total $50.00 or less, lunch for $40.00 or less, and breakfast for $30.00 or less.
3. Student lists food and costs to find actual total.
4. Students determine the amount of change due to them and record the amount of change on their answer sheet.
5. An example of recording chart is:

Food for Thought Record Sheet

BREAKFAST		**LUNCH**	
FOOD ITEMS	COST	FOOD ITEMS	COST
1.	$_____	1.	$_____
2.	$_____	2.	$_____
3.	$_____	3.	$_____
Total	$_____	Total	$_____
Change from $30.00	$_____	Change from $40.00	$_____

DINNER	
FOOD ITEMS	COST
1.	$_____
2.	$_____
3.	$_____
Total	$_____
Change from $50.00	$_____

ACTIVITY: Fishing for Time

Objective: Match clock times with correct notation

Materials:

30 blue index cards with clock faces stamped on each

30 green index cards with times written on them that match each clock face on blue cards

Directions:

1. Students work in pairs.
2. The cards are placed in two piles face down between the players. One pile contains the clock face cards and the other pile is that of the times.

3. Each student draws three cards from each pile to have a hand of six cards in all.
4. The remaining cards are placed in the "clock pot" placed between the two players.
5. Each student checks to see if there are pairs of matching cards in the hands drawn. If the student finds a match between the blue clock face card and the time written on green card, that pair of cards is placed next to that student.
6. After pairs are placed next to a player, the game begins with the first student asking the other player if she is holding a time that matches a clock face in the first player's hand. For example, the first player would ask, "Do you have a 4:15?"
7. If the other player has the requested card, it is given to the "asker."
8. If the other player does not have a match, the asker takes a card from the pile of cards between the two players.
9. Each player takes a turn until all cards are gone and one player has more matched pairs of cards than the other.

ACTIVITY: Time Enough

Objective: Read clock times and those before and after

Materials: Game board with clock faces stamped on the playing surface (see diagram)

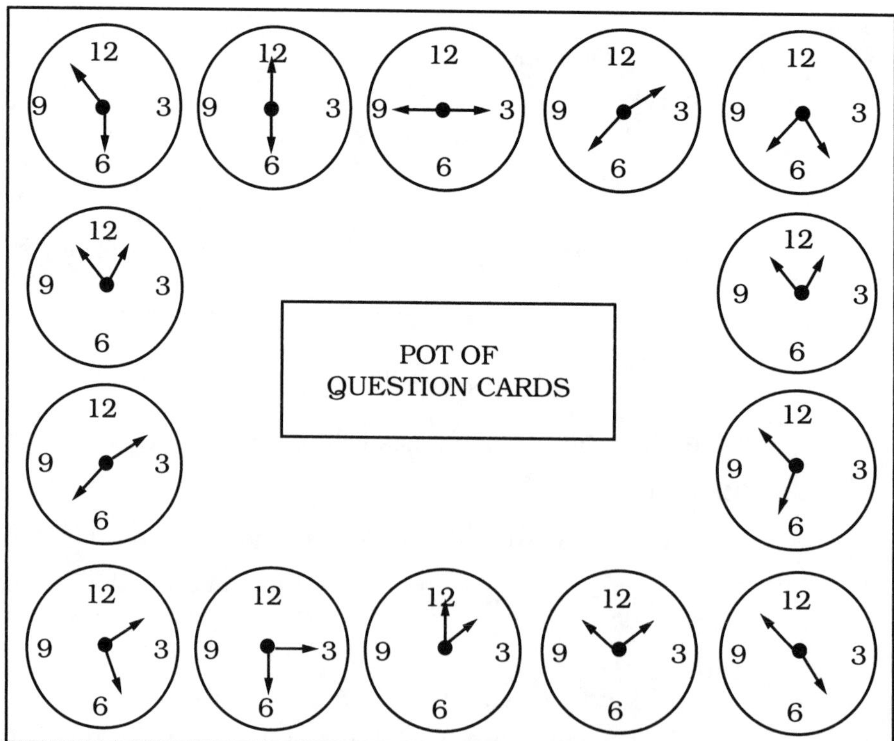

20–25 cards that state questions such as:

What is the time 15 minutes after the clock time you landed on? Move 1 space.

What is the time 10 minutes before the clock time you landed on? Move 2 spaces.

What is the time 1 hour after the clock time you landed on? Move 3 spaces.

What is the time 2 hours and 30 minutes before the clock time you landed on? Move 4 spaces.

What is the time 25 minutes after the clock time you landed on? Move 2 spaces.

Counters or markers to move around game board

Number cube or die

Directions:

1. Students play in small groups with one game board.
2. Players place their movers on the first clock square on the game board.
3. The first player rolls the die and advances the number of spaces indicated by the number shown.
4. The player then draws a card from the pot and responds to the question.
5. If the player is correct, according to other players, he moves the number of spaces indicated on the card.
6. The first player to the Clock Tower wins the game.

Discussion Questions

1. Why is the determination of measures of time and money more difficult for students than the determination of weight, mass, capacity, or length? Provide examples for each measure.
2. Why is the system of coins not entirely based on the base-10 system?
3. What is an activity that helps students count change, using a hundreds chart?
4. What are the number bases involved in reading a clock? What base group is used for minutes? Hours? Explain how you can help students understand that the clock is not a base-10 system.
5. Why are everyday experiences critically important to understanding time and money measures?
6. Design an activity based on having students create a menu that would list dinner meals that include choices for entrées, salads, side dishes, and desserts so that a student could make a selection not costing more than $30.00. Students would total their expenses and change received. Describe your directions for student work.
7. Describe an activity for students to use their hand-made clock to associate before and after times, such as 9:45 with 15 minutes before 10:00 and 5:20 with 20 minutes after 5:00. Explain how you would connect the times to everyday experiences.
8. Identify all computational processes involved with making change. Why does making change present challenges to students?
9. Write a process problem for students to solve that involves an everyday student activity and counting days between calendar dates over three different months.

References

Brenner, M. E. (1998). Meaning and money. *Educational Studies in Mathematics, 36,* 123–155.

Brownell, W. (1935). Psychological considerations in the learning and teaching of arithmetic. In *The teaching of arithmetic.* New York: Bureau of Publications, Teachers College, Columbia University.

Carlsson, G., & Cohen, R. L. (2002). *Mathematics, grade four.* New York: Macmillan/McGraw-Hill.

Carraher, T. N., & Schliemann, A. D. (1998). Using money to teach about the decimal system. *Arithmetic Teacher, 36,* 42–43.

Guberman, S. R. (2004). A comparative study of children's out-of-school activities and arithmetical achievements. *Journal for Research in Mathematics Education, 35*(2), 117–150.

National Council of Teachers of Mathematics. (2000). *Principles and standards for school mathematics*. Reston, VA: Author.

Nunes, T., Schliemann, A. D., & Caaraher, D. W. (1993). *Street mathematics and school mathematics*. New York: Cambridge University Press.

Reys, R. E., Lindquist, M. M., Lambdin, D. V., Smith N.C., & Suydam, M. N. (2004). *Helping children learn mathematics*. Hoboken, NJ John Wiley & Sons, Inc./ Jossey-Bass Publishers.

Yang, S., & Olson, M. (2007). Supermarket math. *Teaching Children Mathematics, 7*(13), 376–377.

Appendix A

Sample DAS and MIP Tables

Templates for the data analysis sheet (DAS) and mathematics improvement plan (MIP) are provided on pages 250 and 251.

Data Analysis Sheet

Student:							
Team Members:							
Context	**Content Assessment**	**Process**		**Behavior**		**Reinforcement**
		Input	Output	Academic	Social	
+	+	+	+	+	+	+
	Learned Concepts ***Learned Concepts***					
–	–	–	–	–	–	–
	Error Pattern I ***Error Pattern II***					

Note: The + symbols indicate strengths and the – symbols indicate areas of concern.

Mathematics Improvement Plan

Time				
Context				
Content				
Process	Input			
	Output			
Behavior	Academic			
	Social			
Reinforcement				

Note: The + symbols indicate strengths and the − symbols indicate areas of concern.

Appendix B

Suggestions for Planning Academic Content Lessons

The following suggestions are provided as options for instructors to consider in planning academic content lessons. Strategies for considering the learning process and for dealing with student behavior are also included as general checklists.

Academic Content

Teaching and Learning Materials

1. Use graphics to help clearly explain concepts and ideas, but don't have one picture do too many things.
2. Have learners complete a few problems at a time. Once you are satisfied that they understand something, move on.
3. Don't reuse materials that have already proven unsuccessful with the special learner. Always note the things that work.
4. Check with the learner's lower-grade teacher to see what materials work best. Don't be reluctant to ask for assistance from the resource teacher and other effective teachers.
5. Be sure the print size and clarity is suitable for learners.
6. Let students see, hear, touch, and write about new or difficult concepts.
7. Provide a quiet area for the learner to study the material. Such learning should occur in the regular classroom; teachers should choose an area close to the classroom if that location is acceptable.
8. High-interest/low-vocabulary materials are desirable when teaching concepts, theories, facts, or principles.
9. Avoid giving too much new material at too fast a rate. Three or four problems are enough for the learner. Follow the exercise with another small set of problems.

10. Utilize materials that address present learner needs (budget techniques for mathematics: food containers for reading, mathematics, and science). Allow the entire class to become involved in this learning exercise. This helps learners realize they can interact successfully with peers.
11. Emphasize materials comfortable to the learner's environment or interest level, such as graphics on sports, home living, and hobbies.
12. Allow learners to develop their own story problems.
13. Use simple numbers to explain a mathematical operation, then move to the more complex level.
14. Encourage the use of communication skills through the use of puppets. Let the learner talk through the puppets.

Alternative Curricular Approaches

1. A life skills curriculum adapts functional skills into everyday living situations. Adolescents desire the ability to care for themselves and this curriculum supports that desire.
2. Career education stimulates involvement in academic skill areas. Several career education programs move from occupational interest to skill development areas.
3. Simple discovery method techniques stimulate and encourage the learner to experience the skill along with the learning of the skill.
4. Technology applications allow the learner to study independently without fear of adult observation.
5. Public utilities, such as the telephone and gas companies, have curriculum and equipment systems to encourage curricular skills.
6. A current event curriculum using local newspapers and magazines can include visuals, low-level reading materials, and pre- and posttest activities.
7. Utilize central idea (theme) approaches to teaching concepts. Research games that require reading, writing, and conversing.
8. Encourage hands-on approaches with students as new concepts are introduced.
9. Combine discovery-based curriculum programs with fact-oriented ones.
10. Introduce the learner to a unit with a small number of activities.
11. Select community individuals to strengthen a curricular activity: guest speaker, teacher for a day, or individual tutor.
12. Let the learners create plays from the stories.
13. Keep learners physically involved as they learn new concepts (role-playing, demonstrating definitions or words, etc.).

14. Keep the experiences of the classroom simple and directed toward the task you are teaching.
15. Frequently review the task through auditory/visual and physical activities.

Process

Methods of Instruction

1. Stand close to learners who have problems as you explain the material.
2. Let the learners investigate materials before they use them. Let them explain to you the purpose of the materials.
3. Cue learners to proper answers and advise them as they work toward a solution.
4. Set up your physical environment to support learning activities (reading center, math center, etc.). Equip those centers with materials that complement the skill levels of your learners.
5. Let activity areas encourage discovery among your learners. Give them the opportunity to talk about each small discovery.
6. Analyze the material when a learner is having a problem. Choose or design new materials that directly address the problem.
7. When reteaching, be as consistent as possible, using vocabulary similar to that used in the initial presentation.
8. When you repeat the instructions, be sure the learner is quiet and is listening to you.
9. Be excited about your topic and show that excitement. Remember that boring people are boring to be around.
10. Intersperse short lectures with a work task, followed by a brief evaluation of the learner's work.
11. Encourage group projects. Combine successful learners and special learners; encourage the involvement of all your learners in each group. Peer encouragement is most effective.
12. Panel discussions encourage learners to contribute, even with a small bit of knowledge.

Behavior

Behavior Strategies

1. Learners must know, in precise words, what is expected. Classroom rules should be brief, posted on the wall or chalkboard, and discussed frequently.

2. Do not assume anything; rules and expectations must be explained in words that the learner can understand.
3. Explain in the same manner what they can expect from you (how you will behave). Be positive.
4. Take time to listen. The special learner takes longer to express a thought. Patience indicates a sincere interest in the learner and the situation.
5. Set up group sessions about social or behavioral issues. Set up rules for the group session and set a time limit.
6. Reward small accomplishments of the learners with honest social reinforcers (smiles, verbal statements).
7. Reinforce the positive behavior of the learners who sit close to the difficult child.
8. Ignore minor infractions and remember to positively reinforce acceptable behavior when it occurs.
9. Stay in the environment of the learner who is under stress.
10. Encourage the learner to describe the inappropriate behavior and to explain the consequences of this behavior and how it is affecting others.
11. Identify and reinforce a behavior in the learner that prevents the occurrence of a negative behavior.
12. Utilize oral and written contracts with your learners. Contract for a small task and begin by using a brief written contract.
13. Develop a total class point system for outside interests, exploration time, or time to work on a high-interest activity.
14. Specify rules early in the year and review the rules on a weekly basis if necessary. Follow this review with positive reinforcement for those learners who are trying to comply with the rules.
15. Use peer models in discussions with special learners about their problems; however, don't use peer models with students who have chronic behavior problems.
16. Clearly explain to the learner the consequences of both acceptable and unacceptable behavior. Be sure the consequences have been approved by the necessary authority of the school and be prepared to follow through with the consequences.
17. Exclusion should be the last step in management. Allow the learner to have alternatives that permit a return to the classroom.
18. When problems occur, analyze the environment in order to understand the nature of the difficulty. Be sure that you are not the source of the problem.
19. Discuss the problems and possible solutions with the students' parents whenever possible. Encourage the parents to be part of the solution.
20. When the problem significantly decreases, encourage and reinforce the learner for being in control of the actions and behavior.

21. Physically use your presence to control behavior. When a problem decreases, move away from the learner so that you communicate that your closeness is a signal for the learner to establish self-control.
22. If the learner is easily distracted, establish a work area with a minimum of stimulation and distraction. However, it is also important to avoid a sterile environment. Balance is the key.
23. When stress occurs in a student, permit a break in the task. Allow the student to complete an errand for you before returning to the task.
24. **Remember:** The management of behavior and curriculum *must* occur simultaneously.
25. Approach the problem from the position of finding a solution—not magnifying the problem. We need answers, not more questions!

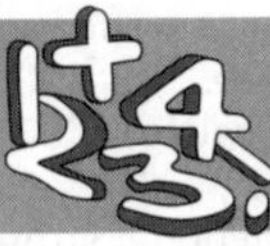

Index